INDIGENOUS PEOPLES' RIGHTS
IN SOUTHERN AFRICA

Edited by
Robert Hitchcock and Diana Vinding

IWGIA
Document No. 110 - Copenhagen 2004

INDIGENOUS PEOPLES' RIGHTS
IN SOUTHERN AFRICA

Editors: Robert K. Hitchcock and Diana Vinding

Copyright: IWGIA 2004 – All Rights Reserved

Cover design, typesetting and maps: Jorge Monrás

Proofreading: Elaine Bolton

Prepress and Print: Eks/Skolens Trykkeri,
Copenhagen, Denmark

ISBN: 87-91563-08-9

Distribution in North America:
Transaction Publishers
390 Campus Drive / Somerset, New Jersey 08873
www.transactionpub.com

**INTERNATIONAL WORK GROUP
FOR INDIGENOUS AFFAIRS**
Classensgade 11 E, DK 2100 - Copenhagen, Denmark
Tel: (45) 35 27 05 00 - Fax: (45) 35 27 05 07
E-mail: iwgia@iwgia.org - Web: www.iwgia.org

*This book has been produced with financial support from
the Danish Ministry of Foreign Affairs*

CONTENTS

THE REGION

INDIGENOUS PEOPLES' RIGHTS IN SOUTHERN AFRICA: AN INTRODUCTION

Robert K. Hitchcock
and Diana Vinding

I ndigenous peoples in Africa and their rights have been the focus of much deliberation and debate in recent years.[1] These discussions have taken place in academic institutions and journals in Africa, Europe and North America, as well as within the European Union, the World Bank and the United Nations.

A major area of dissent has been whether the concept of "indigenousness", and hence of specific "indigenous" rights, could be used in an African context. Most African governments have until now maintained that all their citizens are indigenous or, alternatively, argued that there is no such thing as an indigenous group in their country. Some researchers and social scientists have stressed that the problems faced by certain ethnic minorities have more to do with poverty than cultural differences and the problems they face should therefore be alleviated by welfare and development measures (see Saugestad, this volume).

There is no single, agreed-upon definition of the term "indigenous peoples" but, as Saugestad mentions in her Overview (this volume), the four most often invoked elements are: (1) a priority in time; (2) the voluntary perpetuation of cultural distinctiveness; (3) an experience of subjugation, marginalisation and dispossession; (4) and self-identification. Often, the term indigenous is used to refer to those individuals and groups who are descendants of the original populations (that is, the "first nations") residing in a country. In the case of Africa this raises particular problems. Africa is the continent with the longest history of human occupation, and it contains the greatest range of human genetic and cultural diversity. In many cases, it is difficult to determine antecedence since a variety of populations have moved into and out of local areas over time. There have been complex interactions between "first peoples" and newcomers, often with the result that the former groups are marginalized. In no country in Africa are indigenous peoples in control even at local government level, and far less in positions of power at national level.

However, an important criterion for "indigenousness" is the identification by people themselves of their distinct cultural identity. Most people prefer to reserve for themselves the right to determine who is and is not a member of their group. There exist in Africa a number of population groups who define themselves - and are defined by others - as "indigenous" i.e. they feel that they are culturally distinct from their neighbors and the dominant ethnic groups and, as a result, share a common experience that includes dispossession of land and natural resources, impoverishment, discrimination and human rights abuses.

An important number of the people, who in an African context, define themselves as indigenous, live in southern Africa and while some countries in the region, such as South Africa, have taken important steps toward recognizing their rights, others have abrogated these rights, with members of indigenous groups being discriminated against, dispossessed of their ancestral lands and deprived of their rights to resources.

This book aims to look at some of the complex issues relating to the situation of these indigenous peoples. It examines their human rights in the broad sense, taking into consideration their civil and political rights, their social, economic and cultural rights, as well as their rights to development, participation, a healthy environment and peace. More specifically it deals with land rights, gender issues, natural resource management, education and with some of the efforts being made by indigenous groups and their supporters to defend and promote these rights.

Attention is focused primarily on six countries, where ethnic groups, who historically have been characterized as indigenous, still live.

These populations used to be called Bushmen and, in the case of Botswana, Basarwa, while others were known as Nama or Hottentot (Schapera 1930, 1933). Today, they are usually generically known as San and Khoe respectively but use of the names they give themselves is becoming ever more prevalent. Khoe and San peoples are found in Angola, Botswana, Namibia, South Africa, Zambia, and Zimbabwe (Barnard 1992; Suzman 2001a). There are also other groups who claim indigenous status such as, for example, the Himba of Namibia and the Vadema of Zimbabwe (see the chapters by Daniels, Harring and Akpan et al.).

In all six of these southern African countries, the San and Khoe are numerical minorities, though there are regions within the boundaries of the states where they outnumber other groups. There are also smaller indigenous groups, like the Ju|'hoansi of north-western Botswana and north-eastern Namibia, who overlap national borders. The transboundary nature of many indigenous peoples puts them in a special position vis-à-vis nation-states, many of whom are concerned about their sovereignty and security and are attempting to prevent movements of people and goods across their borders. Zambia is a case in point since its government does not recognize the San living in the country as being Zambian citizens but sees them primarily as refugees or immigrants from Angola, as noted by Akpan et al. (this volume).

The claims of indigenous peoples in southern Africa are relatively similar to those of indigenous peoples in other parts of the world: they wish to have their human rights respected; they want ownership and control over their own land and natural resources; and they want the right to participate through their own institutions in the political process at the nation-state, regional and international levels. However, as this book documents, they live in a region where discrimination and human rights abuses have been rife and where they are still dominated by a mainstream society that deals with them "injudiciously and with impunity at the three levels of the individual, the community and the state" to quote Mazonde (this volume).

The Issue of Identity

As noted by several authors, indigenous peoples in southern Africa are highly diverse. They range from small communities of foragers (hunters and gatherers) to sedentary agro-pastoralists and peri-urban factory workers in the industrial economies of southern African states. The vast majority have diversified economic systems, combining small-scale agriculture and livestock production with natural resource procurement and business activities.

However, a common feature is that they have been, and still are, viewed as representing "a form of primitivity" (Taylor, this volume) that must be overcome to give way to development. In the past, with the expansion of agro-pastoral populations and, later on, explorers, hunters, miners, settlers and others, there were instances where they were simply murdered, tortured or enslaved (see Saugestad, this volume; Skotnes 1996:17-21). In other cases, San and Khoe groups were either displaced by cattle farms that were established and allocated primarily to white farmers or they were incorporated as farm hands and domestic workers. This situation of dispossession and marginalisation continues to this day. As Taylor (this volume) remarks, "the removal of San from the Central Kalahari Game Reserve can essentially be understood as a civilising project towards the segment of Botswana's population considered to be the most 'backward'." As a result, an increasing number of San and Khoe end up as 'hangers-on' around towns and villages and many today live in townships where they depend on handouts and cash obtained through odd jobs (see the chapters by Harring, Taylor, and Hitchcock, Johnson and Haney).

During this process, many Khoesan people have given up their customs and traditions and have been more or less assimilated into the dominant society although most of them remain at the bottom of the social ladder. In the case of Botswana, as Mazonde (this volume) underlines, this is to a large extent the result of deliberate government policies seeking to integrate the San into the culture of mainstream Batswana, notably through the formal education system.

Some Khoesan people, on the other hand, wish to continue to practise their culture and hold tightly to their beliefs, values and customary practices. Sensing that language is a crucial element of cultural identification, indigenous groups in southern Africa are today struggling to retain or revive their mother-tongue languages. So far, only Namibia - and South Africa to a lesser extent - ensure mother-tongue and culturally appropriate education for the first three years of school for San and other minorities. While this is commendable, it can also be argued, as Hays does in her chapter on education, that formal classroom-based education has many detrimental consequences for the San and their identity. Instead, she advocates for the need, "To look carefully at what education is, what it means to peoples like the Juǀ'hoansi, and what options are actually available to them." And to give them the right to refuse or accept these options.

Land Rights in Southern Africa

Indigenous identity is intimately related to land. Indigenous peoples view land not only as an economic resource but also as one that has social, political and spiritual dimensions. Taylor (this volume) notes, "To have a small tract of land gives people a sense of standing in the wider social economy that landless San cannot achieve" and quotes Roy Sesana, a San leader from Botswana, who said, "Our human rights are our land. They cannot do anything for us if they take us off our land." Yet, being taken off their land is exactly the fate that many - if not most - indigenous peoples have faced in southern Africa.

Traditionally, southern African societies managed their land on a communal - or group - basis. Under this tenure system, land could not be bought or sold and individuals were only allocated land rights insofar as they were members of a group or, in some cases, through provision by a tribal authority (e.g. a chief, a clan elder). Individuals and groups could also obtain land by moving into an unutilized area and establishing themselves. Conquest was another way of acquiring land but, more often than not, this happened at the expense of indigenous groups.

In some cases, people had to demonstrate continued usage of their land in order to maintain their rights of access. This was not easy in the case of hunting and gathering societies, and one way to mark their landscapes was to leave behind traces of their campsites.

Segments of African societies were associated with discrete areas. This was the case, for example, of the Juǀ'hoan San of Namibia and Botswana, whose ancestral territory was divided into a number of smaller units known as *n!oresi*. Each *n!ore* (sing.), or land and resource unit, had people with long-standing rights to that area - also known as *n!ore kxausi* - whom outsiders had to approach if they wished to camp or use the resources. Rights were handed down from one generation to the next, and people were generally aware of who had what rights to specific areas. The territories could also be subdivided further, depending on the types of resources available in them; those places that were rich in certain kinds of nut-bearing vines, for example, were considered to be gathering areas of segments of communities. Sacred areas or ones that were important ideologically (e.g. burial or ritual places where, for example, initiation rites were held) were often set aside specifically for groups rather than individuals.

Most of these traditions are still alive among contemporary indigenous peoples. The Himba case discussed by Daniels and Harring (this volume) provides a good illustration of this situation: because they consider the Epupa Falls on the Cunene River sacred and because many of their ancestors are buried in areas close to the river, the Himba of Namibia and Angola have struggled for years to stop the building of a dam at Epupa. Claiming "Heritage Rights", i.e. rights to culturally and ideologically significant property such as sacred sites, places on the landscape that are viewed by local peoples as important, is increasingly becoming a new aspect of the indigenous peoples' struggle for cultural recognition (see Chennells and du Toit for relevant examples from South Africa).

With colonization, land became an important commodity and the privatization of land was seen as a key approach to the agricultural and economic development of the European colonies in southern Africa. Turning tribal or communal land into private leasehold or freehold (private) land would provide, it was argued, individuals with the incentive to invest more labor and capital and, at the same time, to manage and conserve resources. An examination of the land-holding structure in southern Africa after the establishment of colonial governments is revealing (see Table 1): in none of the southern African states did the colonial governments leave even half of the land to the Africans, who made up the majority of the population.

Instead, much of the land was given to European immigrants or private companies. This commercialization of land resulted in a dramatic increase in landlessness for indigenous peoples as Taylor (this volume) shows with an example from western Botswana where the rights of the San were obliterated by the creation of freehold land and the cession of the Ghanzi Ridge to Cecil John Rhodes at the end of the 19th century.

The land rights situation of indigenous peoples in southern Africa did not improve with the arrival of independence. In Namibia, for in-

Country	Percent of African Population	African Lands as Percentage of Total Area
Angola	94%	40%
Botswana	99%	38%
Namibia	87%	25%
South Africa	80%	12%
Zimbabwe	91%	33%

Table 1.
Amounts of Land Reserved for African Populations in Southern African Countries Data compiled by Bodley (1999) and Hitchcock (2004) from the colonial administration reports in the national archives of southern African states.

stance, Harring notes that only 10% of the Namibian San retain "communal land rights" in a region that is one of the poorest and most remote in the country, and the Nama and Damara are still relegated to the "homelands" that the apartheid regime created in the 1960s and early 1970s in a barren, overgrazed desert.

In virtually all of the countries in southern Africa, indigenous groups have had to face new dispossessions and development-related relocations, often as the result of post-colonial policies based on the same arguments as those used by the colonial governments. In independent Botswana, for instance, the idea of providing incentives in order to thereby ensure economic development was at the core of the Tribal Grazing Land Policy (TGLP), a land reform and livestock development program introduced in Botswana in the mid-1970s. It is also behind the more recent National Agricultural Development Policy dating from 1991 (see Taylor, this volume, for a discussion of some of the impacts of these two programs).

An important exception is South Africa, where the ‡Khomani San and the Richtersveld Nama have been able to get their land claims recognized (see the chapters by Chennels and du Toit and by Chan). Clearly, with the end of apartheid[2] in South Africa, some progress has been made in recognizing indigenous peoples' rights.

Water Rights in Southern Africa

Water rights are intimately related to land rights. Southern Africa is in general a water-scarce region, and a large numbers of southern Africans have difficulty in obtaining sufficient water to meet their needs. This is particularly true for the peoples of the central and south-eastern Kalahari such as the G|ui, G||ana, and !Xoo San, some of whom have to resort to the use of sip-wells[3] in order to obtain moisture from the sands when there is no surface water available. When, in 2002, the Botswana government decided to stop delivery of water (as well as other services) to the residents of the CKGR, it therefore amounted to *de facto* forcing the residents to relocate outside the reserve (see Taylor, this volume), and prompted the spokespersons for the people of the Central Kalahari to argue that "water is a human right".[4]

Over the past decades, and in step with the land privatization process, indigenous peoples have seen their access to water resources greatly restricted, with grave consequences for their livelihood.

As with land, water resources in southern African societies were traditionally associated with social units (families, bands or clans). Under customary law, open surface waters such as rivers and springs were free to be used by anyone. In grazing districts, on the other hand, use of surface water was supposed to be confined to the tribal groups or wards that were granted access to those areas. Individuals belonging to other wards who drove cattle through the grazing areas were allowed to water their animals only after seeking permission from a local overseer (Schapera 1943) and people who watered their herds in another group's grazing area ran the risk of having their animals confiscated. In times of stress, however, many people in southern Africa, including San, followed the rule that individuals in dire need of water for themselves or their animals should be granted access to it.

Changes in water technology in the late 19th and early 20th centuries brought about major shifts in patterns of user rights over water resources. The digging of wells with the aid of dynamite and, later, the drilling of boreholes, led to a shift away from communal access to water resources to a system in which private ownership predominated. Those individuals with the resources to have boreholes dug were able to gain *de facto* rights not only over the water but over the grazing land surrounding the water point as well, and they could deny other people access to that water and nearby grazing. Borehole drilling in drier areas of southern Africa (e.g. the Kalahari Desert, the Namib Desert) facilitated the expansion of the number of livestock that could be kept by ensuring that water was available year-round. But the rising number of livestock and the reduction of their mobility contributed to a process of overgrazing and environmental degradation. As a consequence, both chiefs and the colonial administrations began to call for the privatization of land in order to counteract what they saw as problems of communal land and water access. The impact of this policy, which has been continued and further developed by the governments of post-colonial Botswana, is described by Taylor in his chapter on Land Rights, where he also remarks that few San have the capital to sink a borehole.

But restrictions on indigenous peoples' access to water can also take other forms. As Mazonde and Hitchcock note in their chapters, water resources in the RAD settlements that were originally meant for the domestic use of the San have, in many cases, been appropriated by dominant groups who use them for watering their cattle.

Conservation Policies and Indigenous Rights

There is reason to believe that the process of land dispossession will continue. Land, which in the past was often viewed as an unlimited natural resource, is becoming a scarce and valuable commodity. In some parts of southern Africa, there is intense competition for land and other natural resources, especially in those places where there are high demands due to population growth, agricultural intensification, urbanization, industrialization and environmental degradation (see Akpan et al., this volume)

However, it is conservation concerns that have created some of the heaviest demands on land and it is the creation of national parks and game reserves all over southern Africa that has dispossessed the largest number of indigenous peoples. As Hitchcock (this volume) remarks, most of the people required to leave their homes and resettle have been hunter-gatherers and part-time foragers and data indicates that many of them consider themselves worse off than was the case before they were relocated.

As a rule, resettlement is a complicated process, and only in a few cases has there been relatively large amounts of compensation paid to people for the losses of their homes and other assets, one case being that of the residents of the Central Kalahari Game Reserve (see the chapters by Hitchcock and Taylor, this volume). However, the main conclusion to be drawn from the discussions in this volume is that resettlement projects - with or without compensation - in general have failed to restore the livelihoods of people affected. In a number of cases they have even made people worse off, one reason being that planners tend to focus attention on loss of residence (i.e. homes) rather than on loss of access to means of production, especially land, grazing resources and the wild resources on which people depend for subsistence and income. As shown in the chapters dealing with Botswana, this has also been the case with the ambitious Remote Area Development Program (RAD), which was aimed in part at mitigating the impact of the Tribal Grazing Land Program. Instead of promoting development, moving to settlements has created dependency, deteriorated people's livelihoods and seriously undermined the status of indigenous women.

A less recognized aspect of forced relocation out of conservation areas is the way it has all too often exacerbated problems of poverty and environmental degradation, and has created situations of social conflict and violence. In the course of state efforts to promote conservation, national conservation legislation has placed legal restrictions on hunting, fishing and the gathering of certain wild resources (see the discussion on this issue in the chapters by Hitchcock and by Hitchcock, Johnson and Haney). Such legislation has not only reduced local people's access to natural resources but also resulted in individuals and sometimes whole communities being arrested, jailed and, in some cases, tortured or even killed for having allegedly been poaching or for being in areas where wildlife department personnel, police or the military were engaged in anti-poaching operations. Security rights, which include the rights to freedom from torture, execution and imprisonment, have thus become a major concern for indigenous peoples. In this respect it is interesting to note that the Convention against Torture and Other Cruel, Inhuman or Degrading Treatment or Punishment has been signed by most southern African countries, with only two countries in the region, Angola and Zimbabwe, failing to do so.

Only Botswana and Namibia have allowed local people to hunt and gather for subsistence purposes. As noted by Hitchcock in his chapter on community-based natural resource management (CBNRM), a special game license for hunting by subsistence-oriented households was introduced in Botswana in 1979. It did not, however, prevent people from being harassed and even arrested as suspected "poachers" by game scouts. It was abrogated early in the new millennium. Today, only community trusts receive hunting quotas and only for a certain period each year. The trusts may choose to either use these quotas for their own hunting purposes or sell them to safari operators. In Namibia, the Ju|'hoan San in Tsumkwe District East are allowed to hunt specified animals as long as they use traditional weapons and techniques (pursuit hunting on foot with bows and arrows and spears).

For many indigenous peoples, denial of the right to hunt and gather is not only a restriction placed on their subsistence rights, it is also a restriction on their cultural rights. Indigenous peoples realize full well the need for conservation of wildlife, plants and other resources. At the same time, they feel that they should be able to live according to their traditions if they so wish and to exploit resources as long as they do so sustainably.

There have been efforts made in recent years to combine conservation and economic development. As described in several chapters (see Daniels, Paklepppa, Mazonde, Taylor, Akpan et al. and Hitchcock), community-based natural resource management (CBNRM) projects are today implemented in most southern African countries. The results so far have been mixed: some projects have brought great benefits to the indigenous communities, others have failed or been appropriated by dominant groups within the community. As Hitchcock remarks, the projects are not easy to implement. They need to be monitored close-ly, diverse interests in the communities should be taken into account and transparency as well as a more participatory approach is recom-mended in order to ensure greater chances of success. CBNRM projects, however, represent an important attempt to meet the interests of in-digenous groups and have the potential to contribute to greater wel-fare for at least some of the indigenous communities.

The Future of Indigenous Peoples in Southern Africa

With the exception of Zambia (1964) and Botswana (1966), independ-ence came to the other four southern African countries - Angola, Na-mibia, Zimbabwe and South Africa - after prolonged armed liberation struggles, which were often followed by inter and intra-group strug-gles which, in the case of Angola, lasted for well over 25 years. As dis-cussed in Akpan et al. (this volume), indigenous people in these coun-tries have been exposed to mass killings, torture and detentions without trial, and have witnessed massive human rights violations that could be described as either physical or cultural genocide or both. The prolif-eration of land mines in a country like Angola has turned huge blocks of agricultural, grazing and foraging land into no-go areas for years to come. Many indigenous people have been forced from their homes, been internally displaced or have crossed international borders and become refugees.[5] All of the countries in southern Africa have had to cope with refugees, establishing large camps such as, for instance, in Dukwe (Botswana) and Osire (Namibia). As documented by Pakleppa (this volume), the establishment of refugee camps can indirectly impact on local indigenous groups and threaten their well-being. But not all refugees are protected under national legislation and given assistance. Instead they are sometimes considered to be illegal immigrants without any rights, as in the case of the San in Zambia (see Akpan et al.).

Today, and with but a few local exceptions, the region is free of armed conflicts. Democracy is developing and countries like Namibia, Botswa-na and South Africa have progressive constitutions based on equality of rights (see Daniels, Chennells and du Toit and Mazonde, this volume). These countries are relatively prosperous, with diversified economies and a welfare system that meets basic social needs. All six southern Af-rican countries considered in this book have signed the African Charter on Human and Peoples' Rights, the International Covenant on Economic, Social and Cultural Rights, and the International Covenant on Civil and Political Rights (see Table 2) and, as noted previously, only two, Angola and Zimbabwe, have failed to sign the Convention against Torture and Other Cruel, Inhuman or Degrading Treatment or Punishment.

	International Labour Organization Convention 169 Concerning Indigenous and Tribal Peoples in Independent Countries 1989 (1991)	International Covenant on Economic, Social and Cultural Rights 1966 (1976)	International Covenant on Civil and Political Rights 1966 (1976)	International Convention on the Elimination of All Forms of Racial Discrimination 1965 (1969)	Convention on the Elimination of All Forms of Discrimination against Women 1979 (1981)	Convention against Torture and Other Cruel, Inhuman or Degrading Treatment or Punishment – 1984 (1987)	African Charter on Human and Peoples' Rights 1986
Angola	Not signed	10 Apr 92	10 Apr 92	Not signed	10 Oct 86	Not signed	02 Mar 90
Botswana	Not signed	Not signed	08 Dec 00	22 Mar 74	12 Sep 86	07 Oct 00	17 Jul 86
Namibia	Not signed	25 Feb 95	28 Feb 95	11 Dec 82	23 Dec 92	28 Dec 94	30 Jul 92
South Africa	Not signed	03 Oct 94	10 Mar 99	09 Jan 99	14 Jan 96	09 Jan 99	09 Jul 96
Zambia	Not signed	10 Jul 84	10 Jul 84	05 Mar 72	21 Jul 85	06 Nov 98	10 Jan 84
Zimbabwe	Not signed	13 Aug 91	13 Aug 91	12 Jun 91	12 Jun 91	Not signed	30 May 86

Table 2.

Status of Ratifications for Human Rights Charters, Conventions and Covenants

Souce: OHCHR 2004

Yet, as this book documents, the indigenous peoples of southern Africa - with only some exceptions - enjoy few of the rights enshrined in the constitutions of the countries in which they live and which, in most cases, are enjoyed by their fellow citizens, i.e. the right to retain their own cultural identity and be respected, the right to land and to water, the right to subsist and benefit from the natural resources that surround them, and the right to be heard and take part in the decisions that directly affect their lives.

It is interesting to note, in this regard, that none of the six countries have signed Convention No.169 of the International Labor Organization concerning Indigenous and Tribal Peoples in Independent Countries. In other words, none of the southern African governments have subscribed to the only international human rights instrument that deals directly with the rights of indigenous peoples.

As several authors (e.g. Saugestad, Mazonde) underline, one of the misunderstandings of southern African governments with regard to indigenous peoples' rights is the idea that protecting the rights of indigenous peoples necessarily means that a government would be giving special rights to one group over another. Indigenous peoples are quick to point out that they are seeking equitable treatment, not special treatment. They want the same rights as other groups: the right to be protected from arbitrary arrest and mistreatment, the right to organize and take part in the political process, and the right to benefit equally from development projects.

A second misunderstanding with regard to the indigenous peoples' rights movement in southern Africa is the idea that it will lead to ethnic conflict because of the promotion of what some government officials describe as "tribalism". Virtually all indigenous groups are in favor of multiculturalism. They do not want independence but rather autonomy to make their own decisions at the local or regional level.

An important draw-back for the San and the Khoe is that their leadership structures are not recognized by the dominant groups. And where the San have elected chiefs to represent them, as in Namibia (see Daniels, this volume), the government still reserves the right to recognize them formally. But, as shown by Pakleppa, even recognized San leaders do not easily get themselves heard and respected by the authorities.

Because of this, the indigenous groups of southern Africa are seeking to organize and to lobby in defence of their human rights. In doing so, they are employing a variety of innovative strategies that range from use of the Internet and media to conflict resolution and negotiation techniques. One recent development has been the creation of a San Council in South Africa (September 2001) and, more recently, in Namibia in March 2004 (see Saugestad). They have also resorted to legal means to obtain recognition of land and resource rights not only in South Africa, as already mentioned, but also in Botswana where a group of San and Bakgalagadi whose land access rights in the Central Kalahari Game Reserve were extinguished by the Botswana government (see the chapters by Saugestad; Hitchcock, Johnson and Haney; and Taylor) have taken the government to court in order to reclaim their land and resource rights.

Indigenous representatives have, since the 1990s, taken part in international fora on indigenous issues held by academic institutions and indigenous peoples' human rights and advocacy organizations, 6 and they have attended the meetings of the United Nations Working Group on Indigenous Populations (WGIP) in order to seek support for respect of their human rights and their land and resource rights. In the light of the international development on specific areas of rights, such as Intellectual Property Rights and Biological Property Rights, they have started to include these rights in their claims for recognition and respect. They have sought to have governments, international organizations and multinational corporations recognize their intellectual property rights and compensate them for the exploitation of culturally significant knowledge (see Chennells and du Toit, this volume). They have also made efforts to have the bodies, body parts and cultural property of individuals who had been taken to Europe for display or analysis returned. The two best-known cases of these repatriation efforts are those of El Negro and Saartje Baartman.[7]

While the indigenous movement is still in its infancy in southern Africa, steps are being taken toward establishing Africa-wide indigenous peoples' networks and promoting indigenous peoples' rights at the continental and regional levels, one example being the Indigenous Peoples of Africa Coordinating Committee (IPACC).[8]

As this book attempts to demonstrate, indigenous peoples in southern Africa are making some progress in their efforts to promote human rights and social justice. However, as Mazonde rightly remarks, real progress will first be achieved when a change in attitude has been initiated among the "blacks". It is therefore a significant landmark that the African Commission on Human and Peoples' Rights adopted and circulated a report on indigenous peoples and communities in November 2003 and, subsequently, set up a Working Group with a mandate to examine the concept of indigenous people, to study the implications of the African Charter on the human rights and well-being of indigenous communities, and to consider recommendations for the monitoring and protection of the rights of indigenous communities (Saugestad, this volume). It is therefore important that indigenous groups and their supporters are vocal about the discrimination they are coping with, and that they and their supporters put pressure on their governments to commit themselves - not only on paper but in deeds - to the elimination of all forms of racial discrimination. While they still have a long way to go, the indigenous peoples of southern Africa are convinced that their rights will be recognized and that they will be able to enjoy the fruits of development, democracy and social justice.   ❑

Notes

1   See Kuper (2003) and the discussions following his article in the section entitled "The Return of the Native", *Current Anthropology* 45(1):261-267, 2004; the discussions on African indigenous peoples in the journals *American Anthropologist* (e.g. Hodgson 2002), *Indigenous Affairs*, in the annual reports of the International Work Group for Indigenous Affairs entitled *The Indigenous World*, and reports by Survival International and the Minority Rights Group. For additional information, see Barnard and Kenrick (2001) and Kenrick and Lewis (2004).

2   The term apartheid means "apartness" of separate development in Afrikaans. The apartheid period in South Africa lasted from 1948 (election of the Nationalist Party) until 1994, when a democratic election was held in South Africa and the African National Congress (ANC) and its leader, Nelson Mandela, came to power.

3   Sip-wells are hand-dug wells in sandy places in the Kalahari Desert where San and other local people suck water out of the ground using their mouths as a kind of vacuum. These are highly labor-intensive water facilities; it sometimes takes a woman 5-8 hours to get sufficient water to meet her family's daily water needs.

4   This was noted by Roy Sesana, one of the leaders of First People of the Kalahari (FPK), in discussions with the media concerning the relocation of people out of the Central Kalahari Game Reserve in 2002.

5   Refugees are those persons who, owing to a well-founded fear of being persecuted for reasons of race, nationality, membership of a particular social group or political opinion, are outside the country of their nationality.

6   One example has been the conference on indigenous peoples of eastern, central and southern Africa held in Arusha, Tanzania (1999) and organized by the International Work Group for Indigenous Affairs (IWGIA) and the Pastoralist Indigenous Non-Government Organizations Forum (PINGOs Forum), Tanzania.

7   El Negro, a southern African man whose body was stolen from his grave in the early 19th century, was for decades on display in a small museum in Banyoles, Spain. His remains were returned to Botswana in 2000. Saartje Baartman, also known as the "Hottentot Venus", was exhibited, while alive, in France and England in 1810-1815. After her death, her skeleton, preserved genitals and brain were placed on display in the Musée de l'Homme in Paris, France. Her remains were repatriated to South Africa in 2002, after protracted and complex negotiations between South Africa and France (Parsons 2002; Davies 2003).

8   OIPA - the Organization of Indigenous Peoples of Africa - is another regional umbrella organization, with headquarters in Tanzania.

THE INDIGENOUS PEOPLES OF SOUTHERN AFRICA: AN OVERVIEW

Sidsel Saugestad

M yth and facts combine to give a special place to the indigenous peoples of southern Africa, known as Bushmen, Khoe, San, Basarwa and, more recently, by a number of specific group names. Myth has given them a special place in the origin and evolution of mankind, hailing hunter-gatherer San as the representatives of the way all mankind lived at the dawn of history, and Western thoughts have spanned the extremes of seeing them as "brutal savages" as well as "harmless people". Little of these debates affects, and even less benefits, the average San person in Botswana, Namibia and South Africa.

The contrast between the international attention of media and research, and the struggle they have in drawing attention to their everyday concerns is striking, and this is part of the justification for this volume. This overview will be divided into three parts. The first will focus on the region and give a brief historical background leading up to the contemporary socio-political context. The second will look at the international debate on indigenous issues and current codifications of indigenous rights, and trace the emergence of representative organisations in the region. In conclusion, some areas of controversy in the current debate will be examined. This overview provides a background to, and hopefully also justification for, the need for constitutional reforms and recognition of the resource rights that are the topic of subsequent chapters.

The Conundrum of Ethno-Linguistic Concepts

But first a clarification of terminology that is of some significance for this volume. As no single term of self-reference is shared by all Khoe-San languages, it is difficult to follow the preferred convention of using a group's own terminology. The most commonly used term is *San*, which has been adopted by San organisations as the best generic term (WIMSA 2003), and is also widely used by anthropologists (Lee and DeVore 1976). San refers to the descendents of the aboriginal population of the subcontinent, chiefly (but not exclusively) characterised by a hunting-gathering adaptation. In Botswana the official term is *Basarwa* and, for a time, the supposedly neutral term *Remote Area Dweller* (RAD) was used, although deeply resented by those to whom the term was applied. The term *Bushmen* is also widely used. There has been much debate over which terms have the most derogatory connotations but this debate has focused largely on the etymological and historical origin of the different ethnic labels, and not on their use. As any term takes on a derogatory meaning if it is used to express negative attitudes about a group of people, it is the social context, and as far as possible the wish of the people being named, that should guide the use of the terms.

Recently there has been a debate over the term "Khoesan", a term coined to refer to all Khoe-San languages, and to Khoe and San people. Khoe means "a person" in many languages and is also the name of the largest of the three families of languages (see Appendix on languages).

However, as an ethnic (not linguistic) label it has been used to refer to people who come from a mainly herding tradition (Schapera 1930; Barnard 1992). In South Africa many people who reclaim their indigenous ancestry after having for generations been labelled "coloured" use the term *Khoe*, *KhoeKhoe* or *Khoesan* (Bank 1998). Khoe people span a wide diversity from educated Griqua and Nama to destitute urban proletariat, and it is argued that in a socio-political context it is not always expedient to lump together Khoe and San in one category. WIMSA recommends that where researchers wish to refer to common gene type or to the communality of languages, the spelling Khoe-San should be used. Khoi is the English spelling; Khoe is the correct Khoekhoegowab spelling.[1]

The Southern African Region: Some Historical Background

At the World Archaeological Conference in Cape Town, January 1999, a popular joke was that there should have been a banner at the airport wishing those arriving "Welcome Home", to remind everyone that South Africa was the "cradle of mankind", as evidenced by the recent discovery of human fossils spanning 3.5 million years of human evolution. The artifacts of the Blombos Cave in South Africa, east of Cape Town, indicate that people living there 70,000 years ago were not only anatomically modern humans but were also creating weaponry and tools with engraving that must have had some symbolic significance (d'Errico et al. 2001). It might be tempting to identify San presence over an equally long period of time. However, for our purpose, which is to understand the relevance of history for the contemporary situation, we need to link the Bushmen's presence to past expressions of society and culture that demonstrate continuity with modern-day inhabitants. Such records are in the form of rock art, paintings and engravings, and sites associated with Late Stone Age tool assemblages. From about 25 to 20,000 years ago, there is evidence of cultural practices that were until recently still being followed by southern African hunter-gatherers, such as the making of ostrich eggshell beads, shell ornaments, bows and arrows and rock art. Some of the most recent rock paintings date back to the mid 19th century. San hunter-gatherer presence covered the whole African sub-continent from north of the Zambezi River in Angola and Zambia south to the Cape (Lee and DeVore 1976, Hitchcock 1999a).

Bantu-speaking pastoral people moved into the region, mainly along the eastern parts of the sub-continent (present-day Mozambique) around two thousand years ago, and along the western coast (present-day Angola into Namibia). In between those two strands of migration, the vast expanses of land adjoining the Namib and Kalahari deserts and stretching south to the Cape remained the area of San hunter-gatherers, and the closely related Khoe herders/pastoralists. Modes of adaptation were flexible, and reflect the ecological variations within the territories. Along the Cape coast, as well as in the northern regions, around the great Okavango Delta (present-day Namibia and Botswana), fishing was combined with hunting and gathering, and there is evidence of salt and copper production in the Makgadikgadi Pans near Nata (present-day Botswana).

The relative autonomy of the individual bands did not mean a lack of contact and trade relations. Relationships with the Bantu tribes in pre-colonial time included warfare on a smaller scale, but also coexistence and intermarriage. Assimilation with Bantu-speaking groups in the eastern part of present-day South Africa is demonstrated in a legacy of click sounds in the modern Zulu and Xhosa languages. Wilmsen (1989) documents early trade and exchange routes extending into the most remote areas of the Kalahari, and linked to exchange networks to Great Zimbabwe and the eastern coast. Integration in the global economy following colonisation led to extensive economic transactions, either directly or through Bantu chiefs as intermediaries between Bushmen who provided valuable goods such as hides, ostrich feathers and ivory in exchange for tobacco, guns and other consumer goods.

The Dutch colony established at Table Bay in 1652 led to extensive changes. The early encounters with the Khoe semi-nomadic herders of the Cape area, and later encounters with inland San hunters and gatherers, rapidly escalated from interaction and exchange into a tenacious appropriation of land, a process of gradual decay, reinforced by epidemics, diseases and drought. There are indications of a social hierarchy ranking hunters (Sonqua/San/Bushmen) below herders (Khoekhoe/Hottentot) (Smith 1999) but such differences were soon overshadowed by the unequal relationship between new settlers and the natives, which created a distinct class of people in a position of permanent dependence, cut off from their traditional means of production and livelihood, and barred from participating in the emerging, economically dominant, settler society. It is estimated that San probably numbered 250,000 – 300,000 before colonisation (Lee and DeVore 1976:5).

Annexation of land was a common feature of all relationships between colonisers and the native peoples of South Africa but relations with the San people were marked by an attitude of hostility and contempt probably not matched in attitudes to Bantu-speaking peoples, even during the worst periods of apartheid. Records abound of the way they were regarded as ultimate savages, in look and lifestyle. The words of the missionary Robert Moffat exemplify how Bushmen were regarded during the 19th century:

> Harsh is the Bushman's lot, friendless, forsaken, an outcast from the world, ...We can scarcely conceive of human beings descending lower in the scale of ignorance and vice (Robert Moffat, cited in Dowson 1992:3).

The following appeared in the British Parliamentary Papers in 1835:

> Regularly every year, large commandos, consisting of 200 and 300 armed Boors, have been sent against the Bojsmen, and ...generally many hundreds Bojsmen were killed by them, amongst which number there were perhaps not more than six or ten men, and the greatest part of the killed comprised helpless women and innocent children (cited in Dowson 1992:3).

Added to the social, economic and physical onslaught came an extreme linguistic prejudice: from the first contacts, there was a persistent attitude "that the language was utterly bizarre, unpleasant, inarticulate and not human" and further, "that the language was unlearnable" (Traill 1995:5).

Throughout the encounters with the incoming Bantu, and in the eyes of the European colonisers, there were three dimensions of contrast: the language (Khoe-San versus Bantu), physical type (the light skinned more slender versus the "black people"), and the mode of adaptation (combinations of hunting, foraging and herding in contrast to agro-pastoral tribal structures). Over the years, the contrasts have blended: many have lost their original Khoe-San language or are bilingual, intermarriage has modified genetic distinctions, most San are landless agricultural workers, or unemployed. However, the sociological contrast remains, albeit with different implications in the countries of the region.

Regional Variations

Trade routes, followed by missionaries and administrators, gradually penetrated the entire region. However, European settlement was concentrated in areas with good soil and climate, and it accordingly affected present-day South Africa and parts of Namibia to a larger extent than Botswana. The historical differences between the three countries are significant for understanding the contemporary situation.

Botswana: some 50,000 San, some Khoe

Except for some trading expeditions, Botswana did not attract many white colonisers looking for quick fortunes. The social structure of Botswana was shaped by the well-organised Tswana tribes that moved in from western Transvaal, from the period around AD 1200 (Tlou and Campbell 1984). For many centuries, Tswana presence was concentrated on the land on both sides of the current border along the Limpopo River. Developments within South Africa, pressure from white settlers, and the population explosion in around 1800 led to more extensive movements of Tswana tribes into the territories that now make up Botswana. The history of origin and arrival of contemporary Tswana and other Bantu-speaking people in Botswana is thus relatively short: apart from in the south-easterly part, it spans little more than two centuries.

The tribes that established themselves in the then Bechuanaland Protectorate were well organised, stratified structures, each with a chief or king. Through the control of land and cattle, the chief was able to distribute assets and privileges among his followers, according to their relative social position. These kingdoms, the most powerful ones later to be codified as the "eight main tribes" in the Constitution of 1966, found their place through dispersal, feuds and conquests, and were by early 20th century in control of most of Botswana. The exceptions were present day Chobe, Ghanzi and Kgalagadi, which remained sparsely populated, and came to be designated *Crown Land* by the colonisers.

British impact was minimal, and the Tswana chiefs suffered relatively little interference in their internal affairs. The changing fortune of the San population was thus determined by their relationship to the dominant groups in the country, a relationship that was not much modified by colonial rule. The Protectorate administration created *Native* or *Tribal Reserves* (roughly corresponding to the Districts after independence), generally assuming that land belonged to the tribe occupying an area, and tribal leaders retained considerable autonomy. To the extent that the colonial administration considered the rights of non-Tswana communities, they were conveniently assumed to be subject to the Tswana land use regime.

In the 19th century population density was low, and interaction between the San and other groups appears to have been fleeting, consisting largely of trade. In the more densely populated southern and eastern parts of the country, the indigenous Bushman population was gradually integrated within a semi-feudal relationship, while the dry savannah expanses of western Botswana were conquered as late as the second half of the 20th century, when improved borehole technologies opened up new expanses for cattle ranching. As incoming Tswana groups expanded, the San and other minorities were gradually incorporated into the stratified social structure of "Tswanadom". Social status was derived from cultural and kinship proximity to the chief (*kgosi)* and his family, while non-Tswana groups were incorporated into three broad classes in descending order: commoners, foreigners and serfs.

Most of the formal aspects of this structure disappeared long ago. Serfdom has been abolished, and the authority of the chiefs has been considerably modified since independence. However, the *marginalised position* described above is still a defining feature of the social context. This unequal relationship has had some obvious economic advantages for owners of property, as working conditions for many San, especially at cattle posts, are still of a semi-feudal nature, with terms of employment running from barely tolerable exploitation to benevolent paternalism. As water rights are granted to cattle owners (in other words, those who can afford to drill for water), and with a new fencing policy, the previous users of the territories become "squatters on their own land" (Bishop 1998) who must ask for permission to stay. Their hunting rights are restricted or have been abolished. In return for their cheap labour, the San are integrated into the economy at the very lowest level of the wider, economically stratified society.

The Khoe (or Nama), who may number up to 4,000, are found mainly in the southern and south-western part of the country. They are Khoe-speaking people who in the past were primarily pastoralists but now live on cattle farms.

Namibia: some 35,000 San, 100,000 Nama

Development in South-West Africa, now Namibia, was more similar to that of South Africa although, like in Botswana, the less fertile parts of the country were of less interest to the white settlers' commercial interests. German occupation matched the Boers in attention to racial details, creating an elaborate hierarchy of tribes, with a Bushman's life considered to be worth even less than that of a black person's. Gordon quotes headlines in the settler press from 1911 referring to the "Bushman Plague" and the "Bushman Danger" (Gordon 1992:57). The transfer from German to South African rule brought little change, as both assumed that disappearance of the Bushmen, i.e. assimilation into more civilised tribes, was only a matter of time.

Namibia's San include the Hai‖om and Ju|'hoansi as the largest groups, who are today found on white farms, in urban areas, in former government sponsored settlements such as Tsumkwe, and in small communities where people make their living through a mixture of foraging, herding and rural industry (Suzman 2001b). The apartheid legacy of creating *homelands* led to the identification of some of the traditional land of the Ju|'hoansi as *Bushmanland*. Even if there have, since independence, been problems in asserting traditional land rights, and even if this piece of land can only provide a livelihood for a small part of Namibia's Bushmen, the symbolic significance of the limited control exercised is significant.

South Africa: some 7,500 San, a considerable number of Khoe

A legacy of colonial rule in Namibia is the 4,000 !Xun and Khwe people who worked for the South African Defence Force, and who were airlifted from Namibia during the final days of South African occupation in 1990. Since then, these people have been located in a provisional tented army camp near Kimberley, and are only now being settled in proper living quarters. They make up the largest existing Bushman settlement of any country, most untypical in the way that this settlement was established but typical indeed in falling outside of the regular format of welfare provisions set up by a modern state to care for its inhabitants.

The few descendants of the South African Khoe and San groups who were not physically exterminated during the 18th and 19th century, or who did not perish from disease or poverty, disappeared within the apartheid category "coloured". They became doubly invisible, as the drama of South African politics was dominated by the overriding black-white dichotomy, with "coloured" a residual category of diverse individuals lumped together for administrative purposes. Apartheid politics towards the black, and the land use regulations creating the *Bantustans,* dominated the picture. In the new South Africa, the deconstruction of the category "coloured" has brought about a Khoe-San revival and a new recognition of the remaining San, adding further diversity to the contemporary picture of indigenous peoples (Robins et al. 2001, SASI 2002). There are also smaller populations of San in Angola, Zimbabwe and Zambia, as demonstrated by the Regional San Assessment (Robins et al. 2001), although the numbers are very uncertain.

San woman, CKGR. Photo: Diana Vinding

San, Angola. Photo: WIMSA

San boy, Botswana. Photo: Arthur Krasilnikoff

Himba woman. Photo: Mark Hakansson

Angola: some 3,500 San

Several thousand San, mainly !Xun and Khwe, used to live in the southern part of Angola. For more than 40 years living conditions were primarily determined by war, first employed by the Portuguese to fight the liberation armies in Angola, and later by the South African Defence Force to fight SWAPO in Namibia. A majority has now migrated south to Namibia, and a few into Zambia. Today, little remains of the natural resource base, or the cultural skills to utilise the environment. In 2002, representatives of Angola San participated for the first time in the Annual General Meeting of WIMSA, and efforts are underway to establish some sort of representative organization (see WIMSA 2003).

Zimbabwe: some 2,500 Tyua San

An estimated 2,500 Tyua (Shua, Chwa) live in the western border area of Zimbabwe and are related to the Tyua on the Botswana side. They were relocated out of the Hwanke National Park in the 1920s and 1930s. They rely on a mixed economy, combining subsistence crops, some cattle and goat rearing and some foraging. Many Tyua work for other people, including Ndebele and Kalanga, as herders or agricultural labourers.

Zambia: some hundreds

Zambian San live in the western borderlands region, having moved across the border from Angola during the civil war. Some small communities of Khwe were recognised as refugees in the 1970s, while larger groups (some 300) have moved across the border in recent years. The Khwe are not recognised as Zambian citizens, and they are thus not entitled to drought relief. They are also excluded from other government services, and depend on support from a Catholic Mission (Brenzinger 2000).

Present Policies

Despite the many similarities in the situation of the San across the sub-continent, there are significant differences in national policies. This is to a large extent related to the different processes of transformation from colonial rule and apartheid to independence and democracy. In southern Africa, negative stereotypes of the San were not abolished with the demise of colonialism and apartheid but were to some extent replaced by new ones, expressing the sentiments of the new regimes.

Botswana is almost unique in Africa in not having been through a liberation struggle. The transfer from old to new regime was peaceful, and the position of the traditional chiefs was recognised alongside the new structures (Parliament and District Councils), as was a House of Chiefs alongside the regular Parliament. The new Constitution guaranteed the "Protection of Fundamental Rights and Freedoms of the Individual...whatever his race, place of origin, political opinions, colour, creed or sex". In the 1960s, as a neighbouring state of apartheid South Africa, this was a courageous and visionary statement.

However, the strategy chosen in Botswana has been to over-communicate an image of a non-racial, non-ethnic homogenous state. The political rhetoric ignores the *de facto* cultural diversity of the nation. In effect, this has meant that the culture and language of the numerically dominant Tswana people have become the dominant symbols for Botswana as a nation. The social divide between majority and minority is acted out in daily interactions that reinforce the differences and inequalities. In Botswana, the moral force behind this negation of cultural diversity has probably been a major obstacle for San emancipation. San/Basarwa does not exist as a category in legal documents and public policies. Ironically, this professed liberal and non-discriminatory negation of the distinct culture of the Basarwa can be seen to have had a damaging effect on their self-image and their potential for self-realisation, very similar to the blatant discrimination of the apartheid system further south.

Independence in Namibia was brought about by an entirely different process. A successful war of liberation brought in a new regime in 1990, many of whose members had spent several years abroad, and who were returning with new ideas about good governance and democracy. Moreover, the heterogeneous ethnic composition of the country, without one single dominant majority, could not be ignored so that, from the outset, Namibia adopted a policy that recognised a diversity of cultures and languages. Finally, the new government's opposition to the racist policies of the previous regime made for a very liberal and open attitude to the challenges of ethnic diversity, very similar to the political climate in South Africa post-1994 but in marked contrast to the regime in Botswana.

A case in point was the two Regional Conferences on Africa's San Populations, held in 1992 in Windhoek and 1993 in Gaborone respectively. The initiative taken in Namibia expressed the progressive attitude of that time, encouraged by a close relationship with the international donor community (SIDA and NORAD[2]), which funded those conferences. On both occasions elected San representatives met with

Government representatives and NGOs, and passed a number of resolutions on education and culture, land, health and social welfare, employment and economic opportunities, water and communication. The preamble to the first conference in 1992 described the event as charting "an ambitious path towards goals of social equality and dignity for San peoples, as well as a sustainable future for them as participating citizens of several new African states" (Namibia 1992:2). It was a diplomatic coup to arrange the first one as a cross-border conference that obliged Botswana to organise a follow-up the next year (Botswana n.d.; Saugestad 2001a). This was one of the very few occasions when the Botswana government met with San representatives on an equal footing, but there was no follow-up to the resolutions passed.

In Namibia, recent developments show a more mixed picture. Significant progress has been made in some aspects of legislation, in terms of facilitating mother tongue education, recognising traditional authorities, and economic promotion though the establishment of community-owned enterprises and conservancies. A more negative development has been the unrest in the Caprivi Strip, where some groups of Khwe felt threatened by stronger groups and took refuge in Botswana. The situation was aggravated by the civil war in Angola spilling over the border into Namibia. There has also been relentless pressure on the small piece of land set aside for the Ju|'hoansi by Herero repatriates from Botswana, while government plans to transfer 20,000 refugees to the area, hardly able to cope with its current 6,000 inhabitants, was eventually abandoned.

It is an illustration of the rapid changes in South Africa that there were no San present at the two regional San conferences of 1992 and 1993. At that time, the "visible" San community was the !Xun and Khwe airlifted from Namibia, and cross-border diplomacy made travel difficult. By the end of the century, the presence of the San had been rediscovered. Important stages in this process were the Miscast exhibition in 1996 (Skotnes 1996) and the large Conference on Khoesan Culture and Identity in Cape Town in 1997 (Banks 1998), and the spectacular legal case in 1999 restoring parts of the Kalahari Gemsbok national park to the traditional inhabitants, the ‡Khomani San. Like in Namibia, the new regime in South Africa brought with it entirely new ideas about representation and participation. It is the only African country that has so far even considered adopting ILO Convention No.169 (IPACC 2003/4). Activities in South Africa reflect many aspects of the International Indigenous Movement, and we shall consider some of the international trends before examining some of the implications for policy and organisational development in southern Africa.

International Perspectives on Indigenous Issues in Southern Africa

During the 1970s and 1980s, indigenous organisations and advocacy organisations put forward an understanding of indigenous development that proposed an alternative to withdrawal, submission or assimilation. The practical applications of such new perspectives on indigenous development comprise some of the major topics of this volume. The international movement is based on a recognition that the problems of being indigenous, as experienced in South Africa, Namibia and Botswana, are similar to those in New Zealand, Australia, the Americas, Scandinavia and a great many other places. Despite regional differences, the common criteria of indigenous peoples are the same: numerical minority, non-dominance, i.e. no influence over policy formulation in the respective nation states, and a relationship to land that is not reflected in the regulations for land use as laid down by the nation states. In the new movements, old characteristics and new dimensions blend.

A combination of attitudes characterises this situation: a generally disparaging attitude on the part of the majority, often combined with discrimination and/or stigmatisation, acted out in practice even if not upheld in any formal laws or regulations. The premises for interaction are laid down by the majority, and the knowledge and competence of the indigenous people are not considered as qualifications either within the education system, or in working life, or in the political system. Beyond internal differences, indigenous peoples have two things in common: their experience of being disadvantaged in relation to the national majority, and the recognition that this disadvantage is related to their structural position within the state.

Indigenous organisations began forming in Western countries in the 1970s, with American and Canadian Indians, Inuit, Saami, Maori and Aboriginals among the pioneers. The early phase was characterised by a "politics of identity", and the development of organisations that claimed recognition of cultural distinctiveness. For instance, one of the first objectives of the World Council of Indigenous Peoples was to be given NGO status at the United Nations. The 1980s and 1990s moved on to what one might call a legal phase: the preparation of international conventions within the UN system, and epoch-making legal decisions such as the Mabo case in Australia, the recognition of Nunavut in Canada, and national political debates leading, for instance, to Saami parliaments in Norway, Sweden and Finland.

This process has been instrumental in changing the international landscape. The most important events have taken place within the United Nations system: ILO Convention No.169 concerning indigenous and tribal peoples in independent countries in 1989; the UN Year of Indigenous Peoples in 1993 and the subsequent decade 1995-2004; the process around the annual meeting of the Working Group for Indigenous Populations, attracting around 1000 indigenous representatives, activists and academics to Geneva for one week in July; the UN Draft Declaration on the Rights of Indigenous Peoples which is now on its cumbersome way through the UN system, and the opening of the UN Permanent Forum on Indigenous Issues in New York in 2002. Moreover, public funds and support structures such as Survival International, Cultural Survival and the International Work Group for Indigenous Affairs (IWGIA) provide logistic and financial assistance so that indigenous representatives can participate in the multitude of fora that debate these issues.

The legal basis for claiming indigenous status is still weak. The only legally binding statement about indigenous peoples is found in ILO Convention No.169, which so far has not been ratified by any African country. There is a long way to go before the United Nation's Draft Declaration on the Rights of Indigenous Peoples is put before the General Assembly, and many African states are among the strongest opponents to the declaration (IWGIA 2003). However, the significance of concern for indigenous issues cannot be measured solely by its weak legal status. The very formulation of these international instruments, described by some as "customary international law" (see Anaya 1996), introduces a moral standard and sets a new agenda. This moral standard is not a matter of degree, and cannot be measured by number of ratifications alone. In other words, even if legal implications are at the core of the concept, we must also look at its sociological significance. The need to balance general ideals of equal rights for all against the special protection needs of the minority is a challenge for all democratic states with indigenous minorities within their borders, and is part of a broader liberal dilemma as to how to handle differences.

Both indigenous organisations and the UN system argue strongly against a very strict definition of who is indigenous. The diversity of peoples and situations is such that a universal definition would inevitably exclude some peoples. Moreover, it is cautioned that many governments may use a strict definition as an excuse for not recognising indigenous peoples within their own territories. However, even if there is no binding definition, the way the concept is being used within the United Nations system, particularly in the Draft Declaration, has had a tremendous impact, highlighting the following elements: a priority in time; the voluntary perpetuation of cultural distinctiveness; an experience of subjugation, marginalisation and dispossession; and self-identification.

First and foremost, "indigenous" is a relational term: a group is only indigenous in relation to another encompassing group that defines the dominant structures of the state. The meaning thus depends on context but one can reasonably conclude that ILO Convention No.169, and the UN Draft Declaration are rather precise, *not* in a strict listing of criteria and a definition of form but in a persistent focus on the *relationship* between indigenous peoples and the encompassing national state. The core feature of this relationship is the recognition of the nation-state - or rather *its lack of recognition* - of the distinct background and therefore distinct needs of the indigenous population. The relationship between a state and an indigenous minority is one of unequal distribution of power. The concept is coined to describe this inequality. It is also designed as a tool to change this inequality.

A highly interesting and promising process is currently being initiated by the African Commission on Human and Peoples' Rights. In 2000, the African Commission adopted a resolution concerning the promotion and protection of the human rights of indigenous peoples and communities in Africa. A Working Group was subsequently set up with a mandate to examine the concept of indigenous people, to study the implications of the African Charter on the human rights and well-being of indigenous communities, and to consider recommendations for the monitoring and protection of the rights of indigenous communities.

Bearing in mind that the African Commission has never before dealt with issues of human rights for indigenous peoples, the adoption of this resolution is a remarkable step forward. The Working Group was set up as a small task force of people, in their personal capacity as experts. A final report was submitted to the Commission in May 2003, and it was adopted at the 34th session in The Gambia, November 2003. The report includes an analysis of the human rights situation of indigenous peoples in Africa, including a discussion of the criteria for describing indigenous peoples in Africa, an analysis of the African Charter on Human and Peoples' Rights and jurisprudence of the Commission with a relevant bearing on the promotion and protection of the human rights of indigenous peoples and concrete recommendations to the African Commission (http://www.iwgia.org/sw371.asp).

San Indigenous Organisations

San organisations had started in Namibia before this current trend, with support from anthropologists who had been working in Bushmanland, where a sizeable Ju|'hoansi population had been left on a tract of land large enough to allow for the establishment of a territorially based development organisation. The *Ju/wa Bushman Development Foundation* was founded in the early 1980s to develop subsistence farming in the face of a lack of water, insecurity of land tenure, and the threat of predators. In 1991 the organisation was renamed the *Nyae Nyae Development Foundation of Namibia*. Political awareness and economic self-reliance have become important aspects of the work undertaken, and have been backed by the Nyae Nyae Farmers' Cooperative, later renamed the *Nyae Nyae Conservancy*. The aim has been to re-establish traditional land-use patterns, based on right of access via kinship and marriage to water points and the resources surrounding them, the *n!oresi*, and to develop a modern sustainable version of subsistence farming.

In Botswana, the longest and most sustained effort to mobilize the San has been through the work of the *Kuru Development Trust* in D'Kar. Projects were initiated to address the problem of unemployment among the large numbers of destitutes settling on the farms in Ghanzi. The Trust was founded in 1986 as a community-based organisation, initiating skills training, language and income-generating projects. In 1996 Kuru officially became a peoples' support organisation and during the early years of this century the organisation has reorganised once more, into what is now called the *Kuru Family of Organisations*, which has offices in Ghanzi and Ngamiland, and a number of separate organisations.

The San-based interest group *First People of the Kalahari* (FPK) was registered as a trust in October 1993. The main objectives of the organisation were listed as: to work for the recognition of the N|oakwe as one people and to advocate the rights of the N|oakwe people vis-à-vis the Botswana Government and the public; to create a National Council for the N|oakwe through duly elected representatives, and to work for the recognition of land rights; and to invigorate the culture as well as individual identification with the culture of the N|oakwe. (N|oakwe is a Naro term of self-reference, meaning literally "the red people"). The FPK suffered a severe setback when its first charismatic leader, John Hardbattle, died in November 1996. Its main activity has been to support the residents and former inhabitants of the Central Kalahari Game Reserve, and to facilitate the court case planned for 2004 which, it is hoped, will reclaim land and resource rights for the people who have been dispossessed.

The NGO follow-up to the resolutions of the Second Regional San Conference (1993) gave networking across the national borders high priority. A new organisation, the *Working Group of Indigenous Minorities in Southern Africa (WIMSA)*, was established in 1996 to provide a platform for San communities in Namibia, Botswana, South Africa, Zambia and Zimbabwe. WIMSA's mandate is to advocate and lobby for San rights, to establish a network for communication and exchange, and to provide training and advice to San communities on administrative procedures, developmental issues, land tenure and tourism (WIMSA 2003; www.wimsareg.iafrica). Education is another priority area (Le Roux 1999). WIMSA is looking for successful rural development models that could guide the implementation of income-generating and cultural projects. The challenge, as WIMSA defines it, is to steer development in a direction that builds on the culture of the people concerned and their concept of development, and at the same time relates in a realistic manner to the expectations raised by economic development, consumer patterns and material wealth that are spreading to remote parts of the countries. WIMSA has a main office in Windhoek and a small office in D'kar, WIMSA Botswana.

The *South African San Institute* (SASI), a support organisation founded in Cape Town in 1996 has, over the years, achieved some spectacular results in terms of capacity building, human resource development, language development and culture and heritage management. In Botswana, *Letloa Trust* was formed in 2001 as a similar service and support organisation for the organisations belonging to the Kuru Family of Organisations.

In collaboration with WIMSA, a South African San Council was formed in 2001. It aims to promote the rights of San communities at local, regional and national levels and to coordinate development plans, programmes and awareness raising campaigns among San communities. Its main achievement has been to secure San intellectual property and heritage rights against commercial interests that have sought to profit from San knowledge of the succulent Hoodia plant, in one instance, and the San rock art heritage site in the Drakensberg, in another. In 2000 a Khoisan National Forum was formed, calling on the government to implement measures to address their "vulnerability as an indigenous minority" and asking for representation of traditional leadership at central, provincial and local government levels. There is also a national Khoe and San Coordinating Council that unites Khoe and San Groups.

A Namibian San Council held its first constitutional meeting in 2004. Its ten members are elected by communities in the different Districts, according to a number of criteria for nomination. Among these are: to be literate in either English or Afrikaans, to speak at least one San language fluently, to be respected by one's community and show proof of being able to "stand up" for the community, and to have traditional leadership skills, understanding both San culture and basic customary rules.

It is a paradox that the San of Botswana, making up more than half of the world's total San population, have not yet been able to organise themselves into a Botswana San Council, although there are plans to achieve this before the end of 2004. There may be many reasons for this but a brief overview of public policy in Botswana shows how extreme poverty, ignored identity and denied legitimacy combine to make conditions for organisational development exceptionally difficult.

Areas of Contention: Identity, Poverty and Legitimacy

Communality among the San was to a large extent *ascribed* to them by Bantu neighbours and European explorers, later by scientists, according to such shared features as physical type, language and hunting-gathering as mode of adaptation. Earlier stereotypes of the wild and inhuman were replaced (as they became physically depleted) by romantic stereotypes of the noble savage. The commercial value of exotic, photogenic and beautiful people is still considerable, as is the market for coffee-table books and adventure stories on exotic Bushmen, trance dances, and magic healing sessions.

One may well ask what the relevant criteria for contemporary self-identification are. Modern theories of ethnicity and identity formation recognise the subjective and eclectic nature of selecting criteria for self-ascription: there is almost no limit to the criteria that may be used to signify communality within a group, and its contrast with others. Among relevant diacritica may certainly be physical traits, language and mode of adaptation, but there is no objective way of deciding their relative importance. There is a growing indigenous insistence, globally, that ethnic identity and status should be by self-ascription and no longer be determined by the ascription of others. Acceptance of this position, however, is less than universal, and the concluding part of this paper will consider some areas of debate in southern Africa.

Poverty

Some argue that the best way to assist San in their quest for empowerment is to concentrate on their almost universal poverty. In an assessment of the regional situation of the San, produced for the European Union, Suzman argues that the demonstrable poverty of the San groups should be justification enough to initiate special development measures:

> However, given the current political and economic climate in southern Africa, addressing the status of the San by way of appealing to rights pursuant to their status as "indigenous people" is not the wisest strategy at the moment. The evidence presented in this assessment suggests that there are adequate grounds for arguing that the marginalised and impoverished status of the San is so clear-cut that irrespective of questions pertaining to their status as an "indigenous minority", special measures should be adopted to improve their status relative to others (Suzman 2001a:34)

This is a valid point. Why challenge a sceptical government regarding the use of a controversial term when, perhaps, a term such as "marginalised minority" could be used to single out the most deprived section of a population equally well? It is a regrettable fact that most indigenous peoples in Africa - however defined - also find themselves in a situation of poverty and deprivation, lacking in resources, scoring low in education, often suffering from bad health, apathy, alcoholism and despair. Southern African governments, particularly Botswana, argue that one should not focus too much on the contentious and abstract issue of "indigenousness" but rather address the immediate and concrete situation of poverty. Development organisations, concerned with human suffering, might be inclined to agree with this and play down the political issue. Whether this is a wise strategy to follow or not depends on your objective. Clearly indigenous peoples' problems almost always include problems of poverty, which can be alleviated by welfare. The danger is that this may remove the symptoms but not the cause. A case study from Botswana, where the government has for many years run a welfare programme called the Remote Area Development Programme, may serve as illustration. The target group in this case is not identified by cultural or ethnic criteria but by a list of social problems that the programme seeks to remedy. The San, who make up the majority of the target group, are not described in terms of the culture, tradition, skills or other specific qualities that they possess. Rather they are identified by what they are lacking: *by not* having a tribal structure with formalised leadership positions, *by not* living in established villages, *by not* speaking the majority language, *by not* having access to a number of resources, and so on (Saugestad 2001a). The design of the programme is that of a welfare programme, and relieves some of the gravest social problems. But it is a programme that creates clients, rather than empowerment.

Norway was a main donor to the Remote Area Development Programme but pulled out around 1996. Later, as the controversy over the Central Kalahari Game Reserve hit newspaper headlines in Europe and the USA, the British High Commissioner to Botswana offered to call a conference on "Poverty Alleviation among Remote Area Dwellers", thereby subscribing to the official policy of addressing people in the marginal areas in relation to their capacity of being poor and in need of welfare. Newspapers reported that "The British promise to offer a solution to Basarwa problem" (*Mid-Week Sun* 04.03.98). The initiative was seen by San organisations as a severe step backwards compared to the Regional San Conference in Gaborone in 1993, which brought promises for consultations with San representatives that have yet to be honoured. The First People of the Kalahari and Kuru Development Trust, with the support of a dozen local NGOs, expressed considerable resentment at another top-down conference being planned without confronting the problems as the San people themselves perceive them, and the conference never materialised.

Identity politics may appear less radical than economic analyses challenging the economic mechanisms that almost inevitably relegate indigenous people to the bottom of society. However, and paradoxically, a focus on economic deprivation, even class conflict, appears to be more acceptable to many governments because it easily implies a tacit acceptance of the view that the problem of indigenous peoples is one of *poverty alone*. This is also why a more neutral concept of "marginalised minorities" may be correct enough as a description but still fails to serve as an instrument for social change.

Legitimacy

For all political movements, *recognition* is a key objective. In Africa, recognition of indigenous status represents special conceptual challenges. The historical roots of the concept identify indigenous peoples as the descendants of those who occupied a given territory that was invaded, conquered or colonised by white, colonial powers. Strikingly similar problems were created in places as diverse as the Americas and Australia. The racism of colonial powers left all of black Africa in a subordinate position which, in many respects, was similar to the position of indigenous peoples elsewhere. Compared to the colonial powers, all native Africans were first comers, non-dominant and different in culture from the white intruders. However, and in contrast to Australia, America and elsewhere, white colonial forces eventually *withdrew* from Africa. Subsequently, national politicians argued that all Africans are indigenous or, alternatively, that this is a distinction that does not apply to the African continent. Neither position helps us to analyse the complex internal relationships in parts of Africa *after* the liberation from colonial dominance.

Unless there is recognition of the way the San minorities have historically suffered from various forms of exploitation and domination within the national economic and political structures, their claim for recognition of special needs will easily be seen as going against the general democratic ideals of equality. One should also bear in mind that the claim for affirmative action goes against all bureaucratic preferences for clear and unambiguous target groups, and is generally seen as cumbersome.

Indigenous organisations argue for fairness, not special favours. In order to have their special needs recognised, they must engage in three types of relationship: between the organisation and the people they represent (the "constituency"); with the state and its administration, the target counterpart for negotiations; and with the international networks of similar organisations.

The speed of events in southern Africa this last decade has to some extent overtaken the organisations when it comes to local mobilisation. This leaves them wide open to accusations of a lack of representativity when they raise concerns in the political arena. Precisely *when* an organisation or a community-based structure becomes representative is not an easy question to answer. What we know is that at the same time as trying to continue a dialogue with the constituency they represent, the leaders of the new organisations must establish a platform for negotiations with national authorities. This involves the paradox that in order to defend their own cultural values they have to behave in ways which, in many respects, break with the norms and values of their culture. The more effective they are on the national and international scene, the less typical and "authentic" they will be. Such cases of "damned if you do and damned if you don't" at times impose a tremendous personal strain on people in leadership positions, a fact that governments may use strategically to weaken their position.

The chapters that follow will illustrate in greater detail many of the debates and dilemmas touched upon in this chapter. Indigenous peoples in southern Africa started their struggle later than their sisters and brothers on other continents. They face considerable challenges. This book helps us to understand how they are being dealt with and what they are themselves doing to enhance their lives. ❏

Notes

1   See the website http://sanculture.org.za/history_terms.htm
2   SIDA: Swedish International Development Cooperation Agency;
    NORAD: Norwegian Agency for Development Cooperation. –Ed.

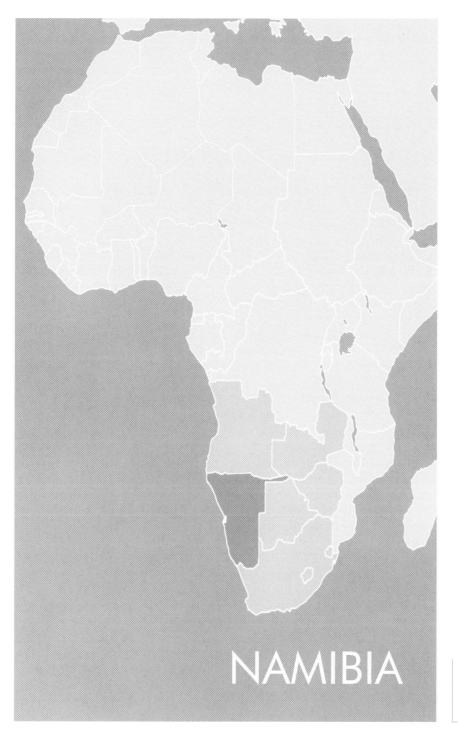

NAMIBIA

INDIGENOUS RIGHTS IN NAMIBIA

Clement Daniels

N amibia gained its independence in March 1990 after a period of colonial rule spanning more than 100 years and an armed liberation
struggle that lasted twenty-four years. After years of colonial domination characterized by a "divide and rule" policy in which "ethnic"
identities were emphasized, independent Namibia adopted a policy of
national reconciliation as a tool for nation building, discouraging the
use of "ethnic", "tribal" or traditional identities.

In reality, and although the Constitution prohibits discrimination
on the grounds of ethnic or tribal affiliation, ethnic identities are difficult to ignore and tribal affiliation still plays a very prominent role
when it comes to the redistribution of wealth and national resources.
It is also sometimes politically expedient and convenient to use tribal
and ethnic allegiances.[1]

The 11 major ethnic groups that compose Namibia's population of
1.8 million inhabitants - the Ovambo, Kavango, Herero, Nama, Damara,
Baster, Subia, Mafwe, Tswana, Himba and San - are highly diverse in size
and face very different socio-economic and political conditions. This chapter focuses on the socio-legal status of the Himba and the San communities, two of the most marginalised indigenous minorities in Namibia.

The Himba[2] is an independent pastoral society of approximately 20,000 people who live in the rocky terrain of north-west Namibia.
They are politically organized into four chieftaincies along the Kunene
river basin (Bollig 1997:13). According to this author, the Himba pastoralists were engaged in various forms of economic diversification
before 1920. They traded with Portuguese and Ovambo communities,
fought as mercenaries for the Portuguese colonial army, and entered
wage employment with traders, hunters and farmers. From 1920 on,
and for decades, the Himba have lived in relative isolation and even
the successive colonial administrations rarely interacted with them:
the South African colonial administration placed restrictions on the
movement of livestock and cut off opportunities for trade and wage
labour; and the Portuguese also constrained the economic activities of
the Himba on the Angolan side of the Kunene river. Bollig accordingly believes that the subsistence economy, which characterises Himba
communities today, was artificially created and enforced by the colonial administration. But he also describes the Himba as one of the
most successful and economically independent subsistent farmers in
Africa (ibid.:9).

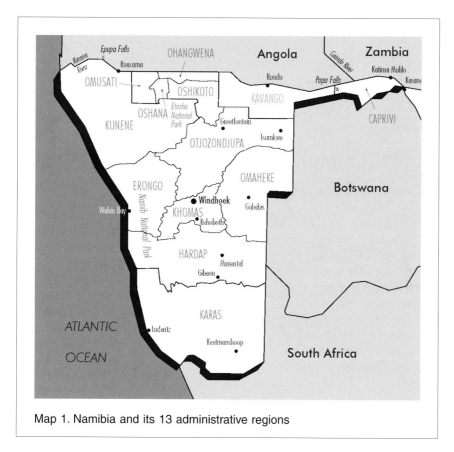

Map 1. Namibia and its 13 administrative regions

More recently, the Himba's main contact with outsiders has been with soldiers during Namibia's liberation struggle from South Africa and, recently, tourists and scientists have frequented the area.

The San consist of a number of socio-linguistically diverse communities of between 32,000 [3] and 38,000 [4] people who are settled throughout much of the north-east and east of the country. The ancestors of many of Namibia's contemporary San people were once the sole occupants of much of southern Africa. Indications are that these people lived in small, flexible and dispersed groups located in areas with sufficient natural resources to make settlement viable. For the most part these groups hunted and gathered, developing a formidable knowledge of their local environment and how to exploit its resources but, on occasions, they also traded with one another (and, later, with others) in addition to raising livestock (Suzman 2001b).

Soon after independence, the government showed a willingness to resolve all San-related issues and problems, such as matters relating to land rights, education and culture, social welfare and economic issues. A number of initiatives to improve the situation were implemented but very few have yield positive results. Many San are arguably worse off in some important ways than they were immediately before independence and, unlike the Himba who are relatively wealthy and successful pastoralists, the San constitute a highly dependent, impoverished and marginalised minority who, in terms of a broad range of socio-economic and development indicators, are considerably worse off than any other Namibian language group.

The Namibian Constitution

At independence, Namibia adopted a liberal constitution as the basic law and its system of government is generally described as a multi-party constitutional democracy.

The Constitution provides for a separation of powers between the executive, judicial and legislative branches of government. This is, however, not always observed in practice since Namibia has a dominant majority party, which enjoys almost eighty percent of national support. There are three tiers of representative government, namely, a national parliament, which consists of the National Assembly and National Council, regional councils in each of the 13 political regions and local authorities in the form of local municipality, town and village councils.

Before independence, the colonial administration applied policies of racial discrimination against the local population in almost all areas of social, economic and political life. A vast number of people were dispossessed of their land and restricted to certain parts of the country, the so-called communal areas (reserves). These areas were neglected, with the state providing very little or at times no development assistance to ensure the sustainable development of these communities. Private ownership of land and resources in the communal areas was severely restricted. The Constitution has perpetuated the situation by explicitly stating that the land, water and natural resources of Namibia belong to the state, if they are not otherwise lawfully owned.[5] This provision has further dispossessed the majority of Namibians from ownership of land and has limited their capacity to participate in the national economy.[6]

There is no specific recognition of the rights of indigenous peoples or minorities in the Constitution and neither is Namibia a signatory to any of the international conventions recognizing the rights of indigenous peoples. The definition of "indigenous peoples" is problematic and many countries have avoided it. Namibians popularly define "indigenous" by reference to European colonialism and ascribe indigenous status to almost anyone born in Africa, who is of an African bloodline. *The*

Traditional Authorities Act[7] defines all Namibian traditional communities as "indigenous". This certainly creates a problem for indigenous minorities in Namibia and there is accordingly a need to develop criteria to recognize indigenous minorities and provide for a form of "affirmative action" to address the special needs of such minorities.

The Constitution of Namibia, adopted by the Constituent Assembly in February 1990, is founded on five basic principles:

- Namibia is a secular and unitary state;
- Namibia is a multi-party democracy with universal franchise;
- The state shall uphold the rule of law and justice for all;
- A separation of powers between the three branches of goverment; and
- An enshrined bill of fundamental human rights and freedoms.

The Constitution is the supreme law and, amongst others, it recognizes the right of all citizens to practise their respective cultures, subject to the rights of others and the national interest of Namibia.[8] All people, including indigenous minorities, are entitled to and protected by the same rights guaranteed under the Constitution. It is, however, difficult and sometimes impossible to enforce rights on the ground. The existing liberal democratic legal system makes it virtually impossible for poor people to access the courts and the justice system. Equality before the law and justice for all remain principles on paper, since most individuals and communities lack the capacity to use the law effectively.

The Namibian Constitution is unique in that it provides for the automatic application of international treaties in the domestic legal system, once they are ratified by parliament.[9] Namibia acceded to the International Covenant on Civil and Political Rights during 1994.[10] The International Covenant on Civil and Political Rights accordingly forms part of the domestic law of Namibia. Under the Covenant, all people have the right to self-determination, as well as the right to "freely determine their political status, freely pursue their economic and social development and to freely dispose of their natural wealth and resources". Namibia is also a signatory to the Covenant on Economic, Social and Cultural Rights and the Convention on the Elimination of Racial Discrimination, which indirectly addresses the rights of indigenous peoples, and which they could use to lobby for their own interests.

Namibia is a member of the International Labor Organisation but, like all other African countries, it is not a signatory to ILO Convention No.169, which is the only legally binding international convention dealing with the rights of indigenous peoples.[11] In southern Africa, the issue of minority rights has always had a bad connotation, since it is linked to the claim by "whites" that they are entitled to protection as a minority and have the right to self-determination.

Indigenous Peoples and Mainstream Politics

The participation of all citizens is necessary to maintain and nurture the newly established democratic order in Namibia. Like many other Namibians, the overwhelming majority of the San and Himba communities do not understand their rights and obligations in the new political dispensation. Their recent experiences of the democratically elected national government have also not convinced them of the virtues of democracy or its ability to protect their interests. Many San are apathetic about mainstream politics. As a small marginalised minority, they feel that they have little or no influence over national issues and developments. The Himba, on the other hand, seem to have their own understanding of government's role and have the confidence and courage to engage government (even the President) in a very confrontational manner with regard to the protection of their rights and interests.

The Constitution provides for the devolution of limited powers and an "advisory" role to Namibia's "traditional authorities". This constitutional provision recognizes the important role of traditional leaders in certain parts of Namibia and tries to incorporate them into the civil and political structures of government.

The colonial system of divide and rule and the creation of tribal reserves had revived (or in some cases reinvented) "traditional" leadership structures among peoples such as the Herero, Mbukushu and Kwangali.[12] However, the majority of San were dispossessed of their land and their largely vulnerable leadership structures, which had evolved in reaction to the presence of outsiders, were effectively dismantled during the colonial period: the fragmentation of social groups at all levels of organization through the loss of land and the need to provide labour in exchange for a livelihood undermined the very integrity of San leadership.

Despite the general lack of interest in mainstream party politics, in the ten years since independence some San community leaders, such as the late Kipi George, the Ju|'hoansi leadership of Nyae Nyae and others have developed an increasingly sophisticated understanding of mainstream political processes. They have utilized public support and national NGOs to articulate their concerns and are asserting what they consider to be their rights and, indeed, others' violations of these rights (Suzman 2001b:105). In the 1999 Parliamentary Elections, the

first San Member of Parliament, Kxau Royal |O|oo, was elected to the

National Assembly on the ruling party ticket.[13] But so far only two of the six established San traditional authorities, those of Tsumkwe East (Nyae Nyae) and Tsumkwe West, have been formally recognized by government.

The Himba community, on the other hand, has remained well organized with strong traditional leadership structures with effective control over their land and natural resources. Most of their leaders are recognized by government and have some political influence in the Kunene region, in particular their area of jurisdiction.

Some Himba from the broader Kunene region are represented at various government levels, but the communities from the Kunene river basin are not directly involved in national or regional politics. They are normally invited to and participate in regional ceremonial events, but are not involved in political decision-making. The leadership is respected as part of the Herero tribe. They normally express their views and lobby for support through the Herero leadership, which is well represented at all levels of government (Bollig 1997:56).

The Khwe's Struggle for Recognition as a Traditional Authority

The Traditional Authorities Act requires traditional authorities to apply for recognition from the state and must be recognized as such before they can assume their legally mandated roles and receive remuneration from the state coffers. In West Caprivi, the Khwe Traditional Authority is one of the most established San traditional authorities in Namibia. While the social and political structures of the San were under threat elsewhere in Namibia, Khwe were in the process of establishing a more centralized traditional authority. In the 1950s, the Khwe traditional authority emerged in response to increasing pressure from their neighbours in West Caprivi. According to oral histories, the former chief of the Khwe, Kipi George,[14] was elected in Omega in 1987 to succeed his grandfather, Tlaxa Ndumba. The community formally installed George as chief of the Khwe following Ndumba's death in 1990.

During the initial registration of Traditional Authorities immediately after independence, Chief Mbambo of the Mbukushu indicated that Kipi George and his people were Mbukushu subjects and, by virtue of this, that the lands they occupied were Mbukushu traditional lands. In doing so, Mbambo laid claim to the entire West Caprivi from the Okavango River to the Kwando River. At the same time the Mafwe chief (see Harring, this volume), Boniface Mamili, also made claims over the Khwe and the lands of West Caprivi. He claimed that Kipi George was a Mafwe councillor. Few Khwe consider themselves subjects of the Mbukushu or Mafwe Traditional Authorities and written historical sources support this notion unequivocally (Brenzinger 1997). The Khwe Traditional Authority also submitted a separate application for recognition as a traditional authority.

In March 1998, the government announced that 31 leaders, and hence 31 Namibian "traditional communities" had been formally recognized.[15] Not one of the six traditional authorities from San communities that initially applied for formal recognition was listed. Following a formal complaint, the government requested that they submit their claims in writing, which they did. These claims were submitted to the Investigating Committee on Tribal Disputes for assessment. This committee recommended that only the two traditional authorities that retained an autonomous land base should be recognized and that further consultations would be required regarding the four outstanding applications.

After the Namibian government allowed the Angolan Armed Forces (FAA) to operate against UNITA from Namibian soil in 1999, the Kavango and West Caprivi region became insecure due to increased banditry activities on the part of the UNITA rebel movement. The increased presence of the Namibian security forces and the Angolan government's armed forces also contributed to the insecurity of the area.

The San communities living in West Caprivi have suffered large-scale harassment at the hands of the Namibian security forces during this period of insecurity, and their traditional leadership believes that they are being victimized because they were used in the 1970s and 1980s by the former South African government forces in its military operations against SWAPO's liberation fighters.

The government finally decided not to recognize the Khwe Traditional Authority at the end of 2001. The community has accordingly instructed the Legal Assistance Centre to proceed with legal action for the recognition of their traditional authority and leadership, as well as their ownership of the disputed land. After an application was lodged, the President referred the matter back to the Council of Traditional Leaders for further investigation. The outcome of this investigation, which was apparently given to the President in November 2003, has not been made public despite several written requests from the community. The matter will now proceed to court in late 2004 or early 2005.

The Traditional Authorities Act makes specific provision for "traditional communities" that may not have had formal leaders in the past or for communities whose leadership structures were ignored and destroyed by the colonial regime. The Act[16] states that "every traditional community shall be entitled to have a traditional authority". From a legal perspective, therefore, the assessment of the San leaders' demands for recognition should be based entirely on whether the different San groups involved constitute bona-fide "traditional communities". There is reluctance on the part of the government to recognize the Khwe as a separate traditional community, entitled to its own leadership structures. The government's attitude reinforces marginalisation, poverty and creates opportunities for other communities to oppress the San.

Socio-economic Rights

One of the major concerns facing post-independence Namibia is the enjoyment of social and economic rights and justice for all people. There are huge income discrepancies and the gap between rich and poor is growing every year. The government has made serious attempts to address the situation by allocating huge financial resources to education, health and job creation. Unfortunately, improvements are very slow. Although more people have access to education and health care, there has been a general decrease in standards of services.

Very few socio-economic rights are recognized and enforceable under the Namibian Constitution. Article 20 of the Constitution provides for the right to education but indicates that only primary education for all children under the age of 16 is free and compulsory. Other socio-economic rights, such as the right to health care, to education in general, to social assistance and employment rights are contained in chapter 11 of the Constitution as Principles of State Policy, and depend on the financial resources of the state. It is accordingly not enforceable through the courts. Marginalised communities are obviously more affected since they lack the social and political clout to access state resources.

Health Care

In terms of the apartheid colonial policy, health care was provided on racial lines with white people receiving the best treatment while the health care of blacks was severely neglected. In the communal areas, very few doctors and hospitals were available. Since independence, there has been a concerted effort to reverse the situation by allocating a bigger share of the national budget to health care and by focusing on primary and preventative health care. A number of new hospitals have been built in rural areas, whilst hospitals and other health care facilities have been made available to all residents. Despite these efforts, many people believe that state-funded health care is deteriorating and, unless individuals have access to medical insurance, they are unlikely to receive proper medical care. The steep drop in the exchange rate of the Namibian currency has further affected the heath care situation over the last few years, since most medication is imported. The fast spreading AIDS pandemic is also causing severe pressure on health care resources. Close to 20% of all Namibians are HIV positive, with the rate of infection increasing every year, thus placing Namibia among the most infected countries of the world.

Among the San community, the human or spiritual world is often understood to play a role in a person's health and, in most cases, spirit mediums are engaged in the healing process. Inside and outside their own communities, the San are seen as very effective traditional healers due to their exceptional knowledge of herbs and traditional medicines. San healers are thought to have special skills and abilities that other traditional and registered medical practitioners lack The San are, however, not averse to Western medicine, which is sometimes seen as the best and only curative solution. The extent to which San make use of existing health services depends on the ailment in question and the availability of health care services.

The health status of the San is intimately linked to their poverty, lack of education and high mobility. Health Unlimited[17] has identified a number of health problems common among San communities, the most pervasive being tuberculosis, malaria and HIV/AIDS. Tuberculosis is the second most common cause of death in Namibia and the most serious health problem among San communities. Its prevalence is related to poverty and also to certain cultural practices that may facilitate its rapid transmission. The proper treatment of tuberculosis in rural communities has been hampered by a lack of transport to implement community-based Directly Observed Treatment Short courses (DOTS), the method recommended by the World Health Organization (WHO) for effective TB treatment world-wide. Amongst the San, the problem is further complicated by economic insecurity and mobility.

San communities are less affected by HIV than many others in Namibia but, due to interaction with other communities and poverty, it is unlikely to remain so for long. Because of the increasing numbers of San squatting around towns and villages in commercial and communal areas, they are at serious risk of HIV infection through alcohol abuse, casual sex, rape and prostitution in these areas. Among the Khwe in West Caprivi, AIDS is an immediate and visible problem and levels of infection within that community are consistent with those of the surrounding communities. Infection rates in the north-east of Namibia are the highest in the country and sexual relations between Khwe and others are frequent.[18]

The Himba have been described as one of the healthiest communities in Namibia due to their lifestyle and diet. Malaria, tuberculosis and sexually-transmitted diseases are the most common health problems.[19] According to recent reports,[20] there was a 78% increase in deaths from malaria between January and March 2001 (N = 24) and the same period in 2002 (N = 108) in the Kunene region. The Namibian Red Cross Society is providing primary health care to the Himba. This includes personal and household hygiene and preventive health education and water and sanitation awareness. They also supply fresh water to isolated households.

The rate of HIV infection amongst the Himba is low (approximately 7%) as compared to the national average (of approximately 20%). The obvious reasons for the low level of infection are the Himba's geographic isolation and marginalisation and strong cultural sexual practices. There is, however, a danger that infection may increase due to the practice of polygamy and the fact that women have no say over their own and their husband's sexuality. Should the Epupa Hydro project proceed, the expected influx of workers from other areas will certainly have an impact on the spread of HIV and AIDS within the Himba community.

Many local and international NGOs are involved in the provision of health care services but, without long-term government resources, these initiatives remain unsustainable.

The Himba and the Epupa Hydropower Scheme

The proposed hydropower scheme on the lower Kunene River, also referred to as the Epupa Dam Project, has focused both local and international attention on the plight of the Himba community in north-western Namibia. The idea of damming the Kunene River was suggested during the German colonial era but it was only after independence, that NamPower (the Namibian parastatal for the bulk supply of electrical power) began to advocate for the construction of a hydropower scheme in the Epupa area.

In the mid-nineties, discussions regarding the building of the dam gained momentum and a major feasibility study was undertaken by the government of Namibia, with support from Norway and Sweden. The first phase of the consultation process commenced in 1991 when Nampower and government officials visited the affected community in the Epupa area. This visit resulted in misunderstandings and most of the Himba were left with the impression that the Epupa dam would be a very small dam for livestock water consumption. The crucial issue of the inundation area was either not addressed or misrepresented by the aforementioned officials.

During the feasibility study in 1997, the Himba were informed of the size of the dam, the inundation area and other important factors that would have a major impact on their community. The Himba were obviously not happy with the misrepresentation.

Due to the difficulties in dealing with government officials and the complexity of the matter, the leadership of Chief Hikuminwe Kapika approached the Legal Assistance Centre to represent the community and to obtain legal advice. The government was not impressed with their opposition and tried to play down the community's concerns, accusing them of being against development and the national interest. The government was very sensitive to the international publicity generated by this issue and tried different means to silence the community, including discouraging journalists and environmentalists from having contact with the Himba, and monitoring community meetings. In July 1997 the police dispersed a first consultation meeting between the community and legal practitioners of the Legal Assistance Centre.

It was only after the Legal Assistance Centre obtained a court order from the High Court that the Epupa community was able to meet with their lawyers without fear of intimidation and harassment from government agents.[21] The police action was clearly in contravention of Articles 21 (d) (Freedom to assemble peacefully); 21 (j) (Freedom to practise any profession); and 13 (Right to Privacy) of the Namibian Constitution but, to date, no action has been taken against the police officers involved in disrupting the meeting.

The disruption of the meeting further undermined the relationship between the Himba community and the government. In February 1998, 26 out of the 32 traditional leaders from the Kunene Region in which the project is situated signed a petition stating that they were opposed to the dam. The government has argued that the Himba's opposition to the dam is a result of manipulation by foreign environmentalists and local tour operators.[22]

The impact of the proposed dam at the Epupa site on the Himba can be summarized as follows (see Corbett 1999):

- The Himba will lose valuable land resources and 110 permanent dwllings.
- The loss of riverine forests - a crucial source of grazing and browsing in dry seasons - will destroy the social and economic status of the Himba.
- The flooding of 160 ancestral graves will be a threat to their culture since a grave is a focal point for defining identity, social relationships and relationships with the land, as well as being a centre for important religious rituals.
- The Epupa site is expected to cause a health risk by producing higher incidences of malaria and bilharzia (schistosomiasis), as well as sexually-transmitted diseases, including HIV.

Discussions around the building of the dam have been on hold for the past three years due to a lack of interest on the part of the Ango-

Part of the Epupa Falls. Photo: Terese Sveijer

lan government.[23] Now that peace has returned in Angola, it is highly possible that the Namibian and Angolan governments may take up the issue of the dam more vigorously.

The San and Resettlement in Namibia

After independence, the government was faced with the reality that a number of people were impoverished and had been displaced as a result of many years of colonial exploitation, the liberation war and the deteriorating economic situation.

In the case of the San, the government showed a willingness to look for a solution to San-related issues and problems. A number of initiatives were taken but, to date, there have been few positive results. In 2001, Suzman summarized the San's socio-economic situation as follows:

- Despite almost universal dependence on the agricultural sector, only around a fifth of San have de jure rights to land. Large numbers of San people are consequently highly mobile and spatially unstable, lack security of tenure and are economically dependent.
- Very few San have adequate access to schooling. Despite the efforts of the government attendance levels are more than 50% below the national mean, while literacy levels are lower than 20%. Only a small proportion of San have attended school and a negligible number of them have completed formal education at school level.
- Per capita income among San people is the lowest in the country. The majority of San lack access to any independent means of subsistence. A sizeable number have no direct cash income and are almost entirely dependent on a single, declining sector of the economy.
- San life expectancy is some 22% lower than the national average, indicating their poor nutritional and basic healthcare status. In addition, a variety of serious social problems have arisen in San communities, including alcohol abuse, high levels of domestic violence, crime, depression and boredom.
- Few San outside of the NGO sector feel that they have any real say regarding their future or the direction their development should take. In almost all government run projects, a highly paternalistic top-down approach has been pursued.
- Dominant perceptions of San are mostly negative and San complain that they are confronted by prejudices towards them and are discriminated against on a daily basis (Suzman 2001b:1-2).

According to Suzman the most far-reaching intervention that can be made on behalf of San in Namibia is the protection and expansion of their land rights. In this regard, the stated aims of the government re-settlement policy that was finally adopted in 2001 directly address some of the key difficulties faced by San communities. According to these aims, resettlement should provide a safety net by allowing landless and impoverished settlers (San, ex-soldiers, returnees from exile, disabled people and displaced agricultural workers) to gain autonomous rights to land and become self-sufficient at a basic subsistence level (Harring and Odendaal 2002). The reality on the ground is, however, very different from the stated objectives.

Only a small proportion of San are beneficiaries of the resettlement programme. At present, approximately 7,000 San are resettled on 11 resettlement projects. Very little assistance is provided and the San are deliberately resettled with other more powerful groups, which creates conflict and leads to further impoverishment. The trend has been to settle large numbers of San in small areas where natural resource limitations restrict the capacity of settlers to become self-sufficient. This problem is most serious at Skoonheid and Drimiopsis, where between five and seven hundred settlers are expected to make a living from a total of 2,762 hectares[24] of land. Under these circumstances it is impossible for settlers to achieve any form of economic self-sufficiency as farmers.

At Skoonheid Resettlement Camp large numbers of other groups, who are not regarded as targeted groups, have settled and continue to occupy 80% of the land to the detriment of the impoverished San and Damara settlers. This is causing tremendous social conflict and is detrimental to the development of all settlers. The government is powerless and unsuccessful in its attempts to evict these illegal settlers through legal channels and the illegal settlers do not see why they should move for the sake of San (Suzman 2001b:99).

The Khwe and the Divundu Prison Farm

Divundu Rehabilitation Centre, a prison farm situated next to the San community-run campsite at Popa Falls, N//goavaca, was built in 1995 on the premises of a defunct government agricultural project. Although the Rehabilitation Centre is located on land under the jurisdiction of the Khwe Traditional Authority, they were not consulted during the planning stages. A letter from them requesting the government to disband the project was ignored. The Khwe wrote the letter because of their concern that the Rehabilitation Centre might have a negative impact on community-based tourism in the region. The building of the

Rehabilitation Centre proceeded with the consent of the Mbukushu Traditional Authority.

After the prison was completed, the government announced plans to extend it into the area currently occupied by the N//goavaca community campsite and the White Sands Lodge adjacent to Popa Falls on the Kavango River and decided that the Khwe living there would be compensated and resettled elsewhere.

The Khwe objected to these plans and, with the assistance of WIMSA, the Khwe Traditional Authority appealed to the government to work with them to find an amicable solution. The government agreed to convene a meeting to try and resolve the land dispute between the Khwe and the Mbukushu. The meeting was convened but, according to the Khwe delegation and other observers, both government officials and the Mbukushu delegation were biased and demeaning towards the Khwe.

At the end of the meeting, the chairperson, Martin Kapewashe, former Deputy Minister of the Ministry of Lands Resettlement and Rehabilitation, made a number of unilateral resolutions:

- The N//goavaca Community Campsite and the White Sands Lodge were illegal and had to be moved;
- An evaluation of compensation for the Khwe would be conducted;
- The Khwe would be allocated another place for a campsite;
- Land allocation in West Caprivi was henceforth to be handled by the Mbukushu Traditional Authority;
- The prison farm expansion would go ahead as planned. (Suzman 2001b:110)

In response, the Khwe leadership sought redress in the High Court in December 1997 and, represented by the Legal Assistance Centre, filed a 15-point motion in which they requested that:

- Their traditional authority be recognised with immediate effect and the contradictory claims of the Mafwe and Mbukushu be disregarded;
- The court declare that they were the owners of the land situated between the Kavango and Caprivi subject to the limitations of law; and
- That plans to expand the Divundu Rehabilitation Centre and evict them from N//goavaca be stopped immediately.

The government initially opposed the above motion but later expressed a desire to resolve it without recourse to the courts. Thus, in early 1998, the Attorney General's Office notified the Khwe leadership that the government had not only revoked its decision to evict the Khwe from N//goavaca but also that it was willing to reconsider the traditional leadership issue and, moreover, that they would defer to a Judicial Commission of Inquiry as far as the land issue was concerned.[25]

As mentioned above, in 2001, the government made a final decision not to recognize the Khwe Traditional Authority and their land claim remains in dispute. The government has, however, not proceeded with the extension of the Divundu Rehabilitation Centre due to the insecurity in the region. The Khwe have now instructed the Legal Assistance Centre to proceed with the above claim. The court application for the recognition of the Khwe Traditional Authority will also address their land claims.

The Hai‖om and the Etosha National Park

The Hai‖om San community were the original owners of the area that is now known as the Etosha National Park, one of Namibia's renowned tourist attractions. Although the park was declared in 1927, the Hai‖om were only forcefully evicted from the park in 1953. They have since been living and working on commercial farms and some resettlement areas in the Oshivelo corridor under extreme poverty and miserable conditions (Suzman 2001b:13).

In 1997, members of the Hai‖om community blockaded the two main entrances to the Etosha National Park. It was the first protest of its kind in Namibia since independence. Armed with bows and arrows, they prevented traffic (and tourists) from entering the park in a bid to draw public attention to their landless plight, as well as to their ancestral claims to areas in and adjacent to the park. The police were called in and broke up the demonstration with teargas and sjamboks.[26] Many of the protestors were arrested and spent a few days in detention, although all charges against them were later dropped.

The government subsequently agreed to negotiate with Chief Aib of the Hai‖om on their claim for alternative land for resettlement, together with certain concession rights to run tourism enterprises in the south-eastern part of Etosha National Park. These negotiations are still continuing, but are hampered by internal leadership disputes.

Conclusion

Marginalised communities in Namibia remain in a state of insecurity due to inconsistent approaches to development and a lack of policies that appreciate the marginalised position of indigenous communities. From colonization to globalization, most countries across the globe have shown a strong disregard for the rights of indigenous peoples, and Namibia is no exception. International efforts to protect the rights of indigenous peoples globally have been undermined by vested corporate and political interests.

There are, however, attempts (and some countries should be applauded for their efforts) to improve the situation of indigenous peoples. There are no easy solutions to the problems faced by indigenous peoples around the world but, by listening and respecting their views and addressing the problems with care and consideration, we can make a difference.

Efforts by the government and various NGOs in Namibia have made no progress in reducing San marginalisation or poverty and it is clear that greater efforts will be necessary to effect any meaningful change to their collective status in the future. San structural poverty is so deeply rooted that the fate of San in Namibia ultimately depends on the success of the Namibian economy as a whole. Those countries where indigenous minorities have been best catered for in recent years tend to have been those where the majority of the population enjoy first-world living standards and hence can afford to be charitable.

The success of any such interventions will be contingent on establishing a suitable policy framework that is cognisant of the causes of San marginalisation and the factors that reproduce it. Should capacity building and meaningful empowerment not be central to these efforts, San will very likely remain a dependent underclass heavily reliant on the State's resources.

The San have continued to experience social and political difficulties since independence and this has hindered their development. In West Caprivi, insecurity over land and leadership issues has been further complicated by the regional political problems that came to a head in 1999. The government has not recognized the Khwe Traditional Authority or their rights to land. San traditional authorities have a symbolic role that exceeds their legal status. Since they are inadequately represented in other public bodies, traditional authorities are expected to represent San interests in a variety of different forums. To ensure that this is effective the following should be implemented immediately:

- Government should recognize the San traditional authorities;
- NGOs should maintain and expand support for existing San traditional authorities with particular focus on capacity building and institutional support; and
- San traditional authorities should themselves work towards strengthening their respective communities, with donors and NGOs providing material support to this end.

The situation of the Himba community and the Epupa Hydro scheme remain unresolved. It has, however, focussed the attention of many Namibians on the vulnerability of marginalised communities when governments are determined to implement major development projects. It has also revisited the debate about the concept and process of development in a constitutional democracy.

The dam controversy has also helped the community to look at other indigenous as well as modern development options for the social and economic empowerment of the people. It has also assisted the broader Namibian society to understand the importance of involving people in the discussion of development projects.

Acknowledgements

This chapter relies heavily on Dr James Suzman's comprehensive study *An assessment of the Status of the San in Namibia* (2001b), and the social impact assessment of the Epupa Project by Dr. Michael Bollig: *Resource Management and Pastoral Production in the Epupa Project Area* (1997). The chapter also draws on cases dealt with by the Working Group for Indigenous Minorities in Southern Africa (WIMSA), an umbrella organization representing most San organizations in the region, and the Legal Assistance Centre, a public interest law center involved in public interest litigation, in particular on land and environmental issues affecting poor and marginalised communities in Namibia. ❑

Notes

1   It is also sometimes politically expedient and convenient to use tribal and ethnic allegiances, as it is a reality that people feel strong loyalty to their ethnic group.
2   The Himba are sometimes called the Red People because they traditionally cover their bodies, hair and the animal skins they wear with a mixture of butterfat and a powder ground from the iron ore ochre. See Ezzell, 2001.
3   Suzman, 2001b:4.
4   Joram I Useb, WIMSA. Address to the 19th Session of the UN Working Group on Indigenous Populations, Geneva, 23-27 July 2001.
5   Articles 100 and 124 of the Constitution.
6   People in communal areas cannot use the land, which they have worked for centuries, as collateral to obtain loans or capital investments because they are not the legal owners. Because of the "red line", a veterinarian cordon fence placed between the communal areas and the so-called "police zone" during the colonial period to avoid the spread of animal diseases from the communal areas, movement of livestock and meat products from the north to other parts of the

country was restricted. The red line still exists fourteen years after independence. Namibians are not allowed to freely sell their livestock in the area south of the line. See the paper by Gottfried Wellmer, Implications of the Red Line on the Namibian Economy, presented at the Civil Society Conference on Land Reform, Windhoek, October 2001.

7   Act 17 of 1995 (as amended in 1997).

8   Article 19 of the Constitution.

9   Article 144 of the Constitution.

10 Debates of the National Assembly, Vol. 41:30.

11 Namibia has not ratified this convention despite the fact that ILO membership is written into the Namibian Constitution.

12 The Mbukushu and Kwangali are subgroups of the Kawango. –Ed.

13 Kxau Royal was only preceded by Geelbooi Kashe, who served in the Constituent Assembly (1989) and the first National Assembly (1990) on behalf of the Democratic Turnhalle Alliance (DTA).

14 Kipi George fled to Botswana from the Caprivi region with some of his followers in 1998. He become very ill and was granted permission to return to Namibia in 2000 by the government. He subsequently died in his home village.

15 Government Gazette, No. 1 828.

16 Section 2 (1) of the *Traditional Authorities Act*.

17 A UK-based NGO that provides preventive health care to rural San communities in the Omaheke and Otjozondjupa Regions.

18 NACP/MOSS reports that infection rates among pregnant women at Andara, Rundu and Katima Mulilo in 1997 ranged between 17.3% and 25.7%.

19 This is according to Abel Augistino, the regional manager and health coordinator of the Red Cross in the area. The Red Cross is the only NGO active in the provision of preventive heath care amongst the Himba.

20 Dr. Naftali Hamata, Director of the North-western Health District, as reported in the *Republikein* newspaper, 11 April 2002:1.

21 *Kapika v Government of the Republic of Namibia* (unreported September1997).

22 Michael Bollig, who conducted the social impact assessment, indicated that the interaction with foreign tour operators and environmentalists is so limited that it is incomprehensible that they could have an impact on the Himba decision-making.

23 The Angolan government had previously indicated that establishing peace in Angola was a national priority as opposed to the building of the dam.

24 This figure is based on the area available to San settlers at Skoonheid rather than the hectarage of the entire farm.

25 See *The Namibian* 6, 9 and 21 January 1998.

26 A sjambok is a strong and heavy whip made out of rhinoceros or hippopotamus hide used in South Africa for driving cattle and sometimes for administering chastisement. –Ed.

INDIGENOUS LAND RIGHTS AND LAND REFORM IN NAMIBIA

Sidney L. Harring

Namibia, independent only since 1990, is a big country – larger than Texas and New Mexico together - with a small population of 1.8 million - two facts that should mitigate the country's indigenous "land problem". While these demographic forces may offer some opportunities for meaningful land reform, Namibia is also one of the most unequal nations on earth measured in terms of the gap between its richest and poorest citizens. There is an awful symmetry to this fact: about 4,500 white families "own" nearly 50% of the arable land, primarily in the form of vast cattle ranches, while over a million Africans share, under customary law, the remaining arable land, largely subsistence plots on communal lands. In addition, Namibia is a difficult land to inhabit: vast tracts of desert lands are unsuitable for agriculture and are owned by the state, held as national parks or in the "Diamond Area".[1]

It is in this context that the issue of indigenous land rights must be analyzed. Namibia's two indigenous peoples, the San and the Nama, adapted to living in this harsh environment over a period of thousands of years. The San, in fact, are a number of distinct linguistic groups: James Suzman (2001b:3-4) identifies seventeen San dialects occurring within five distinct San languages, of between 32,000[2] and 38,000[3] people, who live in distinct communities across much of Namibia but concentrated in the north.

The Nama, a Khoesan people, number about 80,000 in fourteen distinct groups, living in a number of communities, mostly in southern and western Namibia. Like the San, they are ethnically distinct from the Bantu majority - Ovambo, Kavango, Herero and others. The Damara, about 132,000 people who speak a Nama language, are a black people who moved among the Nama prior to the Bantu migrations, and constitute a related but distinct people. There are eleven distinct subgroupings of the Damara. While the Damara are ethnically distinct from the Nama and San, their long occupation in Namibia and their close cultural relationship with the Nama gives them some claim to an indigenous status, derived through the Nama.

These peoples, hunter-gatherers, pastoralists and small farmers, the original occupants of Namibia, were displaced by successive migrations of Bantu peoples from Angola. The Bantu had pastoral economies that were inconsistent with hunting and gathering as cattle depleted natural grasses and disrupted wildlife migration and traditional subsistence food sources. These displacements were sometimes violent, with patterns of cattle raiding and territorial warfare continuing until the twentieth century. The Herero moved first into northern, then into central Namibia. The Ovambo and the related Kavango moved into northern Namibia. These people not only displaced Namibia's indigenous peoples but also currently outnumber them and dominate Namibia's political order, constituting 70 to 80% of Namibia's population (Malan 1995). Thus, the "indigenous" land rights issue pits minority ethnic groups against larger black groups who now hold political power.

This brief description of some of the eleven ethnic groups[4] that make up Namibia needs to be understood within the framework of Namibia's legal structure of land holding. A system of "legal dualism" in land tenure, in common with Zimbabwe and South Africa, means there are three distinct "land rights" issues in Namibia that are interrelated but need to be separated for the purposes of discussion.

Land Rights: Three Distinct Issues

The first land rights issue, as in any colonial-settler society, is the problem of the "stolen lands", the vast white-owned farms averaging more than 8,000 hectares each and, given a majority black political demand for "land reform", the redistribution of those farms to blacks. The white landowners, as in South Africa and Zimbabwe, have a European standard of living in the midst of the poverty and suffering of rural southern Africa. This political demand for "land reform" has assumed an urgency since the land occupations in Zimbabwe in 2000, a country with a similar distribution of agrarian wealth (see Akpan et al., this volume). Without some redistribution of these white-held lands, there simply is no land available to any native peoples to redress either indigenous land deprivation issues, or issues of poverty alleviation and social justice.

A second land rights issue, legally distinct but politically and economically interrelated, is the tenuous legal and economic situation of black, San and Khoesan peoples living on Namibia's vast communal lands, almost 50% of the arable land in the country.

These communal lands are held by all of the "native" people of Namibia, with no distinction made between the "indigenous" peoples and the Bantu peoples who migrated to Namibia in the pre-colonial period. Within these communal lands, the different ethnic groups carry on a wide variety of subsistence activities, largely dependent on their access to the land. Under South African administration, each of these groups was given its own distinct communal area, a "homeland". This policy, named the "Odendaal Plan" after its architect, Fox Odendaal, was designed to both weaken and divide the non-white population of

Namibia, as well as to ensure a permanent and cheap labor force for white enterprises (see Map 2).

While these communal lands are under "native" occupation, the Namibian government claims that the state "owns" these lands, creating serious land tenure issues for all communal landholders. These lands are overcrowded, sometimes poorly managed, environmentally degraded, remote from economic development and impoverished. The average subsistence farm in the communal areas provides no cash income at all and an "in kind" annual production of under Namibian \$200[5] worth of food crops, often distributed among a three-generation family.

Finally, there is an "indigenous land rights" issue, distinct from that of "communal land rights".

The original inhabitants of Namibia, the San and Nama peoples, have only limited land rights in the communal lands. These rights amount to a small proportion of the land that they occupied originally as indigenous peoples, and largely consists of environmentally degraded and very dry desert lands. Only about 10% of all San have land rights in the "communal area" of Tsumkwe District - under the apartheid era known as "Bushmanland" (i.e. the homeland of the Bushmen as the San were called then) - the remaining 90% live outside the District, mostly in either other communal areas, such as Ovamboland, Kavangoland, Caprivi and Hereroland, or on white farms. A much larger but indeterminate number of Nama and Damara have "communal land rights" in Namaland and Damaraland. Some of these peoples claim "indigenous land rights" distinct from the "communal land rights" of the Bantu peoples who settled Namibia after about 1600.

Therefore, the question of "indigenous" land rights in Namibia involves some complexity, as there were conflicts between African tribes prior to German and Afrikaner colonization, as well as considerable physical movement from one area to another. In addition, different peoples used their lands in different ways and during different seasons, providing for overlapping indigenous land rights claims. For example, the San carried on their traditional hunting and gathering by moving away from the pastoralists, who moved cattle into their lands, retreating into desert lands when the grass was lush, then returning to these grazing lands after the cattle had moved on. Some San and Nama groups jointly occupied the same lands. Herero, Ovambo and Kavango who migrated to Namibia up to 400 years ago also claim to be "indigenous" and entitled to land based on their long occupation.

These parallel land rights issues require very distinct political and legal approaches. There are conflicting claims arising among the different ethnic groups of Namibia that require careful legal analysis. The fact that white commercial farmers hold almost 50% of the arable land is a distinct "land reform" issue, requiring another framework for analysis. The call for "land reform" is meaningless without a clear understanding of "who benefits" from the acquisition and redistribution of those lands. Therefore, the "land reform" issue is dependent on addressing the "indigenous land rights" issue.

Indigenous Land Rights in Namibia: the Legal Framework

Namibia, like most countries in Africa, does not legally recognize an "indigenous" land title, nor any "native title" in the communal lands. This common resolve in new African states with very distinct legal and colonial histories reflects a strong nationalistic pragmatism: these are poor and weak nations, often with a number of different tribal and ethnic groups and sub-groups, with diverse and even competing historical claims, defining a precarious existence against both existing power structures – the chiefs and councillors who control the communal lands, as well as the new power structures, composed of urban black elites (Barume 2001). The legal manifestation of this, in Namibia, is the government's claim that, based on Article 100 of the Constitution providing that "Land, water and natural resources…shall belong to the State if they are not otherwise lawfully owned", all lands that are not held in what is known as fee simple (the white-held farmlands) are state property. This includes all of the communal lands, the lands occupied by more than 80% of Namibia's population, as well as the national parks, and all unused desert lands. The clause, if it has this meaning, would also deny all indigenous land rights.

A claim to "indigenous land rights" is a claim to land rights under natural law, common law, or international human rights law based on an historical occupation that precedes both Bantu and white settlement and is not dependent on any particular legal action formally granting that right. "Communal land rights", on the other hand, stem from a legal occupancy in the former "homelands", designated by statute as "communal areas", with the land held in trust by the state and allocated to individual families by a "traditional" tribal governing body, a chief and councillors, legally empowered by the state to administer the "communal lands". Therefore, although "indigenous" and "communal" land rights stem from different legal foundations, both rights are apparently denied on the same basis by the Namibian Constitution.

The modern Namibian state also claims legal ownership of the communal lands through a title derived from the South African state's title to native trust lands. Schedule 5 of the Constitution transfers to the Government of Namibia "all property of which the ownership or control immediately prior to the date of Independence [was] vested in the Government of the Territory of South West Africa, or in any Represe ntative Authority…" The various Native Authorities in the com-

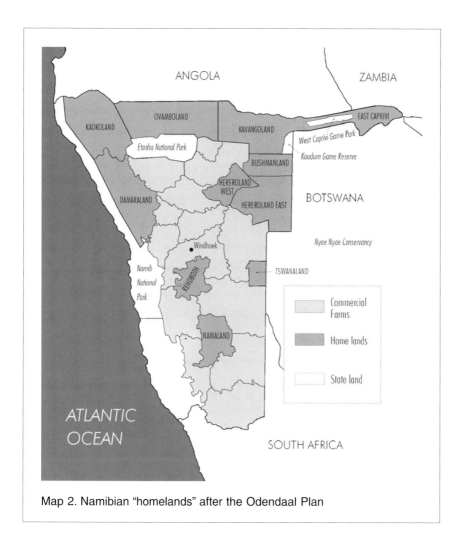

Map 2. Namibian "homelands" after the Odendaal Plan

munal areas were such "Representative Authorities" and this provision may include the communal lands. While these "Native Authorities" and their communal lands are expressly recognized in the Constitution, there is no constitutional mention of any "indigenous rights", the rights of the original peoples of Namibia to legally occupy lands independently of the state or the communal authorities. In this sense, those holding "communal land rights", which implicitly exist under the Constitution, may stand in a stronger position than those holding "indigenous land rights", which are not even mentioned.

This matter is extremely complicated but some have suggested that the state has an inadequate legal basis for its claim to these lands based on apparent conflicting language within different sections of the Constitution. Namibia's claim to legal title to the communal lands derives from South Africa's apartheid-era title, a statute providing that the underlying title to "native trust lands" is vested in the state. Besides the obvious racism in this claim, Article 16 protects "all forms of property", which would apparently in its plain language apply to both "trusts" and "communal property rights" – both of which are " property". The Preamble to the Constitution renounces apartheid and declares the policy of the Namibian government as one of abolishing all vestiges of apartheid. This would also appear to renounce any legal theory that would apply Article 16 to white-owned private property but not to black owned communal property. However, it is not clear what force in law the Preamble has: it may be simply a "policy statement". None of these constitutional issues have been fully litigated in Namibian courts so the whole question of the legal nature of communal land rights is ultimately unknown and could take many years to resolve (Harring 1996:467-484).

While "communal land rights" were known and recognized in Namibia at the time of the making of the Constitution, the legal status of "indigenous land rights" as distinct from "communal land rights" at that time is more complex. It is difficult to argue that South Africa recognized any such right but it may have existed in international or common law at that time, even if unrecognized by the South African state. If such "indigenous land rights" did, in fact, exist under South African or international law, the same argument that they are implicitly recognized under Article 16 would also apply.

Finally, Article 10, providing that "all persons are equal before the law" and that "no person shall be discriminated against on the grounds of sex, race, colour, ethnic origin, religion, creed or social and economic status" may also have an impact on land rights. This language clearly makes most forms of discrimination illegal, and makes it clear that every person in Namibia is equal under the law. But, the potential issues raised by Article 10 in the context of any program of land reform or redistribution are many. Ironically, Article 10 may well be used to protect the rights of the white landowners against the government. But, at the same time, it may also, by implication, protect the land rights of "indigenous" peoples. If they could not hold land title legally under South African rule, then they stand on an unequal basis before the law. Thus, to legally recognize a form of land title, fee simple, that is open to whites but closed to indigenous peoples, may violate the spirit – if not the letter - of Article 10.

However, Article 10 may not be used as an obstacle to affirmative action. Article 23 not only specifically provides for affirmative action "for the advancement of persons…who have been socially, economically or educationally disadvantaged by past discriminatory laws or practices" but also provides that "nothing contained in Article 10 shall prevent Parliament from enacting" affirmative action legislation. This makes it clear that there is no constitutional impediment for the Namibian government to recognizing indigenous land rights, or communal land rights, and to giving those land holders preferential treatment over other Namibians, black or white, in order to ameliorate past injustice.

While the Constitution is the supreme law of Namibia, other laws may apply as well. The National Land Conference in 1991 adopted a resolution asserting that "the restitution of ancestral land rights is impossible under existing conditions", which is now clearly government policy, enacted in national land reform legislation (NEPRU 1991). While the full meaning of this policy is unclear, in plain language it states that the nation's land policy should not be based on the restitution of historic land rights, obviously referring to indigenous land rights. This was aimed at the ambitions of some tribes to recover their ancestral lands. While this provision may have been directly aimed at the Herero, who have consistently demanded the return of the "ancestral" lands they occupied at the beginning of the German colonial period, it also impacts directly on the indigenous land rights claims of the San and Nama, dispossessing them of the right to assert these claims to their indigenous land rights.

In immediate policy terms this means that the Namibian government's "land reform" program resettles people without regard for their ancestral land rights, a policy of putting poor people on land wherever land is available (Harring and Odendaal 2002). This policy has worked to the disadvantage of the San and Nama because the Ovambo majority, who occupy an overcrowded and degraded communal area, are resettled all over Namibia.

While there are several provisions in international law that might apply, such provisions have never been applied to a domestic indigenous land rights claim in Africa. Briefly stated, International Labor Organization (ILO) Convention 169 states that "aboriginal title" derives from their historic possession and does not depend on legislation. It further recognizes the right of indigenous peoples to hold their lands as a group, protecting a broad range of their cultural and political rights as a people. The United Nations Draft Declaration on the Rights of Indigenous Peoples affirms indigenous peoples rights to "own, develop, control and use lands they traditionally owned or otherwise occupied or used". The International Covenant on Civil and Political Rights in Article 27 protects certain cultural rights of minorities, including indigenous peoples, but does not directly protect land rights. Article 26 of the same document protects all peoples from all forms of discrimination, again a provision that applies to indigenous groups (Barume 2001:103).

Potentially, international law may be more applicable in Namibia than in many other countries both because of its history as a nation created by the United Nations after repeated recourse to international law against South Africa, and because Article 144 of the Constitution stipulates that "unless otherwise provided by this Constitution or Act of Parliament, the general rules of public international law and international agreements binding upon Namibia…shall form part of the law of Namibia". Thus, general principles of international law apply in Namibia – unless Parliament decides otherwise, a so-called "saving clause". At this time, there is no indication of the application in Namibia of any principles of international law on indigenous land rights, but the legal position of indigenous groups in Namibia may be stronger than in other countries in Africa because of this constitutional provision.

Because Namibia has only been an independent nation since 1990, its courts have not yet defined the full legal scope of any of these provisions concerning either indigenous or communal land rights. This means that many principles of Namibian law in relationship to indigenous rights have yet to be established. Legal principles are not decided by courts as abstract theoretical matters: they must be brought as lawsuits by injured parties. Thus, the Namibian law of indigenous rights will be established if and when these cases are brought. Some of the emerging cases are discussed in the next section.

Land Rights in the Communal Areas

Communal land rights are not indigenous land rights, but some issues overlap. The communal areas in Namibia are lands that were left to Africans by German and South African law. While "indigenous land rights" stem from ancestral occupation, "communal land rights" stem from a colonial law that placed most Africans in a communal area simply on the basis that they resided in Namibia. Unlike the vast dislocation of native people in South Africa and Zimbabwe, both the German and South African governments left many Namibians on their traditional lands, the lands that they occupied at the beginning of German settlement, especially in the northern regions. For the Germans, this took the form of their creation of a "police zone" for German settlers that left blacks, outside of that zone, under the authority of traditional chiefs. The South Africans took over this system and, under apartheid, used the system as the base for drawing the boundaries of ten "homelands"[6] in Namibia under the Odendaal plan (1964) – homelands that included both traditional black areas but also redrawn boundaries that enlarged former reserves, buying hundreds of white farms for reinclusion in these "homelands".[7] Although the homelands were abolished at independence, the communal lands within those former areas remain in African possession, with individual plots of land allocated by chiefs and councillors. Most people in Namibia, including many Nama and Damara, and a few San, continue to occupy communal lands, so they have some right to land under customary law.

The communal lands, therefore, are colonial constructs, placing particular groups of native people on particular lands, as the system served colonial political and economic interests. Some of these land allocations conformed to existing indigenous land use. The San, for example, were allocated a "homeland", "Bushmanland", in the northeast, which included some of the lands that they had occupied historically. While some Ju|'hoan San still occupy this area, it is but a fraction of the lands that they occupied formerly (approximately 9%). Some of the land in what used to be the Ju|'hoan area was allocated to the Herero and became Hereroland, while areas in the northern portion of the Ju|'hoan range were allocated to the Kavango. A portion of the Ju|'hoan territory was turned into the Kaudum Game Reserve, and the land on which Tsumkwe (or Tjum!kui) - the administrative center of Bushmanland which was set up in the late 1950s - sits, is open to any group. Similarly, Nama were placed in "Namaland", a vast tract of what some see as worthless desert in central Namibia. Again, while Nama traditionally occupied these lands, they are but a fraction of their former lands.

The legal status of these communal lands is not clear. These lands are occupied "communally", under the authority of traditional chiefs and headmen. This authority is recognized by statute, making the chiefs low level governmental administrators, a role that they are paid for performing by the Namibian government. Communal landholders hold a "use-right", a "usufruct" that may pass on through their family for generations but does not grant them "ownership" in fee simple. Under ordinary circumstances, this is a sufficient title because it will rarely be challenged or alienated, but the combination of tribal politics, overcrowding, and the needs of the modern Namibian state is a continuing threat to these occupants: they can legally be moved against their will without compensation. This basic lack of legal protection for the "communal" landholders applies to all of the communal lands in Namibia and thus is a major issue of concern for the occupants of communal areas.

As mentioned previously, there are at least eleven distinct tribal groupings in Namibia who can claim some kind of communal land rights although, because of different patterns of traditional use, the forms of these claims differ (Malan 1995; Hahn, Vedder and Fourie 1928).[8] Some discussion of land issues in the different regions is instructive.

The San

The legal rights of the San to their lands are among the most threatened. There are a number of distinct San peoples in Namibia, and they originally lived almost everywhere in the country. As more tribes from the north moved into Namibia, the San moved to more remote parts of the country, but continued to occupy their formal lands as they moved with the cycles of water and grass, staying away from the cattle herds of the Ovambo and Herero. This means that, until well into the twentieth century, the San occupied much of their traditional lands, roaming over much of Namibia in search of food.

The South African authorities, reflecting some consciousness of the special difficulties of the San, created a San "homeland" in 1964 called "Bushmanland". The San, however, at that time still lived over vast expanses of Namibia, particularly in the northern half of the country. Until the 1960s, for example, Bushmen still hunted in Etosha National Park, and moved back and forth across the Angolan border between Ovamboland, Kavangoland, Caprivi and Angola.

Bushmanland was the poorest and most remote of the homelands. It is a vast stretch of desert in north-eastern Namibia, adjacent to the Botswana border, today still inhabited by only a few thousand people, including perhaps 3 to 4,000 San who live scattered in several hundred remote settlements. This area – traditionally inhabited by !Kung (in the western part) and Ju|'hoansi (in the eastern part) - is the major area in which the San hold "communal land rights" - but only about 10% of Namibian San hold rights here. These people have a large land base, and have organized nature conservancies to protect their traditional use of the land and keep out squatters from other tribes and their cattle. The San are traditionally hunters and gatherers, travelling vast areas of desert following traditional migration patterns in search of game and bush-food, although they can no longer maintain themselves in this manner, even in the Nyae Nyae Nature Conservancy, a large area some 9,000 km in extent, under the control of the Ju|'hoansi in line with Namibian government conservation legislation.

The creation of "Bushmanland" did nothing for any of the other groups of San, who did not know of these lands, and had no traditional occupation there. Still, San from other areas, primarily !Xun (also known as !Xû), some Hai||om and a few Khwe, were resettled in West Bushmanland, leaving East Bushmanland to the Ju|'hoansi, the indigenous occupants. All these groups currently have "communal land rights" in the former Bushmanland, now Tsumkwe District in the Otjozondjupa region, but not "indigenous land rights".

Other San groups in Namibia, including the Hai||om, the largest San group in the country, most often lack a land base, even in the form of "communal land rights". Today, the majority live in isolated camps on the "communal lands" of other groups, or on commercial farms, including white farms. The land occupied by the remaining 90% of all San thus legally "belongs" to somebody else. When that land is held "communally" by some other group, for example, large numbers of San live in Ovamboland, Kavangoland, and Hereroland, the Namibian state claims to "own" San lands, just as it claims to "own" all communal lands. This means that "land claims "in Namibia actually involve overlapping layers of claims, with the San claims competing with Ovambo, Herero, or other" native claims, or claiming commercial farmlands.

At the same time, the land currently occupied by the San in Tsumkwe District consists simply of "communal lands", held on exactly the same legal basis as all communal lands are held.

Because the San are politically the weakest people in Namibia, and because they do not commonly engage in cultivation, the Namibian state has seen what was Bushmanland as "empty" and suited to resettlement by other groups. This practice ignores the fragility of San society as well as the level to which Bushmen are exploited and abused by other peoples. Some two thousand people, many of them San but members of other groups as well, have been resettled in Tsumkwe District West by the Namibian state. Because these settlers attempt subsistence farming activities, they have transformed the face of "Bushmanland", with the main road lined by these impoverished settlements.

In the past, Herero cattle herders were resettled in eastern Bushmanland, especially in the area to the south, near /Gam, and more recently they have also brought their cattle herds into "vacant" lands in both Tsumkwe District West and East, with and without the approval of the government. In 1991, the Ju|'hoansi, with the support of the Namibian government, were able to convince the Herero to leave with their herds. More recent efforts of Herero to move into the region have resulted in agreements being made between local San and Herero to allow the Herero to keep their cattle in the area.

The fact that most of Namibia's 30,000-plus San still live in dispersed settlements throughout the northern half of Namibia, including many on white farms, raises difficult issues of shared communal land rights. The concept of "shared" land rights also denotes some idea of equality which, in reality, is not the case. San were often driven off their lands by other groups who, because they were herders or agriculturalists, claimed some kind of superior right to the land. Even today the San ordinarily will not resist the movement of Ovambo and Herero onto San lands but simply withdraw, either because they are afraid of attacks, or because they culturally wish to be left alone. Thus, the Namibian state, when it fails to protect the traditional land rights of San in their communal area, stands by while the San are displaced by more powerful ethnic groups (Suzman 2001b).

And the Namibian state is not ordinarily even "neutral" in the displacement of San from their communal lands. A resettlement camp for 20,000 Angolan refugees was recently proposed for Tsumkwe District West (see Pakleppa, this volume).[9] Tsumkwe, the administrative center of the Tsumkwe District, is occupied in part by Ovambo, Ka-vango and government functionaries. A San village in West Caprivi was forcibly moved after the Namibian government granted a per-mit for a safari camp on the same site, moving the Khwe San to make way for a tourist operation. There were also efforts to establish a pris-on farm on the site, which is near Popa Falls on the Okavango Riv-er. The Khwe sought to have these decisions reversed but with little success (see Daniels, this volume).

There are overlapping layers of legal problems here. At the out-set, as long as the Namibian state claims that it "owns" all communal lands, the San are disadvantaged in the same way as all other peoples holding communal lands. But, the San people's lack of political pow-er, in effect, means that it is easier for the Namibian state to displace San from communal lands because they have less political ability to resist. Similarly, legal redress for injury requires access to law and the San, by virtue of their isolation, lack that kind of access.

Because many San still prefer to live in isolated settlements accessible to what remains of their traditional lands, their land-use patterns are in-consistent with the agricultural and grazing practices of their Ovambo, Kavango and Herero neighbors. San lands look - to their neighbors - to be "unoccupied". Few legal forms are adequate to protect San lands. The nature conservancy is one such form but it is politically difficult for the San to organize and control such complex legal entities as it requires ac-cess to political and legal machinery that the San do not have, as well as some legally recognized land base. Only in the Nyae Nyae region and in Tsumkwe District West do the local San control enough land to establish such conservancies. Thus, there is a de facto discrimination against them rather than the de jure discrimination prohibited by Article 10.

The Himba

Perhaps the best known Namibian government threat to the tradi-tional land rights of tribal groups in the communal lands has been the on-going threat to erect a large dam at Epupa Falls, displacing hundreds of Himba and disrupting their traditional way of life. The Himba, like the San, are a small tribe, numbering only about 20,000. Unlike the San, however, the Himba are a Herero people, linking them politically with the powerful Herero tribe, probably the lead-ing rival to the Ovambo, and traditionally supporting opposition political parties. The Himba are also a cattle-herding people, with well-demarcated cattle pasturing grounds, hundreds of thousands of cattle, and living in permanent villages. Therefore, their histori-cal claim to their lands is easy to document: although they are not

Nyae Nyae, Tsumkwe District East. Photo: Diana Vinding

"indigenous" to Namibia, they have occupied their present lands for hundreds of years.

The government of Namibia, through Nampower, a para-statal electric power company, completely denied that the Himba had any right to their lands at Epupa. Cost estimates for the hydro-power project included nothing for the purchase of Himba lands and noted that resettlement costs would be low because the Himba were poor and had little personal property. Government officials offered small bribes to Himba chiefs to facilitate removal, then threatened them with wholesale expulsion if they refused to move. Ovambo were resettled on Himba lands and took the position that they favored the construction of the dam because it would develop their remote region. The Himba were portrayed as "backward" and their culture denigrated as the government threatened to impose a "right to development" on the Himba even against their will.

The Himba, proving great political acumen, took on the Namibian government, even sending a delegation of chiefs to Europe to protest the dam and their treatment by the government. This became a public relations debacle for the Namibian state as the proposed dam and Himba opposition became the most well-known Namibian issue abroad at a time when the country's international image was important. At present the whole Epupa project is "on hold", an implicit victory for the Himba whose political activities have seriously undermined both the economic feasibility of the project as well as the governments' ability to raise funding in Europe and America.

More importantly, the Himba have openly taken the position that they and not the Namibian state "own" their lands, challenging the government's title to the communal lands. Because they have lived on their lands uninterrupted for more than a hundred years, they are in a strong position to litigate the whole issue of "communal" land rights in northern Namibia; and in a weaker position to litigate "indigenous" land rights based on their longstanding occupation (Harring 2001).

The Rehoboth Basters

To date only one land rights case has been fully litigated by the Namibian courts and it is somewhat idiosyncratic as a "land rights" case, and therefore probably not very important as a precedent. Still, it is the major land rights case that has been litigated, so it bears discussion. The Rehoboth Basters brought a lawsuit against the government to stop the alienation of their communal lands. They not only lost but their communal area is now majority Ovambo and their traditional community has been weakened.

The Basters are people of mixed white and African descent, with a good deal of Nama blood, who moved to Namibia from South Africa in the 1870s and formed an alliance with German authorities receiving, in return, recognition of their land rights over a large tract of land fifty miles south of Windhoek, in the center of the country.[10] Thus, they are neither traditional landholders nor "indigenous peoples" although they claim such rights through long-standing occupation of their lands and through recognized communal land rights. The Constitution of Namibia specifically transferred their lands to the state on independence in 1990. Relying on that transfer, the Namibian state resettled thousands of blacks, mostly Ovambo, in Rehoboth. Because these lands were well suited to settlement, and close to Windhoek, they were quickly resettled. The *Baster* case, decided by the Namibian Supreme Court in 1995, turned on narrow legal technicalities and did not require the Court to decide anything fundamental about either communal land rights or indigenous land rights in Namibia as a whole.[11] However, the Supreme Court's narrow and technical interpretation of the law is an indication that they may be unreceptive to broad assertions of indigenous or traditional land rights. The Basters were bitter over this loss of their land and their political autonomy, but lost their lawsuit. Their traditional rights to their communal lands were overwhelmed by the Namibian state and, while it is too early to determine what will become of the Baster people, it seems clear that their way of life has been diminished.

The Mafwe and the Caprivi "Insurrection"

It is impossible to discuss the concept of indigenous land rights in Namibia without discussing the volatile situation in Caprivi. The Mafwe, a small and indigenous tribe living in Caprivi, in the extreme northeast of Namibia, have been decimated by the Namibian police and army following the repression of a small insurrection in 1999. Although it is still unclear exactly what occurred, a small group of Mafwe attacked the police station in Katima Mulilo. Seven people were killed in the following shoot-out. More were killed as the government hunted down the alleged perpetrators and perhaps a thousand Mafwe were jailed, although most have since been released. A treason trial for more than a hundred defendants is in progress but has been repeatedly delayed.[12] At a minimum, these events show a great deal of resentment by the Mafwe of their treatment as a tribal minority within the Namibian state. The tribe's leadership is either in jail or in exile, and the government is seeking life sentences for the defendants.[13]

Caprivi, a former communal area and home to about 90,000 people, lies in an area that is underdeveloped, with substantial agricultural potential. It also offers great potential as a tourist region.[14] The Mafwe uprising, while there are numerous underlying causes, is linked to the instability of their minority position in the region.

The Nama

The Nama are a Khoesan people, among the original inhabitants of Namibia. They, like the San, distinguish themselves by their lighter skin color and smaller stature from the Bantu peoples who dominate Namibia. The Nama, at Gibeon in south central Namibia, and the Damara, a Nama speaking people living in western Namibia, who are distinct from both the Nama and the Bantu peoples, occupy what may be the most dismal lands in the country. The Damara "homeland" was almost entirely recreated by the apartheid era state in the 1960s, which repurchased more than 300 marginal and bankrupt white farms and created these homelands in a barren, overgrazed desert (see Rohde 1993; Sullivan 1996). Neither people have rebuilt viable agricultural economies in the forty years since. Both these communal areas are occupied primarily by old people and children because poverty forces the adults to work far away, and generate even less income from agriculture than is possible in Ovamboland. Any meaningful process of land reform will require the purchase of additional – and better – land, as well as massive environmental reclamation work to combat decades of erosion and drought.

Other groups of Nama live in small villages across western Namibia, including deep in the Namib Desert. Some of these, like the San, have been removed from national parks without being compensated for their lands. A few still live in isolated settlements in Namib National Park, with an unclear legal right to the lands they occupy.

This brief survey of some of the ethnic communities that make up Namibia makes it clear that land is a major issue in each case, even though the tribes are very different and have very different land issues. Most of the peasants in Namibia have access to land, but it is access to small plots of environmentally degraded land. But none of these people have any legal right to their land and hold tenure only at the will of the traditional authorities. Even this land must be rehabilitated and enriched before it can sustain improved agricultural practices. Others, especially the Himba, Herero and Kavango have some wealth and better access to land. But even these peoples lack any legal right to their land, and can be displaced at the will of the state.

Indigenous Land Rights

Namibia, like Botswana and most other countries in Africa, does not recognize "indigenous" land rights as distinct from the land rights of all the other native peoples in Namibia. All these peoples stand on the same legal footing: they hold "communal land rights" to just under 50% of the arable land in the country; and potential additional land rights in various "land reform" regimes that will acquire existing commercial farm lands for redistribution.

This *de jure* denial of "indigenous land rights" reflects the political reality of post-independence Namibia with the Ovambo, Herero and Kavango, the three most powerful Bantu groups, approaching 75% of the population, and each currently occupying lands only recently used by San or Nama peoples and all in different levels of conflict with other groups – especially the San – over the land they currently occupy, or may ultimately claim.

Thus, just as in Botswana, the indigenous land rights of the San and the Nama are not recognized, in the name of a "national unity" ideology that also serves the needs of the groups in power. While all of the native groups in Namibia suffer from unclear legal rights to their "communal lands", the political weakness of the San - together with the sparseness of their communal land rights - puts the San at a great disadvantage: more than 90% of them are essentially landless.

No existing legal regime in Namibia is capable of either recognizing this "landlessness" as a problem, distinct from San and Nama poverty, or of recognizing additional San land claims based on their "indigenous" status. Existing models of land reform focus on establishing "resettlement schemes" that simply settle individual impoverished San in camps dominated by other ethnic groups such as the Tswana, Herero, Damara and others, without regard for their ethnic status – basic welfare schemes. These camps are most often little more than rural slums and destroy the culture of the San. Thus, the redistribution of the commercial farmlands to the various ethnic groups in Namibia will do nothing to improve the status of the San and Nama in terms of access to the large expanses of land that they will need to maintain their cultures and earn a living.

Conclusions

Namibia has some of the elements of an African success story. The country is relatively prosperous, with a diversified economy. Basic social needs are met, with most children in school and basic medical care freely available. Democratic traditions are reasonably well respected. The white minority population is willing to support reasonable land reform initiatives and the black majority has shown a commitment to a multi-racial state that includes continued white ownership of a substantial number of farms and businesses. But there are a number of causes for concern.

The existing state does not recognize the land rights of indigenous peoples. Therefore, the road that "land reform" is taking is simply as a welfare scheme, redistributing land from rich whites to poor blacks, without regard for ethnicity or culture. Because the San and Nama are so small in number and so weak politically, they are getting only marginal land, most often resettled with other ethnic groups in remote "camps", as seen, for example, on the Gobabis Farms in the Omaheke region in eastern Namibia.

In addition, the indigenous land holders, in common with the communal land holders, have no legal title to their lands and apparently, can be dispossessed of their lands by the state without compensation. Thus, even if some indigenous people live on their traditional lands - as some do - they can be removed to make way for various government projects. The government's incursions into San lands in former Bushmanland and in Caprivi are examples of this. Indigenous people already on their lands need to be protected by formal legal recognition of their land rights.

While these difficulties are serious enough, there can be no resolution of the problem of "indigenous" land rights without first a general regime of land reform. The existing commercial lands must be acquired from the few white owners and redistributed fairly to members of other groups regardless of their ethnic background. The Namibian government has begun this process, purchasing and resettling about eighty farms in every part of the country. These efforts are commendable, accomplished peacefully through the "willing buyer, willing seller" principle but too little land has been redistributed. The slow pace of land redistribution may ultimately see the process overtaken by political demands for faster and more meaningful land redistribution. In the spring of 2004 the Namibian government recognized this and announced that it would begin to legally expropriate white farms, although it has not yet done so. Land reform also requires extensive social support, which has not been the case: the individual resettlement projects are most often rural slums, degenerating into poverty. Poor people cannot be moved from one pocket of rural poverty to another, often hundreds of miles away, without serious social consequences. Alcohol abuse, family violence, unemployment are all side effects of this process (Harring and Odendall 2002).

But this land redistribution is only a first step. Native people, whether indigenous or more recently arrived, have no legal right to the land they occupy within any of the communal areas. Even if fee-simple, European style property regimes are not ideal in all societies, there must be basic mechanisms to protect the land rights of poor blacks. This may be possible under some regimes of tribal or customary law, but appropriate legal measures must be taken. Tribal Africa has also undergone rapid social change and it is not clear that traditional authorities can adequately represent the interests of all peasant farmers. Land tenure means little if it is associated with grinding poverty, and moving to shantytowns and squatter camps is as common an option in Namibia as it is in South Africa and Zimbabwe.

Traditional Africa in some ways can be seen as tribal. African tribes are powerful forces for social stability. Yet the place of the tribe in the modern nation-state has been a difficult one. The distinct tribes of Namibia have very different political, economic and social experiences that color their relationships with the state and with each other. The "land problem" is a different problem for each tribe, reflecting their specific colonial and apartheid-era experiences. These experiences have some common elements but may also pose the interests of one tribe against another: the San against the Herero, the Ovambo against the Himba. In other words, land problems are rooted in the colonial experience and in the original deprivation of blacks from their lands by white settlers, but they are now more complex, involving distinct tribal interests. Within tribes, the "traditional" authorities have been structured by a hundred years of colonialism to represent certain kinds of interests. What is now called "indigenous", "traditional" or "customary" law is more rooted in the colonial experience than it is in tribal custom, and may not uniformly benefit every person within the tribe, nor every tribe equally. Among other divisions, these basic divisions also divide Africa. Resolution of the "land" issue is without a doubt among the most complex issues facing Africa. None of the underlying problems are simple. But one way to start is by recognizing the basic land rights of the indigenous people.   ❑

Notes

1   For more information on the general state of the land reform issue in Namibia in the mid-1990s and for data that describes the general state of the land holding in Namibia at that time, see Adams and Devitt, 1992; Donna Pankhurst, 1996; Adams and Werner, 1990; Werner, 1977.

2   Suzman, 2001b:4.

3   Joram ǀUseb, WIMSA. Address to the 19th Session of the UN Working Group on Indigenous Populations, Geneva, 23-27 July 2001.

4   The 11 major ethnic groups are: Ovambo, Kavango, Herero, Himba, Damara, Nama, San, Mafew, Subia, Tswana, Baster. These basic ethnic groupings also have sub-groupings. –Ed.

5   At the time 1 NAD = US$0.15. –Ed.

6   The South Africans created ten "homelands", one for each major tribe, but putting all the tribes in Caprivi in one "homeland". These ten homelands were Kaokoland, Ovamboland, Kavangoland, East Caprivi, Damaraland, Bushman-land, Hereroland, Rehoboth, Tswanaland and Namaland. Tswanaland was later eliminated as one of the ethnic "homelands" in order to allow the more power-ful Herero to remain in the area. –Ed.

7   These changing colonial era land tenure policies are mapped in van der Merwe, 1983.

8   These basic ethnic groupings also have sub-groupings that may also have distinct customary land rights.

9   The resettlement did not take place because the majority of the refugees were eventually able to return to their original homes in Angola.

10 On their history, see Britz et al., 1999. On their legal position, see Peters, 1993.

11 *The Rehoboth Bastergemeente v The Government of the Republic of Namibia*, Case no. SA 5, 05, delivered May 14, 1996.

12 Werner Menges, in "Legal Aid is Not a Right, says Government", *The Namibian*, Dec. 13, 2001, puts the number of defendants at 128, with others in prison and others being sought by the police.

13 It is still unclear exactly what the nature of this "insurrection" was, but more than 1000 Mafwe fled Namibia, and up to 200 were in prison awaiting trial on various charges, including treason. See Fisch, 1999.

14 The Caprivi has also been the subject of a planning atlas. See Mendelsohn and Roberts, 1998.

CIVIL RIGHTS IN LEGISLATION AND PRACTICE:
A CASE STUDY FROM TSUMKWE DISTRICT WEST, NAMIBIA

Richard Pakleppa
with inputs from WIMSA

Government gave us San the right to use our land, to live under our own control. This will be turned backwards if the refugees come. They will act against the rights we have now.

San traditional leader, Aasvoëlnes community meeting

In October 2000, the Government of Namibia announced its intention to relocate 20,000 refugees from an existing refugee camp to a site located on the land inhabited by a population of 4,500 San people.

These plans were in conflict with the community's claim to the land and their plans for its development. Further, the planned relocation would also directly affect a neighbouring San group consisting of 1,800 people. Yet neither the community nor their traditional leaders had been consulted prior to the decision and, in October, Namibian government officials approached only one single member of the !Kung Traditional Authority, asking him to approve the plans.

The community, traditional leaders, local and international NGOs immediately expressed strong concern and opposition to these plans, and told government officials that they would have to negotiate with all the traditional leaders.

In the following months, the San made repeated efforts to be heard by the government but it was only in late 2001 that traditional councillors from Tsumkwe District West and Tsumkwe District East were finally able to meet with then Prime Minister Hage Geingob. Although he promised that they would be consulted from now on, the government appeared for a long time not to have taken any final decision, instead keeping the project to build a new refugee camp "on hold".

In the meantime, developments in neighbouring Angola after the death of UNITA leader, Jonas Savimbi, in early 2002, created a new situation: Angola's rapid progress towards a lasting peace meant that internally displaced Angolans and Angolan refugees could start to return to their homes.

Given that the majority of refugees in Namibia were from Angola and now could be repatriated within a foreseeable future, the Namibian government no longer had reason to pursue its plan of building a new refugee camp. It was only in 2003, however, that the Namibian government publicly suspended its intention to relocate refugees to M'kata.[1]

Thus for more than two years – from late 2000 to 2003 - the community and its leaders lived in uncertainty as to their future. Therefore, and although the threat of a refugee camp now seems to have disappeared for ever, the case study of Tsumkwe West remains illustrative since, by examining government actions, community and NGO responses and the surrounding legal context, it allows us to reflect on civil rights in legislation and in practice in today's Namibia.

The People of Tsumkwe District

The area the refugees from Osire were supposed to be relocated to is known as M'kata. This hamlet lies in Tsumkwe District West in north-eastern Namibia. Tsumkwe District West, along with neighboring Tsumkwe District East, is part of the Tsumkwe District that used to be known in Namibia during the apartheid era as Bushmanland. Today, the District is part of the larger region of Otjozondjupa, one of the 13 regions in contemporary Namibia.

The Tsumkwe District West community is made up of different population groups with diverse histories of dislocation and resettlement. As such, it is a relatively young community and there is considerable insecurity regarding land rights among the population. Further, the community has relatively limited experience of political organisation and leadership at district, regional and national levels.

The San population in Tsumkwe West consists of !Kung and two !Xun groups, formerly known as the Vasakela and the Mpungu. For the majority of !Kung, the land is their ancestral land and they have hunted and gathered in the district for generations. The two !Xun groups were settled in the area during the 80s. One group - the Mpungu - was moved by the South African Defence Force (SADF) from settlements in Kavangoland, and the other group – the Vasakela - originally came with the SADF from Angola to Namibia in 1976. After first being settled at Omega in the Caprivi Strip, they were eventually resettled in Tsumkwe West. These two groups claim that their forebears lived on either side of the border between Namibia and Angola before the onset of war in the 1970s.

Many San men worked for the SADF in the period prior to independence and most of them, including their families, were moved by the SADF to South Africa during the transition to independence (see Chennells & du Toit, this volume). Those who remained are seen in

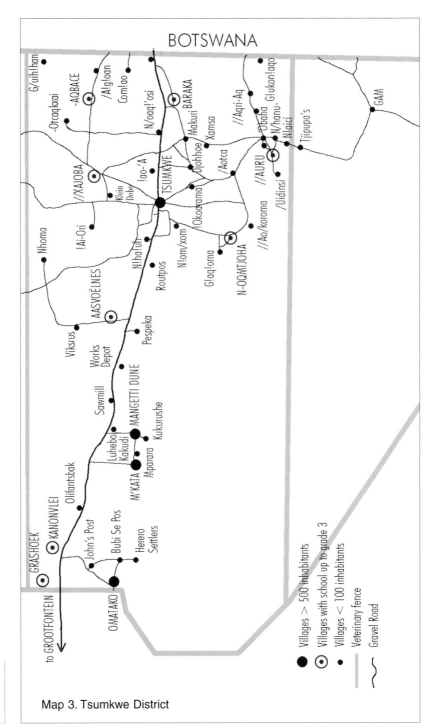

Map 3. Tsumkwe District

some quarters to have fought for the "wrong" side and this is still held against them.

Apart from the San inhabitants, there is also a growing number of recently arrived pastoralists of Kavango and Herero origin in the District. These settlers own herds of livestock, which places added strain on the scarce water, grazing, bush food and game resources. In fact grazing livestock – overgrazing – does also undermine the San's effort to establish income-generating programmes in line with tourism development.

The 4,500 San are settled in a number of small, dispersed villages in the District. Survival in Tsumkwe West is difficult. People gather bush food and medicinal plants such as the Devil's Claw, cultivate fields, keep small numbers of livestock, operate a campsite, market crafts and depend on food aid and state pension payments made to the elderly. There are very few employment opportunities for the population. Rainfall is erratic and harvests of grains are irregular and insufficient.

The community falls under the jurisdiction of the Namibian government in matters of statutory law and common law. It falls under the jurisdiction of the !Kung Traditional Authority in matters of customary law and the settlement of disputes that fall within the ambit of customary law. The Ministries of Regional and Local Government, Home Affairs, Agriculture, Education, Land, Resettlement and Rehabilitation, Health and Environment and Tourism are represented by personnel based in the administrative centres of Mangetti Dune and Tsumkwe.

Like all San communities across southern Africa, the people of Tsumkwe West have endured a long history of displacement, enslavement, oppression and marginalisation at the hands of white colonisers and black pastoralists. While they enjoy equal constitutional rights under Namibian law, they continue to be dominated by stronger groups and their human rights are frequently abused.

Since 1996, the Working Group of Indigenous Minorities in Southern Africa (WIMSA) - a regional networking NGO of San communities and organisations - has been working with the San community of Tsumkwe West to establish a community-based tourism project, co-ordinating training programs for traditional leaders and assisting the community with preparations to form a conservancy in the area. Formation of a conservancy was to give the community rights to jointly manage, use and benefit from wildlife in the area. An application to register a conservancy in the area was submitted in 1998 but had in 2000 not yet been considered by the Ministry of Environment and Tourism (MET). The government's plans for M'kata were therefore seen as the end of the San's dream of a conservancy.

Tsumkwe District West shares a boundary with Tsumkwe District East, which falls under the jurisdiction of the Ju|'hoan Traditional Authority. The Ju|'hoansi are a different San community with a long history of development projects and organisational initiatives that has culminated in the establishment of an officially recognised Conservancy - the Nyae Nyae Conservancy. This community was also likely to be directly affected by the plans to relocate large numbers of refugees into the area.

The Relocations Plans

In October 2000, the community of M'kata -a village of approximately 500 inhabitants - was informed by the Tsumkwe regional councillor that the Namibian government intended to resettle refugees from the Osire refugee camp in central Namibia to a large piece of land in the M'kata area. Subsequent media reports confirmed these plans.

During meetings with government officials at M'kata, comments were made that the inhabitants of M'kata were themselves refugees who had been brought there by the South African Defence Force. These comments were noted with concern and alarm and perceived as thinly veiled threats. People felt that they, too, could face the danger of being moved.

Government officials, who came to meet with the traditional councillor at M'kata, requested that the councillor give his consent to their plans. They were told that such a decision would have to be taken by all the traditional leaders representing the entire community of Tsumkwe West. Up to October 2000, the government had not consulted the officially recognised !Kung Traditional Authority or the broader community concerning this matter.

During January and February 2001, the Chief of Tsumkwe West, John Arnold, and a staff member of WIMSA visited senior officials of the Ministry of Home Affairs and the Ministry of the Environment and Tourism in the capital, Windhoek. In these meetings, the Chief expressed strong concerns about the plans to relocate refugees to M'kata.

The Chief informed the officials that the land of Tsumkwe West was too small to accommodate such large numbers of refugees, that the San population required the existing available land and had development plans for it, that the refugees would pose a serious threat to limited water, grazing, bush food and wood resources in the area and that the peace and security of the district could be threatened. The Chief was told that while M'kata had been identified as the most suitable site, the government had yet to take a final decision on this matter.

In April 2001, Chief John Arnold and a WIMSA consultant visited all the villages of Tsumkwe West. In the context of WIMSA's human rights education program, recent developments regarding the resettlement of refugees were discussed. San traditional leaders, village elders and women and men expressed different opinions as to the possible advantages and disadvantages that would arise from government plans to relocate large numbers of refugees to Tsumkwe West.

The consultations, however, established that the population was united in its opposition to the resettlement of refugees. The following quotation indicates the understanding people in Tsumkwe West had of the problem they faced:

> *They [the refugees] will first look at the land. Then they will extend the fence. They will say they saw that the place was empty. Later you will find them everywhere.*
>
> San speaker, Etameko community meeting

The San are well acquainted with the assertion that they "do not use their land". Settlers with cattle do not recognise the San's hunting and gathering activities as productive use of the land. It appears that government planners, who selected the M'kata site, share this view.

During the community consultation of April 2001, frequent references were made to the bitter memories of subjugation and oppression by other population groups. Since independence in 1990, the San people have acquired rights to live freely on their land. People were very vocal about not wanting to become "enslaved" again by other, stronger ethnic groups.

In April 2001, the !Kung Chief and all the councillors of the Traditional Authority, as well as village representatives and representatives from the Nyae Nyae Conservancy of Tsumkwe East, met at M'kata. The meeting heard strong-worded and well-motivated opposition to government plans to relocate large numbers of refugees into the area. The Chief was instructed to request high government officials to meet with San leaders and representatives from Tsumkwe West and East. The purpose of such a meeting was to demand clarification from the government and to express the strong concerns held by the affected communities. A letter requesting such a meeting was sent to all relevant government agencies. The letter remained unanswered.

In the meantime, the Namibian office of the United Nations High Commission for Refugees (UNHCR) had commissioned a technical feasibility study for the relocation of the existing refugee camp to the new site at M'kata. A water survey had been undertaken and, in the absence of any response to their request for a meeting with the government, considerable concern had grown in the community and within WIMSA.

In September 2001, WIMSA facilitated further meetings of the !Kung Traditional Authority and community meetings in the villages of Tsumkwe West. The developments since April and the government's failure to respond to a request for a meeting were reviewed. Possible proactive measures were discussed. While discussing the possibility of seeking legal advice and taking legal action, some members of the !Kung Traditional Authority rejected such a proposal. Their opposition to the influx of refugees had weakened. They felt that they could not oppose government policy.

After some disagreement between the Traditional Councillors, it was established that the majority of the traditional leaders and their communities wanted to consult legal council. Formal mandates, which empowered the Traditional Councillors to take all legal steps to protect the land, were gathered in all villages. Senior Traditional Councillors of the !Kung Traditional Authority held further meetings with their colleagues of the Ju|'hoan Traditional Authority and with representatives of the Nyae Nyae Conservancy. The leaders of Tsumkwe East agreed to support proactive efforts to counter government plans.

Subsequently a delegation of traditional councillors and leaders from Tsumkwe West and East travelled to the capital, Windhoek, where they briefed a lawyer and had meetings with Namibia's Prime Minister and representatives of the Office of the Ombudsman.

At these meetings, the traditional leaders expressed their concerns and made it clear that they should be consulted on issues that would affect their communities. The Prime Minister assured them that the government would in future consult with the community and its leaders. The office of the Ombudsman undertook to assist the community by ensuring that government agencies would in future consult with them.

Senior Traditional Councillors of Tsumkwe West and the Chief of Tsumkwe East later instructed a lawyer to represent their communities and to mount a challenge to government actions, should this be necessary.

Legislative Framework

Constitutional Rights

Amongst others, the Constitution of Namibia grants the right to freedom of assembly, freedom of speech and the right to influence government policies. Further, the Constitution stipulates that Namibian citizenship can be granted to residents who have lived in the country for a period of 5 years.

Some of the San groups of Tsumkwe West have settled relatively recently in the area. Given the legacies of oppression this community shares with many other San communities in southern Africa, there is an underlying sense of insecurity regarding their citizenship and land rights. It was clarified on a number of occasions that there was no doubt about the Namibian citizenship of the San in Tsumkwe West and that allegations that they were themselves refugees and possibly of questionable citizenship status should be rejected.

The San community of Tsumkwe West had never before held meetings in which land issues with the potential for conflict with the government were discussed. On a number of occasions it was necessary to clarify that not only was there nothing illegal in gathering to discuss such issues but that it was a constitutional right to do so.

The fact that some of the meetings attracted the attention of the local police commander and an agent of Namibia's State Security Service indicates that such fears were not entirely unfounded.

Land Rights

The districts of Tsumkwe West and East both fall within designated communal land. All communal land in Namibia is owned by the state. The legal framework for designated communal land dates back to the founding of reserves by the German colonial state and, subsequently, the various ethnic reserves and "third tier administrations" established by the South African administration prior to independence.

Apart from owning the communal land, the state also has the power to legally appropriate land. *The Land Appropriation Act* makes provision for the state to utilise state or private land in the national interest.

The Namibian Constitution provides for important civil rights and human rights, especially in a context where there is considerable insecurity. These rights have been evoked and explained to communities in the process of working through fears and anxieties surrounding the question of land and land rights.

It should be remembered that, for many San, it is not a given fact that they are equal before the law and that they have human rights that are enshrined in the Constitution and therefore precede the policies of any given government. The overwhelming force of memory and experience has created a very negative image and expectation of authority: authorities are seen to have superior power and should therefore not be challenged. The authorities are still seen by many to have the right to intervene at will into the lives of San subjects.

The Traditional Authorities Act of 1995 and 2000

The Traditional Authorities Act provides for the official recognition of Chiefs and Traditional Authorities that are constituted by the Chief and his Traditional Councillors.

The Traditional Authorities are responsible for implementing customary law and settling disputes. Further, they are responsible for upholding, protecting and preserving customs, culture, language and traditional values. The Act states that implementation of customary law may not conflict with provisions of the Constitution and statutory law or prejudice the national interest.

In terms of the Act, the Traditional Authorities are also obliged to assist the police and other law enforcement agencies in the prevention of crime and the apprehension of offenders and to assist and co-operate with the organs of the central, regional and local government in the execution of their policies by keeping members of the traditional community informed of development projects in their area.

Further, they are tasked to ensure that community members use the natural resources at their disposal on a sustainable basis and in a manner that conserves the environment.

The Act makes provision for the remuneration of the chief, senior traditional councillors and traditional councillors. This means that they receive a regularly monthly salary from the government.

The !Kung and Ju|'hoan Traditional Authorities were constituted and formally recognised in terms of the Act in 1998.

Prior to the promulgation of the Act, neither of these communities had constituted themselves as communities under the central jurisdiction of one Chief. Hunter-gatherer bands and families formed smaller social units, which co-operated with each other on the basis of agreements about land-use rights which extended over large tracts of land.

While the community of Tsumkwe East is culturally and linguistically homogenous and the population of approximately 1800 Ju|'hoansi have long and relatively unbroken connections to their land, this is not the case for all the inhabitants of Tsumkwe West. The majority, the !Kung, who are culturally and linguistically related to the Ju|'hoansi, have longer, unbroken ties to their land but the two !Xun groups have a turbulent history of recent displacement and resettlement.

To some extent, the currently recognised chiefs of the San are modern inventions. However, the customary law that informs their roles and procedures is a continuation of customs formerly associated with the leaders of smaller social units. More importantly, implementation of the Act has brought about an unprecedented recognition of San cultural and political rights. The recognition of the San Traditional Authorities in Namibia has also brought about an historically unprecedented recognition of San rights to the land over which the Traditional Authorities have jurisdiction. It can also be argued that the creation of Traditional Authorities as institutions of centralised representation and leadership provides an important and necessary interface between these indigenous communities and the "modern" face of the newly emerging Namibian state.

Nevertheless, the following statement raises questions about how serious the Namibian government is with regard to the Traditional Authorities it has created:

> *I want to know if all the traditional leaders were informed [about the plans to relocate refugees] and taken to M'kata when this was first discussed. This would not work with other people. Only with San can you come in and make such decisions without asking people. What will happen now to us? To our children?*

San traditional leader, community meeting April 2001

This speaker's rhetorical question points to a contradiction between government actions and policies: while the government formally recognises the San leaders of the !Kung Traditional Authorities, it ignores and snubs these leaders by consistently omitting to consult them in a matter that has the potential to most seriously affect the lives of the communities they represent. This is correctly seen as a continuation of the legacy of disrespect and discrimination afforded to San people.

The government's disregard for the traditional leaders continued up to late September 2001. At this point, the traditional leaders approached Namibia's Prime Minister and officials of the Office of the Ombudsman. The Prime Minister confirmed having knowledge of the letter sent in April by the leaders to - amongst others - his office, with the request for a meeting. He verbally assured the leaders that from now on they would be consulted.

The position of the San communities in Tsumkwe East and West and their leaders would have been considerably weakened had it not been for their recognition under the *Traditional Authorities Act,* and the recognition of the leaders and their communities has in fact bestowed confidence and legitimacy upon the leaders and their communities. They have been included as formally equal players with equal rights in the national framework. They are thus empowered in a manner that strengthens them when approaching government and in their demand that their concerns be heard.

The members of the Traditional Authority are appointed to serve both their communities and the government. While the Act makes it clear that they are elected or appointed by the community it is not clear to whom they should be accountable first and foremost.

In this respect the Act can be interpreted negatively as instituting Traditional Authorities to serve as the central government's instruments of control over indigenous populations in remote areas.

An example of this is that the thinking that informed those !Kung Traditional Councillors who, in October 2001, opposed taking legal action in defence of their rights, was informed by the perception that since they were being paid by the government it was their duty to support the government and its policies. They believed that they therefore could not oppose government policy or be seen to oppose government policy. These councillors expressed the split loyalties the provisions of the Act can create in a situation where there is a conflict of interest between the government and the community.

There is in San communities no body of experience that would indicate to people the constitutionally determined separation of the legal and executive powers of the state. Past experience and perceptions in the present are that the law and the state are one and the same power. So it is incorrectly seen that to take legal action against the state is to take action against the law and this would in itself therefore be ultimately unlawful. Such perceptions are also fuelled by the administrative practice encountered by people on the ground: law enforcement officials and government officials act as if they are the law and cannot be questioned. A human rights culture where such actions are challenged from a position of confident knowledge of one's rights is still very much in its infancy amongst many population groups in Namibia but particularly amongst the San.

The San communities' experience of authority has been predominantly negative. As the most marginalised group in Namibia the San have been dominated, hunted down and abused by various other population groups. It is therefore not surprising that perceptions of the new democratic government are also infused with mistrust and fear.

It is also noteworthy that while the *Traditional Authorities Act* of 1995 and 2000 has brought crucial changes to the official status of San cultural, political and land rights, the practical functioning of these bodies is severely restrained by a complete absence of operational funds required to organise regular meetings, means of communication with government and other agencies and the much required training in administrative and leadership skills. While government pays small salaries to the members of the Traditional Authorities, there is a remarkable absence of any efforts to empower these institutions.

The Nature Conservation Amendment Act

The *Nature Conservation Amendment Act 1996* (Act 5 of 1996) makes provision for the establishment of Conservancies and Wildlife Councils in communal areas.

The Act grants rights to specified groups of people living in communal areas to manage and benefit from wildlife and tourism in these areas. The Act makes provision for the establishment of conservancy boundaries, conservancy constitutions, which will provide for the sustainable management and utilisation of game in a given area, membership and the formation of conservancy committees.

The Act prescribes a strong regulating and monitoring function to the Ministry of the Environment and Tourism. The minister has, for example, the power to recognise or withdraw recognition from conservancies. Before declaring a conservancy, the minister must be satisfied that the conservancy committee is representative of the community residing in the area to which the application applies, that the constitution of the conservancy provides for the sustainable management and utilisation of game and that the committee has the ability to manage funds and has a method for equitable distribution, to members of the community, of benefits derived from the utilisation of game.

The Act aims to increase local responsibility and ownership rights over wildlife while creating the possibility for communities to benefit financially from increased wildlife in the form of trophy hunting, the sale of wild game, income from tourism and income from harvesting quotas agreed by the Ministry of the Environment and Tourism.

In Tsumkwe District West the idea of establishing a conservancy has been discussed over a 4-year period. Conservancy committee members have been elected in every village and there are many concrete plans and hopes amongst the population.

In 2001 many residents of Tsumkwe West were impatiently waiting for their conservancy application to be approved so that conservancy related development plans for the area could be implemented.

> *Our Conservancy is our hope - but the refugee camp will affect our resources - wood, grasses, game, bushfood, the places we need to make camps for tourists.*
>
> San speaker, Etameko community meeting

> *It will not be good for tourists. They come to see wild animals and our traditional culture. They will not find much game. They will mainly see refugees. They will ask, "Where are the San"?*
>
> San speaker, Kanovlei community meeting

The influx of large numbers of refugees was therefore seen as a threat to the development opportunities offered by the legislation that enables the formation of conservancies.In Tsumkwe East the Nyae Nyae Conservancy was already established in 1998. The San leaders of this conservancy were similarly concerned about the negative effects the presence of a large refugee population would have on the development plans linked to their Conservancy.

Legislation regarding conservancies would not have impacted directly on the !Kung and Ju|'hoansi struggle to stop the relocation of large numbers of refugees to their land. However, the fact that this law grants rights to use natural resources and the resulting promise of development opportunities provided a strong incentive for communities to resist plans to relocate refugees.

On another level, the legislation on conservancies and all the process that had gone into preparing communities for this development had given force to the argument that the land in question was neither "empty" nor unutilised. While the government claimed that the site at M'kata was the most suitable land in Namibia for establishing a large refugee camp, its own conservancy-related policies provided strong arguments against this.

Concluding Remarks: Legislation and Struggle

In late 2001, the San communities of Tsumkwe East and West prepared for the possibility of legal action against the government of Namibia if this government should unilaterally confirm its plan to relocate large numbers of refugees to M'kata, Tsumkwe District West.

The first demand of the M'kata community was that it should be consulted, that it should have a say in the matter and that negotiations should occur in good faith. The community and the leaders in the Traditional Authority wanted the opportunity to convince the government not to execute its plans.

Legal action conducted by lawyers in the courts requires the full support and knowledge of the communities. Knowledge of existing legislation and the rights thereby granted is a key factor affecting the unity and resolve of the communities in their struggle to protect their land by all possible legal means.

In October 2000, the San communities and their leaders started attending meetings where reference to the legislation described in this article contributed to clarifying their status in the framework of national politics in Namibia. With an awareness of the rights granted by existing laws, communities and their leaders were in a better position to contest government policy. Reference to this legislation during the Human Rights Education Programs conducted by WIMSA during the same period also contributed to strengthening confidence and resolve amongst the community.

The struggle of the San in Tsumkwe West and East to protect their land has generated important understanding of rights, the functioning of laws and the legal system and the powers of the state amongst the community. For the elected San leaders and the community, the struggle against the planned refugee camp at M'kata brought awareness of constitutional rights, the need to organise unity and the need to challenge government when this is necessary. They also learned, however, that existing legislation enables government to alienate land if this is seen to be in the national interest (the *Land Appropriation Act*).

It is likely that the site at M'kata was chosen precisely because the San populations in Tsumkwe West and East were regarded by a number of government officials as being weakly organised and with little political experience and therefore likely to pose little effective resistance to such policies.

At the time of writing, the communities have to some extent overcome a deeply ingrained fear of and false loyalty to the state. Unity has been strengthened between the communities of Tsumkwe East and West through the co-operation between the two Traditional Authorities involved.

The confidence of the San communities was further improved in July 2003 when the N‡a Jaqna Conservancy was finally gazetted by the government. The official inauguration, jointly organised by the Ministry of Environment and Tourism and WIMSA, took place on 16 December 2003. This joyous event was witnessed by about 400 adult community members from all over Tsumkwe District West.

Another positive step is the envisaged overall co-operation between the management of the N‡a Jaqna Conservancy in Tsumkwe District West and the experienced management of the Nyae Nyae Conservancy. The sense of ownership of all the San members of the N‡a Jaqna Conservancy will be deepened by the detailed community-based land use and development planning currently underway. In addition, the planning exercise will provide a powerful tool that will allow the conservancy membership to take control of the natural resources in the area. Throughout the last six years, WIMSA has never stopped supporting the formation of the conservancy and it has agreed to continue assisting the members of the N‡a Jaqna Conservancy in their effort to ensure sustainable development of the conservancy.

The recognition of San leaders through the Traditional Authorities Act was a radical departure from the past. But it provided a good and advantageous platform for the challenge that faced the community. While people were well aware of the role the peace in Angola played in the resolution of their problem, they also knew that their views were represented by those leaders who "stood up for them", approached the Prime Minister and others and took up contact with legal representatives. However the struggle against the refugee camp also exposed the fault lines that divide the community and make it vulnerable to further division in the future. Not all San elected leaders were of the opinion that it was their duty to sometimes challenge the very government that they were a part of.

The struggle to protect their land and to insist on real recognition of the rights accorded to them by law therefore continues to be part of the San's ongoing project to claim their rightful place as equals in the changing political landscape of southern Africa. ❑

Note

1 While the government's public stance may be seen as a face-saving gesture, it is widely believed that foreign donors at the time were now more than ever unwilling to finance the project and that the Namibian government did not have the cash to spend on a refugee camp that it did not need. In addition, it is possible that pragmatism was helped along by an awareness of the negative publicity that would have ensued should the project have gone ahead.

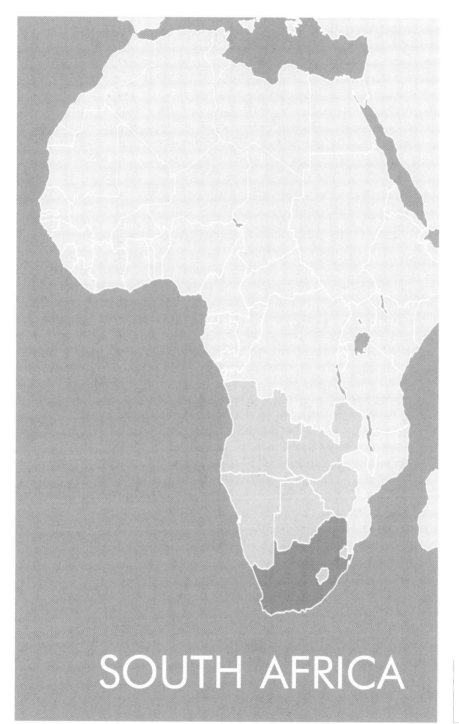

SOUTH AFRICA

THE RIGHTS OF INDIGENOUS PEOPLES IN SOUTH AFRICA

Roger Chennells and Aymone du Toit

When asked by ‡Khomani activists for guidance on what restitution they should be asking for from the government, one elder replied in the ancient language, N|u, "!ão, !haa, //x'am" - Land, Water and Truth.[1]

Defining "Indigenous"

The meaning of the term "indigenous people" is controversial in dis–course worldwide and South Africa is no exception. At present, there is no accepted South African norm. It seems that there exist two parallel definitions, one referring broadly to all South Africans of African ancestry,[2] the other developing along the lines of the United Nations Working Group on Indigenous Populations (WGIP), which refers to non-dominant groups of aboriginal or prior descent with distinct territorial and cultural identities.[3] Within the context of the latter meaning, there is further debate as to which groups would be included.[4]

In this chapter, referring to the second of the two definitions of the words "indigenous people", information relates predominantly to the various San groups, as well as the Nama and Griqua, who are collectively referred to as the Khoe.

The San roughly number 7,500 people and are, principally, the !Xun (4,500 people) and the Khwe (1,500) - the two largest San groups who live at Schmidtsdrift, 80km outside the provincial capital Kimberley;[5] and the ‡Khomani (1,000) who are scattered over an area of more than 1000 km in the Northern Cape Province. Over the past decade, a number of sundry San communities have been identified along the eastern seaboard of South Africa. These some 500 San live in small family and clan groups on the outskirts of Zulu society in KwaZulu-Natal and are often shunned as "Abatwa" or small people. As a consequence, they do not yet feel free to wear their identity openly and the adults are known amongst themselves as the "secret San".[6]

The Nama-speaking Khoe people numbered approximately five to ten thousand in 1999 and live in the Northern Cape, while there were approximately 300,000 Griquas in South Africa in 1999, ranging from impoverished rural farm labour tenants to middle-class urban dwellers (ILO 1999).

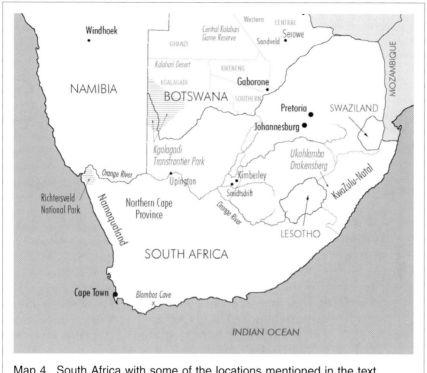

Map 4. South Africa with some of the locations mentioned in the text

The ethnic boundaries are not fixed, and the dividing lines between Khoe, San and other groups are not always evident. The National Khoisan Consultative Conference, formed in 2001, seeks to gather all of the Khoe and San groupings under one loose organisational umbrella. These groupings include the San, Griqua, Nama and Koranna. Identity remains a fluid and evolving concept.

Other groups have in the past and continue today to identify themselves as being indigenous. The substance of the claims of each of these groups varies, and will determine whether they do acquire the recognition they seek. A recent claim by some nationalist Afrikaners for recognition by the UN as indigenous peoples brings into relief the issue of definition, and accounts for a reluctance on the part of the current government to recognize certain associated minority rights, for example the right to self-determination.[7]

The apartheid state of South Africa classified Khoe and San people as "coloured", and racist policies relating to land ownership, group areas and job reservation were of equal application to them. But this classification had the additional effect of denying the existence of indigenous people, and any depictions which there were, for example in school curricula and museums, were profoundly dehumanising in their portrayal of a homogenous, largely static and primitive culture.

Today, there are still no government statistics in respect of indigenous communities, and it is difficult to make an assessment of how levels of education and income may differ from those of other people who were marginalised by the apartheid system. However, there is some indication that, today, these communities still suffer generally from a stigmatized status as a rural underclass and constitute some of the poorest of the poor.

The Current Legal and Regulatory Framework

South Africa's transition to democracy and the adoption of the interim Constitution in 1994[8] augured a new environment for indigenous peoples' rights. Indigenous communities were encouraged to assert their culture and identity and to take their place in South Africa's rich cultural tapestry. In 1997, then President Nelson Mandela noted at the Khoisan Identities and Cultural Heritage Conference[9] that "by challenging current perceptions and enriching our understanding of Khoisan cultural heritage, this conference will contribute to the renewal of our nation, our region and our continent".

In a speech in 1999, on the occasion of the celebration of the ‡Khomani land claim, the then Deputy President Mbeki emphasised the importance of the event, "What we are doing here in the Northern Cape is an example to many people around the world. We are fulfilling our pact with the United Nations during this decade of Indigenous People".

The Constitution makes specific reference to certain indigenous populations, as understood in the narrower sense outlined above,[10] in the context of language rights. Section 6(5) provides the following:

> A Pan South African Language Board established by national legislation must –
> (a) promote, and create conditions for, the development and use of –
> (ii) the Khoi, Nama and San languages.

The *Pan South African Language Board Act*[11] came into force on 4 October 1995. The Act establishes a Board of no fewer than 11 and no more than 15 persons who are appointed for a term of 5 years. The Board has the power *inter alia* to receive complaints of alleged violations of language rights, as well as wide powers of an advisory nature regarding the observance of the constitutional provisions and principles relating to the use of languages. The Board may advise government to provide financial support to individuals or groups who are adversely affected by "gross violations of language rights".

The Equality clause in the Constitution - section 9 - which reflects a substantive conception of equality, is also of significance for indigenous peoples. It recognizes that positive measures are required for the achievement of true equality in South Africa,[12] and that "equality includes the full and equal enjoyment of all rights and freedoms". In general, measures designed for the protection or advancement of people disadvantaged by unfair discrimination, for example affirmative action provisions, would be of application to indigenous peoples who, like the majority of the population, suffered under racist classification during the apartheid era.

What is not clear is the extent to which unfair discrimination experienced by indigenous minorities because of their status as such, as opposed to by virtue of their racial classification by the previous government, would be recognized. It could be argued that the form and extent of discrimination against indigenous minorities were of a particular nature with particular effects, for example forced assimilation in the education system, and that for true equality to be achieved, measures need to be taken to address these effects. A 1999 ILO report refers to an aggressive campaign of assimilation whereby Nama-speaking children were beaten for acknowledging their identity or using their language. This was similar for San children.

The equality clause also prohibits unfair discrimination on the basis of ethnic or social origin, conscience, belief and culture. The prohibition includes that of *indirect* discrimination. Indigenous peoples would have recourse to this right in instances where policies that appear to be neutral adversely affect a disproportionate number of a certain group, even if adopted in good faith.[13]

The inclusion of socio-economic rights in the Constitutional Bill of Rights is integral to a substantive notion of equality and provides a further source of rights for indigenous peoples. In particular, the property clause, which makes provision for land restitution, is of importance since the restitution of traditional land and land reform are seen by many as forming the foundation for the enforcement of other cultural and heritage rights. Whilst the rights of indigenous minorities are not specifically entrenched in this regard, the provisions provide an enabling environment and have been utilized successfully in several instances.

The Constitution provides direct protection for minority rights in sections 30 and 31. They have their history in the political process that led up to the political transition in South Africa. An analysis of indigenous peoples' rights in South Africa, particularly in a constitutional context, must take into account the political issue of "minority rights".

Minority rights, which were championed by members of the past ruling party and other political groups with an interest in protecting the rights of particular ethnic minorities in the new political dispensation, were one of the most controversial areas in the negotiations leading up to the interim and final Constitutions. In light of South Africa's past, the new ruling party was resistant to provisions that would grant special treatment to particular groups. This tension informed the drafting of many of the rights in section 31 of the Constitution, which is more detailed than section 30, providing *inter alia* that persons belonging to a cultural, religious or linguistic community may not be denied the right, along with other members of that community, to enjoy their culture, practise their religion and use their language. The section protects both individual and group interests in cultural integrity. Although the provision gives rise, at minimum, to a negative liberty, it may be interpreted as placing a positive obligation on the state to ensure the survival and development of minority cultures where they are threatened by disintegration[14]. Section 30 provides additional ground for the protection of an individual's interest in using the language and participating in the cultural life of his or her choice.

Outside the Bill of Rights, the Constitution provides for a Commission for the Promotion and Protection of the Rights of Cultural, Religious and Linguistic Communities.[15] One of the primary objects of this Commission, in terms of the Constitution, is to promote respect for the rights of cultural, religious and linguistic communities. The powers of the Commission are governed by national legislation[16] that came into force in 2002. The legislation includes, as one of the objects of the Commission, promoting the right of communities to develop their historically diminished heritage. It also provides for the establishment of community councils in accordance with the Constitutional provision. The Commission may *inter alia* conduct programmes to promote respect for and further the protection of the rights of cultural, religious and linguistic communities; monitor, investigate and research any issue concerning the rights of such communities; and receive and deal with requests relating to their rights and make recommendations regarding legislation that has an impact upon their rights.

In relation to political representation and fair administration, some indigenous communities have indicated an interest in using provisions relating to traditional leaders to ensure a voice in local government.[17] Further, the Constitution requires that municipalities take into account the language usage and preferences of their residents.[18] This would be of particular application in parts of the Northern Cape, where many indigenous people live.[19]

Finally, the Constitution grants significant status to international law, stipulating that a court, tribunal or forum must consider public international law when interpreting the Bill of Rights.[20] Although, South Africa has not ratified ILO Convention No.169, which is the only legally binding instrument protecting the rights of indigenous peoples specifically, this Convention – along with foreign case law - forms part of the body of international law. The Draft UN Declaration on the Rights of Indigenous Peoples is another important development in international law.[21]

In addition, South Africa is a party to several human rights conventions that have a bearing on indigenous peoples,[22] and resolutions adopted at regional conferences may go towards establishing the existence of certain regional norms that amount to the formation of customary international law.[23]

Apart from the Constitution, other aspects of the current legal framework in South Africa present an opportunity for indigenous peoples, for example, new legislation governing national heritage resources. *The National Heritage Resources Act*[24] was passed to transform the system for the conservation and management of South Africa's national estate by giving new participation opportunities to non-governmental heritage organisations and community groups.[25]

However, despite the provisions outlined above, indigenous people in South Africa clearly do not yet enjoy the full benefit of the law. There exists a lack of capacity on their part to enforce the rights that do exist, and a lack of capacity (and in some cases, policy formulation) on the part of government to address the specific problems faced by indigenous people. Much of what is done and needs to be done falls to lobbying and advocacy groups.

Although the Department of Constitutional Development, now the Department of Provincial and Local Government, has been involved in negotiations regarding the constitutional accommodation of indigenous communities in South Africa, in 2001 San and Nama leaders expressed their dissatisfaction with this process and the very slow progress that was being made. A prominent advocacy group was also of the view that the President and Departmental Minister had downgraded the negotiations with indigenous peoples by placing the process under general negotiations relating to the status of traditional authorities in South Africa.

Similarly, San and Nama groups found it difficult to engage effectively with the process of formation of the Commission for the Promotion and Protection of the Rights of Cultural, Religious and Linguistic Communities (SASI 2001).

Some Rights in Practice

Land and Resource Rights

The right to land is often regarded as a foundation right for indigenous peoples. With the assistance of non-governmental organisations, indigenous groups have been effective in using legislation designed for the restitution of rights in land that were lost as a result of past racially discriminatory laws or practices.[26] Although, there is no legislation dealing specifically with land alienated from Khoe and San people on the basis of race, the legislation has been used successfully by these groups in several instances.

The !Xun and Khwe San, who had been living at an army base at Schmidtsdrift since 1990, after serving the South African Defence Force in its war against SWAPO, were granted land at the Platfontein farm near Kimberley (12,900ha) in May 1999. Similarly, by early 2000, the first phase of a land claim by the ‡Khomani San, namely the transfer of ownership and management of six farms in the southern Kalahari (approximately 38,000 hectares), had been successfully completed. During August 2002 the second phase of the land claim was concluded, in which the community received another 25,000 ha in the Kgalagadi Transfrontier Park, together with significant cultural, symbolic and commercial rights in and to an area covering approximately one half of the former Kalahari Gemsbok National Park.[27]

One of the enduring challenges in the area of land restitution is illustrated by the ‡Khomani San land claim. After the successful first phase of the claim, the community struggled to manage their land, calling for urgent government intervention in 2002. It was apparent to the High Court that the community leaders did not yet have the capacity to manage all aspects of their newly acquired land, and that the leadership needed to operate for an indeterminate period under the close supervision and control of the Department of Land Affairs. The ‡Khomani San leadership currently manages the land under a form of benign curatorship, which will be lifted as soon as it is determined that they are capable of proper governance.

Two successful land claims involving Griquas have been negotiated under the restitution of land programme. The first claim was settled with a joint award of land being granted to several Griqua families and the people among whom they had remained when others left the area. The second claim, which overlapped with the first and which was brought by several other Griqua claimants, was settled through the payment of compensation. There has been a further successful land claim in the Free State which, although not perceived as a Griqua claim as such, did involve some Griqua families. Several other Griqua and

Khwe at Smidtsdrift Army Base 1996. Photo: Diana Vinding

Nama claims are currently being processed, which will add to the area of traditional land in the hands of indigenous people.

In December 1998, the Nama of the Richtersveld launched an historic claim for the land rights and associated valuable mineral rights to a large diamond-rich area of land in the barren Northern Cape. Whilst the original action in the Land Claims Court was dismissed, the applicants successfully pursued the case through an appeal to the Supreme Court of Appeal. The case was taken on further appeal to the Constitutional Court, which handed down a watershed judgment on 14 October 2003. The judgment recognized the right of the Richtersveld community to restitution of the right of ownership of the land (including its minerals and precious stones) and to the exclusive beneficial use and occupation thereof.[28] (See Chan, this volume)

An ILO Report in 1999 found that the Department of Land Affairs had actively pursued a policy of redress for San and other rural people and directly encouraged settlement of the Schmidtsdrift and Southern Kalahari land claims. However, it also found that the Department had showed less coherence in its approach to Nama cultural issues in the land resettlement projects at Riemvasmaak and Witbank. The report found further that the Department was reluctant to explore issues of policy regarding indigenous land and natural resource rights.

Language Rights

There are about ten thousand South Africans who speak one of the in-digenous languages - "indigenous" being used in its narrow sense (SASI 2002). In the last two decades, at least four languages have become ex-tinct and the four surviving languages, Khoekhoegowab (Nama), !Xun, Khwedam and the almost extinct N|u language, are all under extreme threat (SASI 2001). Yet, indigenous peoples have thus far struggled to use the relevant constitutional sections effectively to address their needs.

An ILO study in 1999 reported that the Pan-South African Language Board (PanSALB)[29] had at that time made it clear that it did not have the capacity to assist Khoe and San people other than through grant-making. Thus it was found that only well-resourced constituencies with access to researchers, linguists and project managers would be in a po-sition to benefit from the constitutional section.

A lack of coherence in policy at national level seems to be a dimension of the problems being experienced. In the past, the staff of the then Depart-ment of Culture, Science and Tourism had indicated that PanSALB and the Department of Provincial and Local Government were the only Depart-ments/Bodies mandated to deal with indigenous cultural and language rights, whereas both of these have denied this allegation (SASI 2001).

However, a potentially important structure to emerge recently is the Khoe and San National Language Body, which first came into being in August 1999 as part of PanSALB but which initially had very little sup-port from its parent structure. The current members of this body are speakers of various Khoe and San languages in South Africa. An advo-cacy group, the South African San Institute (SASI), and PanSALB funded organisational development training for the members of this body dur-ing 2000 and 2001 and the body has recently begun to test its strength by challenging several government departments, the South African Broad-casting Authority (SABC) and other agencies to clarify what each is do-ing to promote the use of the languages of indigenous peoples. Howev-er the body remains fairly weak, with inadequate technical support and limited internal capacity for budgeting and operations (SASI 2002).

Education

Indigenous children have been found, throughout Southern Africa, to suffer from barriers to learning brought about by language and cultur-al differences. Whereas, there is a new willingness in South Africa to integrate cultural knowledge into school curricula, and emerging pol-icy provides scope for individual adaptation of school syllabi to fit the particular needs and circumstances of children, capacity problems exist for the implementation of innovative methods, especially in rural areas (see Hays, this volume).

A 1999 ILO report found that the national Department of Education did not have policies in place with regard to the education of indigenous people. At that time, there had not yet been contact between the national department and PanSALB and, according to officials, Nama could not be introduced in schools as anything but a foreign language subject, and then only after the approval by the Director-General and the Council of Education Ministers. However, at provincial level, a pilot project was started in 1999 or 2000 in the tiny settlement of Kuboes in the Richtersveld where about 200 learners at a primary school were studying Nama as a school subject. In 2002, this pilot Khoekhoegowab early primary project was expanded to a second school on the Orange River (*The Indigenous World 2002-2003*).

The right to a basic education in the Constitution includes the right to receive education in the official language or languages of one's choice. However, traditional indigenous peoples' languages are not included as official languages. Furthermore, although the state is not precluded from subsidizing any independent institutions that may be established, it is not required to do so.

Many of the issues that arise in the area of education are illustrated with reference to the Schmidtsdrift San Combined School in the Northern Cape. This government school was, in 2002, the largest educational project for San children in Southern Africa (Le Roux 1999). Through the involvement of the !Xun and Khwe Communal Property Association, the school experimented with alternative education programmes to ease the gap experienced by children moving from a traditional lifestyle to formal schooling in a language that is not their own.

Due to the mediation of the !Xun and Khwe and the South African Defence Force (SADF), this school was able to introduce three pre-primary bridging classes in mother tongue with government paid translator aides as well as qualified pre-school teachers (Le Roux 1999).

However, the Northern Cape government stopped using special programmes due to a lack of funding, although the bridging classes continued to be operational. In 2000, the school was rated the poorest school in the Northern Cape on the Norms and Standards for School-Funding Resource Targeting Table for that year.[30] Apart from the translators, who were used in the first grade because of a lack of proficiency in English or Afrikaans on the part of the children, the staff did not speak any of the indigenous San languages. The medium of instruction was Afrikaans. The principal of the school noted in 2000 that many of the pupils failed because of the language barrier. However, the relocation of the school, in 2004, to new buildings at Platfontein following the successful land claim by the !Xun and Khwe community referred to above, was met with enthusiasm.

Among adults, the 1999 ILO Report found that, owing to close associations with military infrastructures, the !Xun and Khwe at Schmidtsdrift had higher than average basic adult literacy in Afrikaans. The ‡Khomani, however, had very low literacy levels, particularly in rural areas and, similarly, Namas' access to adequate education in the Northern Cape was below average. For Griquas, educational standards vary greatly, ranging from impoverished rural farm labour tenants to middle-class urban dwellers.

Despite some of the problems noted above, there is evidence of active government involvement in education on a provincial level. The Director of the Department of Culture in the Northern Cape has supervised San projects to re-establish cultural identity and language and has made funding available for fieldwork for linguistic projects. Similarly, the provincial Department of Education in the Northern Cape recently commissioned a report on the language in education needs of San (!Xun, Khwe and ‡Khomani) and Nama communities.

The Province has also agreed to create a Provincial Language Committee, which must include a representative from the Khoe and San National Language Body. In the last couple of years, the Chairperson of the Khoe and San National Language Body visited outlying Nama communities at Steinkopf, Kubus, Onseepkans and Pella to inform them of the language in education opportunities and the work of the Khoe and San National Language Body. Although many programmes are initiated by lobbying groups, private bodies and individuals, it is hoped that government will continue to develop its role in this area.

Other Constitutional Rights in Practice

The Constitution provides that everyone has the right to health care services, including reproductive health care,[31] and sufficient food and water[32] and that the State must take reasonable legislative and other measures, within its available resources, to achieve the progressive realisation of each of these rights.[33] Many South African indigenous people live in arid to semi-arid areas of the country and inadequate access to clean water is of concern. The 1999 ILO Report noted that while the !Xun and Khwe at Schmidtsdrift had higher than average health care standards (again due to their close associations with military infrastructures), there were regular outbreaks of gastroenteritis in the Kalahari settlements and certain township settlements. Access to health care facilities is below average in the Northern Cape for Namas, while for Griquas, health care standards vary greatly, ranging from impoverished rural farm labour tenants to middle-class urban dwellers.

The ILO report also found that, at that time, the Khoe and San people had not been invited to participate in rural health care programmes, particularly those involving traditional leaders. As is the case for many South Africans, many indigenous people have to walk long distances to get to clinics. Thus, it appears that this right has yet to be realised in practice.

Finally, the Constitution provides the right to: have the environment protected, for the benefit of present and future generations, through reasonable legislative and other measures that prevent pollution and ecological degradation; promote conservation; and secure ecologically sustainable development and use of natural resources while promoting justifiable economic and social development.[34]

However, at least until 1999, the actions of mining companies in Namaqualand were of concern to Nama communities. Although mining companies are by law required to refill and restore open pit mines once the mine is no longer in use, this was not done in practice. This has a negative effect on the tourism potential of the area and would amount to a violation of the constitutional provision. Situations such as these require the continued attention of government and lobbying groups.

Intellectual Property Rights and Heritage Rights

The field of intellectual property rights is, in the discourse of indigenous peoples, often referred to by the broader concept of "heritage rights", which includes the rights to all aspects of heritage and culture, including the legal rights to ideas and aspects of culture (myths, songs, knowledge, images) defined by the term "intellectual property".

This area is in its infancy for indigenous peoples in South Africa and the role of advocacy groups will become increasingly important. It is legally complex and indigenous people suffer from a lack of legal and practical information. Communities, which are disparate and geographically isolated, have lacked a common policy and there are few community-based mechanisms to ensure the protection and management of intellectual property.

Once traditional resource knowledge is in the public domain, it is outside the protection of conventional intellectual property law. Information transfer incorporating expressions of folklore, and traditional knowledge such as medicinal or ethno-botanical information, should be preceded by an agreement regarding its use, distribution and remuneration.

During 2001, the San discovered that the Council for Scientific and Industrial Research (CSIR) had, in 1995, patented the rights to the desert succulent *Hoodia Gordonii*, or *!Khoba*, which had been licensed to Phytopharm in the UK and further sublicensed to Pfizer Inc. for intended trial and eventual commercial release as an appetite suppressant. The

San have used Hoodia for millennia, as a thirst and appetite suppressant, and had freely shared their knowledge with scientists, which led eventually to the patent. The San commenced negotiations with the CSIR in order to ensure that the royalties and other benefits accruing from the commercial drug were equitably shared with the San. In March 2003, the San - in partnership with WIMSA (Working Group of Indigenous Minorities in Southern Africa) and the South African San Institute (SASI) - were finally successful in securing a landmark out-of-court deal recognizing the collective intellectual property of the San over exploitation of !Khoba. The settlement is dependent on the sub-licensee, originally Pfizer, successfully marketing a weight-loss drug derived from the !Khoba's hunger-suppressing compounds, and which could potentially see the San earning millions of South African Rands in profits. During July 2003, Pfizer announced its withdrawal from the license, leading to a further search by Phytopharm for a new sub-licensee. At the time of going to press this had not been finalised. Funds are to be channelled to a San-controlled Hoodia Benefit Sharing Trust, which will assume responsibility for distributing the funds for regional poverty alleviation and development initiatives.

South Africa's estimated 15,000 rock art sites are the most significant and priceless of heritage resources. It is largely accepted that ancient sites with sacred, artistic or other value should be protected on behalf of the nation by national legislation, as they are, to a degree, national assets. However, it is the balancing of the ownership, overall control, management and the associated flow of benefits with the San, descendants of the original artists, that needs to be clearly acknowledged and negotiated. In respect of these rights, the new National Heritage Resources Act, referred to above, is of most direct significance on a national level. During the process leading to the application for the listing of the Drakensberg mountain range, with its internationally recognized wealth of San rock art sites, as a World Heritage Site, the government officials of KwaZulu-Natal inexplicably failed to recognize or negotiate with the recognized leaders of the San as the current custodians of the San heritage. This situation was rectified after WIMSA's urgent intervention and, by the time of the formal opening of the Didima San Rock Art Centre at Cathedral Peak Game Reserve in November 2003, the southern African San leadership had been fully recognized and afforded due honour as key dignitaries at the ceremony.

Finally, regional and national developments in the areas of heritage and intellectual property rights are of singular importance. The Working Group of Indigenous Minorities in southern Africa (WIMSA), which is the collective Council representing all San in the countries of southern Africa, has as its focus the legal protection of San heritage and intellectual property rights. In addition, a review of the shortcomings of international intellectual property law in the context of indigenous peoples, by the World Intellectual Property Organisation (WIPO), is a positive step in the right direction and could have real impact in South Africa given the status granted to international law by the Constitution.

Conclusion

The landscape of indigenous peoples' rights in South Africa is a diverse one. Several successful land claims have represented high points in the short history since the establishment of democracy in 1994. The Constitution grants important political and socio-economic rights that are of application to indigenous peoples, and there exists a growing awareness of the importance of indigenous languages and cultures. Although government policy is as yet unformulated in certain areas, and the continued existence of advocacy and lobbying groups is essential, some progress has been made.

However, it remains to be seen whether the grandchildren of the ‡Khomani elder quoted at the beginning of this chapter will, in turn, ask for land, water and truth or whether we will have met the challenges presented by our past. ❏

Notes

1   International Labor Office, 1999: 3.
2   This is as the term is used in Section 6(2) of the Constitution, "Recognising the historically diminished use and status of the indigenous languages of our people, the state must take practical and positive measures to elevate the status and advance the use of these languages". In this sense, the term is defined by reference to European colonialism.
3   Saugestad, in her Royal African Society lecture (2000) "Contested Images: 'First Peoples' or 'Marginalised Minorities' in Africa", notes that despite arguments that no binding definition exists internationally, the definition in the Cobo study, which first introduced the concept to the UN, has stood the test of time remarkably well. It highlights a priority in time; the voluntary perpetuation of cultural distinctiveness; an experience of subjugation, marginalisation and dispossession; and self-identification.
4   A process of negotiation between the then Department of Constitutional Development and Griqua, Nama and San communities in 1999 identified five constituencies to be researched in order to clarify their membership and claims – Griqua, Nama, San, !Koranna, and the Cape Cultural Heritage Development Council.
5   These two San groups originate from Angola and Namibia. Employed by the South African Defence Force during the independence war, they were moved together with their families in 1990 and resettled on a military camp in Schmidtsdrift.

6   They are in the process of being incorporated in the Pan Southern African San umbrella organisation, the Working Group of Indigenous Minorities in South Africa, (WIMSA).

7   If the term "indigenous people" were to be seen as a relational term, as suggested by Saugestad in "Contested Images: 'First Peoples' or 'Marginalised Minorities' in Africa" (2001: 7), the problem might be alleviated: "A group is only indigenous in relation to another, encompassing group, and thus the meaning depends on the historical context".

8   In 1994, South Africa adopted an interim Constitution for a transitional period. The final Constitution, the Constitution of the Republic of South Africa, Act 108 of 1996, came into force in early 1997 (hereinafter "the Constitution").

9   Held at the University of Western Cape and funded by the Art and Culture Trust – a national funding agency.

10 Note that section 6(2) makes reference to the historically diminished use and status of the indigenous languages and provides that the State must take practical and positive measures to elevate the status and advance the use of these languages. The term "indigenous" in this section is meant in the broader sense outlined above.

11 Act 59 of 1995.

12 Section 9(2) recognises that legislative and other measures designed to protect or advance persons, or categories of persons, disadvantaged by unfair discrimination are integral to the realization of equality, and that "equality includes the full and equal enjoyment of all rights and freedoms".

13 In the context of the *Restitution of Land Rights Act 22* of 1994, the Constitutional Court found, in the landmark judgment *Alexcor Ltd and Another v Richtersveld Community and Others 2003* (12) BCLR 1301 (CC), that certain precious minerals legislation, which had discriminated between registered and non-registered owners of land, was racially discriminatory in that its effect was to discriminate against black land owners who for the most part did not have registered title.

14 Chaskalson et al. (1996) 1999:35-18. Currie notes that constitutional interpretation requires one to look further than the phrasing: "Whilst paying due regard to the language that has been used, [an interpretation should be] 'generous' and 'purposive' and give… expression to the underlying values of the Constitution" – *S v Makwanyane & another 1995 (3) SA 391 (CC)*.

15 Section 185.

16 The Commission for the Promotion and Protection of the Rights of Cultural, Religious and Linguistic Communities Act 19 of 2002.

17 Participation of traditional leaders in local government is now governed by s 81 of the *Local Government Municipal Structures Act* 117 of 1998. An ILO report compiled in 1999 noted that the then Department of Constitutional Development was giving serious consideration to creating equity between Khoe, San and "Bantu" systems of traditional leadership representation.

18 Section 6(3)(b).

19 Note also section 35(4) governing procedures relating to arrested, detained and accused persons. Whenever this section requires information to be given to a

person, that information must be given in a language that the person understands. Note, however, that in *Naidenov v Minister of Home Affairs 1995 (7) BCLR 891 (T)*, it was pointed out that the right to be informed of the reasons for detention in a language that one understands does not mean one must be addressed in one's own language.

20 Section 39(1)(b).

21 These instruments are referred to by some as amounting to customary international law, for example, Anaya, 1997:2.

22 The most significant of these is the UN's Covenant on Civil and Political Rights. Also important is the Convention on All Forms of Racial Discrimination.

23 For example, the Regional Conference on Development Programmes for Africa's San/Basarwa Populations, Windhoek, 1992; the Second Regional Conference on Development Programmes for Africa's San/Basarwa Populations: Common Access to Development, Gaborone 1993; and the Indigenous Peoples' Consultation, Botswana, 1999.

24 Act 25 of 1999.

25 NGOs may nominate people to serve on national and provincial heritage resources councils. The Act obliges heritage resources authorities to develop the skills and capacities of persons and communities involved in heritage resources management. Organisations may apply for financial assistance for heritage resources projects. The Act makes provision for the establishment of a legal contract between a heritage resources authority and another person or body for the conservation of a particular place. Members of the public may register their interest in a particular type of heritage resource so that they may be informed and involved in decision making.

26 Restitution of Land Rights Act 22 of 1994.

27 The agreement, entitled the !Ae!Hai Kalahari Heritage Park Agreement, was formally signed by the Minister of Land Affairs at a ceremony at Twee Rivieren on 31 August 2002.

28 *Alexcor Ltd and Another v Richtersveld Community and Others 2003* (12) BCLR 1301 (CC).

29 The constitutionally mandated structure responsible for monitoring and supporting the achievement of language rights and equitable policy.

30 "One People, many different worlds; the oldest culture in Southern Africa faces huge change if it's to survive". *The Teacher* Vol. 5, 2 (Feb. 2000):12. The school was accordingly earmarked to receive a favourable share of funding from the provincial education department.

31 Section 27(1)(a).

32 Section 27(1)(b).

33 Section 27(2).

34 Section 24.

THE RICHTERSVELD CHALLENGE:
SOUTH AFRICA FINALLY ADOPTS ABORIGINAL TITLE

T.M. Chan

I n 1994, South Africa transformed from an apartheid state into a new constitutional democracy formed on principles of justice and equality. The
government, previously led by and benefiting a small white minority,
shifted to a black majority-led government determined to extend the
franchise and equal protection of the law to all South Africans regardless of race. During apartheid, over 85% of South Africans did not have
the vote and could not legally own land. As part of the post-apartheid
transformation, the right to land of, and the restoration of land to, the
previously disenfranchised were recognized issues of "supreme importance"[1] that captured the attention of the new government. The draft-
ers of the new Constitution ensured equitable access to land and redress
for racially discriminatory land dispossessions by entrenching the principles in the new Constitution and mandating the creation of laws for
the successful application of these principles.[2] As mandated, the Parliament passed the *Restitution of Land Rights Act*[3] (*Restitution Act*) to assist
in efficient and fair land reform. The Land Claims Court was created the
same year and plaintiffs began to bring land claims to the court.

The laws and the courts focused on the immediate and pressing
need to redress injustices from the recent past.[4] The new government
grappled with the tensions surrounding land dispossession from the
apartheid period balancing, on the one hand, the need to prove the
new government's legitimacy by creating substantive laws that would
directly address apartheid dispossessions and that would promote the
principles of justice and equality, and on the other, the practical reality that returning all lands dispossessed during apartheid could create considerable instability that could, in turn, undermine the fragile
new peace.[5]

In the shadow of the complexities created by the apartheid legacy,
indigenous rights to land began to emerge as a growing concern. The
descendants of indigenous communities that had occupied land at the
time of colonization, more than a century before apartheid, were seeking to have their rights to land recognized under the promise of the
new government and their laws. As the movement for indigenous land
rights gained political traction, one of the most topical issues of land
redistribution in post-apartheid South Africa became the role of the equitable doctrine of aboriginal title under the new regime.

Although aboriginal title was recognized in a number of former British colonies,[6] it had not been fully adopted in any country in sub-Saharan Africa prior to the Richtersveld challenge.[7] As developed in comparative jurisdictions, aboriginal title is generally understood to be a common law doctrine based on the principles of justice and equality.[8] Developed outside the statutory paradigm, the doctrine of aboriginal title vests a right in land in indigenous communities who occupied land at the time of colonization.[9] The basic equitable principle is that colonization should not automatically be deemed to have divested indigenous communities of their rights to land, especially in light of the fact that the indigenous communities continued to live on and use the land after colonization without any express act by the colonizing settlers to acknowledge or extinguish such rights.[10]

During apartheid in South Africa, a doctrine of aboriginal title based on fairness and granting rights to colored descendants of indigenous communities was obviously inconsistent with the policies of the government: the doctrine of aboriginal title had neither taken root nor spawned serious consideration. However, following transformation, the principles behind aboriginal title such as racial equality, redress for past wrongs and land rights for the previously disenfranchised, all resonated with the spirit of the new South Africa. The questions emerged: would the doctrine of aboriginal title be recognized to create a right in land in South Africa? Did such a doctrine of equity have a place in the new South Africa and, if so, would there be any real benefits to the descendants of indigenous communities?[11]

In 2000, people from the Richtersveld, descendants from indigenous groups inhabiting the arid northwest corner of South Africa, brought the matter to a head with the first direct challenge in the courts. This chapter follows the Richtersveld case as it moves through the courts. First, this chapter begins by introducing the people of the Richtersveld and their claims under the law. Then it examines the holdings of the courts: from the court of first instance, the Land Claims Court, to the appeal at the Supreme Court of Appeal and to the final appeal at the Constitutional Court. The chapter concludes that the Constitutional Court of South Africa introduced aboriginal title into South African law in the form of "indigenous law ownership".

Background to the Challenge

The following is an introduction to the factual and legal background of the Richtersveld case. As an initial note, any reference to the "Richtersveld Community" throughout this chapter shall mean (1) the present-day inhabitants of the Richtersveld who have been recognized by the courts as the Richtersveld community in the Richtersveld opinions examined herein and (2) the continuous community from which this present-day community has descended and evolved, as the context dictates.

The Richtersveld Community[12]

The Richtersveld is situated within the larger area known as Namaqualand in the Northern Cape Province of South Africa. Namaqualand is an arid region bordering the Kalahari desert and was originally inhabited by the Khoe Khoe and the San people. For centuries, the Khoe Khoe, the San and the merged population of Khoesan occupied the land in a nomadic fashion as pastoralists and hunter-gatherers. Their present-day descendants include the Richtersveld Community, which continues to occupy the land in a similar manner as their indigenous forbearers.

In 1847, the British Crown (the "Crown") annexed a large part of Namaqualand, including the Richtersveld. Although the Crown held sovereignty over the annexed land, the limits of private property ownership rights were not clear. The area remained lightly populated and the Richtersveld Community continued to pursue their pastoral and hunter-gatherer activities. They continued to exercise exclusive beneficial occupation of the land, including the right to exclude and to lease the land to others.

Upon the discovery of diamonds in Namaqualand in 1925, the government clarified its approach: as interest in alluvial diggings increased, the government claimed the land in question (the "subject land") as unalienated Crown land, entitling the Crown to award claims for digging. The Richtersveld people were progressively denied access to the subject land for their traditional uses. In 1994, the ownership of the subject land passed to a diamond-mining company called Alexkor, of which the sole shareholder is the government.

South African Law: the Constitution and the Restitution of Land Rights Act

As discussed in the introduction, land reform was a critical component of South Africa's transition from an apartheid state to a constitutional democracy. The new Constitution embodied a commitment to socio-economic rights, a positive duty on the state to provide basic rights to all.[13] The expansive protection of the new Constitution invited all South Africans for the first time in their history to explore their entitlement to basic rights such as land rights, as embodied in a bill of rights.[14] The new government's aims underscored broad purposes, but the practical reality was that the government was understandably focused on creating laws that eradicated the most immediate injustices of apartheid.[15] Incorporated into the Constitution of South Africa were the principles to ensure equitable access to land and to redress the racially discriminatory land dispossessions of the past. In relevant part to the Richtersveld challenge, Section 25(7) of the Constitution of the Republic of South Africa, as ratified in 1997, provided that

> [a] person or community dispossessed of property after 19 June 1913 as a result of past racially discriminatory laws or practices is entitled, to the extent provided by an Act of Parliament, either to restitution of that property or to equitable redress.[16]

As mandated by Section 25(7), Parliament subsequently passed the *Restitution Act*, which reads in relevant part:

> A person shall be entitled to restitution of a right in land if —
>
> d) it is a community or part of a community dispossessed of a right in land after 19 June 1913 as a result of past racially discriminatory laws or practices, and
> e) the claim for such restitution is lodged not later than 31 December 1998.[17]

To succeed in a claim for restitution under the *Restitution Act*, a claimant would have to prove the following five elements:

1. community
2. a "right in land" prior to dispossession
3. dispossession after June 19, 1913
4. such dispossession as a result of past racially discriminatory laws or practices
5. claim lodged no later than December 31, 1998.

The debate surrounding aboriginal title in the Richtersveld case turned in large part on proving the second element, the "right to land". Under the *Restitution Act*, a "right in land" was defined as

> any right in land whether registered or unregistered, and may include the interest of a labour tenant and sharecropper, a customary law interest, the interest of a beneficiary under a trust arrangement and beneficial occupation for a continuous period of not less than 10 years prior to dispossession in question.[18]

In the Richtersveld case, the question became whether aboriginal title created a "right in land" under the *Restitution Act*.

Prior to the Richtersveld case, the *Restitution Act* and aboriginal title were considered alternative causes of action. Neither the legislature nor the courts had determined whether a doctrine of aboriginal title was part of South African law.[19] But in considering whether it should be adopted, scholars addressed the doctrine as separate from the *Restitution Act*. As one academic paper noted, "[f]or those who cannot meet the requirements of the Restitution of Land Rights Act, aboriginal title . . . will provide an alternative common-law ground of action".[20]

As a separate cause of action, aboriginal title offered another avenue of relief where a deserving claimant might otherwise fail to qualify under the *Restitution Act*.[21] Under the act, a claimant had to prove dispossession occurred due to racially discriminatory laws or practices that occurred after 1913. In addition, the *Restitution Act* limited restitution to claims made before 1998. By contrast, under a doctrine of aboriginal title, a claimant's right to land would not be subject to requirements of proof under the act. In addition, the claimant would not be subject to the 1998 filing date.

The doctrine known as aboriginal title in Canada and Australia, also known in comparative jurisdictions as native title, indigenous title or Indian title,[22] springs from common-law, from a recognition by courts over time that certain indigenous land rights should survive colonization. It should be noted, however, that some jurisdictions have fully embraced aboriginal title within their statutory framework. For example, a number of jurisdictions have recognized aboriginal rights in their respective constitutions.[23] In other jurisdictions such as Britain, however, a doctrine of aboriginal title remains one that is recognized through the precedents of courts.[24]

Despite the variations by jurisdiction, aboriginal title remains consistently based on principles of justice and equality. Where aboriginal title is recognized, it establishes rights in an indigenous community shown to be occupying the land at colonization.[25] In addition, as academic scholars have noted, "[a]ll jurisdictions that have recognized the doctrine of aboriginal title have deemed it to be sui generis".[26] Although each jurisdiction decides on a case by case basis the rights that flow from aboriginal title, several characteristics consistently distinguish aboriginal rights from common law property rights: aboriginal title is held communally, not individually; aboriginal title originates in pre-colonial systems of indigenous law; and once title is established, it is inalienable to anyone except the Crown or state government.[27] General trends to determine the elements of proof of aboriginal title have also emerged from foreign and international law. To prove title, claimants have to show they are a surviving distinct community descending from an indigenous community that at the time of colonization occupied the land. Factors to consider include occupation of the land at the time of colonization, period of occupation, exclusivity, continuity on land, social organization and traditional laws and customs with respect to the land.[28] In addition, to succeed in a claim, the aboriginal right to land must not be extinguished. The general rule is that the state or Crown must show clear and plain intention of extinguishment.[29] If not, the claimant community can successfully claim rights to the land.

Although legal scholars had envisioned aboriginal title under South African law to be a distinct common law cause of action outside of the *Restitution Act*, the Richtersveld challenge in the Land Claims Court presented an alternative approach. The Richtersveld Community as plaintiffs introduced aboriginal title in an incremental step to the courts; rather than arguing for a separate cause of action, the plaintiffs presented aboriginal title as part of the argument for restitution under the *Restitution Act*. They argued aboriginal title as the basis for a "right in land" under the act.

Richtersveld Case Law:
From the Land Claims Court to the Constitutional Court

The Richtersveld Community first brought their claim to the Land Claims Court of South Africa, and then appealed the opinion to the Supreme Court of Appeal of South Africa. The case was then further appealed to the Constitutional Court of South Africa. The following section will examine the three sequential opinions of the Richtersveld case with an emphasis on the courts' interpretations of a "right in land" under the *Restitution Act*. It will argue that the Constitutional Court's finding of "indigenous law ownership" was equivalent to ownership under the doctrine of aboriginal title.

Land Claims Court of South Africa

In 2000, the Richtersveld Community, as plaintiffs, brought two separate claims of action: one in the Land Claims Court of South Africa (LCC) claiming land restitution under the *Restitution Act* and the other in the Cape High Court of South Africa, a trial court of general jurisdiction, asking for an order declaring land rights on the grounds of aboriginal title. The Richtersveld Community subsequently chose not to proceed with the aboriginal title action in the Cape High Court until the final determination of the claim under the *Restitution Act* in the Land Claims Court.

In the LCC, the plaintiffs incorporated aboriginal title as part of their claim under the *Restitution Act*. The plaintiffs asserted that they were a community holding title to the subject land and that such title was not at any time prior to June 19, 1913 lawfully extinguished or diminished. They claimed the Richtersveld Community held a "right in land" under the *Restitution Act* based on the following:

a) ownership;
b) a right based on aboriginal title allowing them the exclusive beneficial occupation and use of the subject land, or the right to use the subject land for certain specified purposes; or
c) "a right in land" over the subject land acquired through their beneficial occupation thereof for a period longer than 10 years prior to their eventual dispossession.[30]

The LCC summarily rejected the first claim. The court found that the government believed it owned the land at the time of annexation and that under the laws of that time, the indigenous Richtersveld Community was insufficiently civilized to own land.[31] The court then turned to the aboriginal title claim and engaged in a lengthy rationale for its rejection of the aboriginal title claim.[32] Despite the fact that the court was created to be a specialized court of expertise in land law and for the purpose of interpreting the *Restitution Act* and any other ancillary laws necessary for the interpretation of the *Restitution Act*, the court stated several times and at length that the adoption of the doctrine of aboriginal title into South African law was a matter for the courts of general jurisdiction.[33] The LCC evaded the legal question of aboriginal title by shifting jurisdiction to other courts.

Although the reason for the court's reluctance to address aboriginal title is unclear, the court gives some insight into its concerns by citing with approval that

> [i]n South Africa, of course, [the extension of the land claims process right back to the time of colonial settlement] would have proven disastrous. Not only would the entire land surface of the country have become subject to claims, but the very ethnic tensions which the land claims process hopes to resolve would simply have been exacerbated.[34]

In addition, the court also included a quote noting that the past colonial land dispossessions were "too complex to reverse, given massive demographic shifts which occurred, the absence of written records and the passage of time".[35]

The LCC also briefly raised and dismissed the idea that the plaintiffs' assertions might more accurately be construed as a "customary law interest". The LCC interpreted the "customary law interest" narrowly as an interest that had to be recognized by the courts, the state or the Crown at the time of dispossession. Based on the LCC's narrow interpretation of "customary law interest", the LCC found no such recognition of indigenous land laws in the Cape Colony and, accordingly, dismissed the idea that the Richtersveld Community would have rights under a "customary law interest" claim.[36] Moreover, the LCC then expressly declined to accept indigenous title as a "customary law interest'." [37]

The court ultimately did find under the third claim that the plaintiffs had a statutory "right in land" based on occupancy of the land in question for over 10 years.[38] The court, however, determined that the rights were not dispossessed as a result of a "past racially discriminatory law or practice" within the meaning of the *Restitution Act*.[39] The court determined that the *Restitution Act* was meant to redress only the discrimination of apartheid, in particular apartheid efforts to spatially segregate by race, and any dispossession of the land in the present case did not take place due to spatial segregation during apartheid.[40] In conclusion, the LCC held that the Richtersveld Community was not entitled to restitution under the *Restitution Act* and dismissed their claim.[41]

Supreme Court of Appeal: Case Summary

In 2003, the Supreme Court of Appeal heard an appeal against the dismissal by the LCC of the Richtersveld Community's claim for restitution under the *Restitution Act*. With respect to a "right in land", the Richtersveld Community, as appellants, contended that in addition to the right to beneficial occupation found by the LCC, the indigenous Richtersveld community possessed rights under indigenous law and, upon annexation, the existing land rights of the inhabitants of the Richtersveld were recognized and protected under the common law. Alternatively, the appellants contended that rights in the land under indigenous law constituted "customary law interest" and as such, the Richtersveld community held "rights in land" for purposes of the *Restitution Act*, regardless of common law.[42]

In response to the LCC, the SCA reframed the issue of "rights in land" under the *Restitution Act*. A "right in land" under the act was defined as

any right in land whether registered or unregistered, and may include the interest of a labour tenant and sharecropper, a customary law interest, the interest of a beneficiary under a trust arrangement and beneficial occupation for a continuous period of not less than 10 years prior to dispossession in question.[43]

The LCC had interpreted the list of specified interests as exhaustive. By contrast, the SCA interpreted the words "may include" to extend the definition beyond those specified interests. Where the LCC asked whether any of the specified interests would qualify the Richtersveld Community for "rights in land" under the act, the SCA reframed the question to ask whether the rights held by the Richtersveld Community would comport with the spirit of the act. The SCA expanded the "right in land" to include broad categories of rights not even contemplated by the laws.[44]

Despite the effort to broadly interpret the statute, the SCA retreated in application, finding a "right in land" based on a "customary law interest", an enumerated right under the *Restitution Act*. In the lower court, the LCC had introduced but summarily rejected a "customary law interest". The LCC had advanced a requirement that a claimant would have to prove that their customary law was adopted or sanctioned by the state, the courts or the Crown in some official manner at the time of dispossession in order for the claimant to succeed in proving a "customary law interest".[45] The LCC's holding would make it difficult for a claimant community to ever succeed under the standard since it is axiomatic that claimants seeking redress for rights unprotected by the state, court or Crown would be unable to prove these rights were recognized by the state, court or Crown. The SCA rejected the LCC's position and instead shifted the test to one that looked at whether a right existed at the time of annexation under indigenous law regardless of state, court or Crown recognition.[46] As noted by the SCA, "[the Richtersveld Community's] right was rooted in the traditional laws and custom of the Richtersveld people. The right inhered in the people inhabiting the Richtersveld as their common property, passing from generation to generation".[47] In addition, the SCA added language that seemed to imply that rights viewed through the lens of indigenous law had to also meet an English and Roman-Dutch standard of "custom" in order to amount to a "customary law interest".[48] Upon review, the SCA found in combination that both parties had conceded that the Richtersveld Community held a "customary law interest" at the time of annexation and that the facts based on indigenous law at the time of annexation satisfied the "custom" requirements.[49] The court concluded that the Richtersveld Community had a "right in land" based on a "customary law interest" at the time of annexation.[50]

The SCA opinion then turned to whether the right in land survived extinguishment before 1913, the cut-off date under the *Restitution Act*. Following an extensive analysis, the court concluded that the Richtersveld Community exercised and enjoyed exclusive beneficial occupation of the whole of the Richtersveld until at least the mid-1920s.[51] In addition, the court determined that extinguishment of title after 1913

122

was a result of "past racially discriminatory laws or practices" as set forth under the *Restitution Act*.[52]

The SCA set aside the orders of the LCC and replaced them with orders granting the Richtersveld Community restitution under the *Restitution Act* "of the right to exclusive beneficial occupation and use, akin to that held under common law ownership", of the subject land (including its minerals and precious stones).[53]

Supreme Court of Appeal: Analysis

The SCA opinion was a partial victory for the Richtersveld Community. They won rights to the land but those rights were not ownership rights. Upon further examination, the SCA opinion is striking in that the court seemed to be struggling with the unrealized wish to recognize ownership rights in land under aboriginal title but settling for the uncomfortable fit of a "customary law interest". One sign of the tension can be seen in the manner in which the SCA attempted to massage a "customary law interest" into fitting the paradigm of aboriginal title. For example, the right the SCA granted based on a "customary law interest" was one the court described in its order as "akin to that held under common law ownership". The addition of "akin to that held under common law ownership" stretched the rights under "customary law interest" to include non-common law communal property rights based on pre-colonial indigenous law. The additional "akin to common law ownership" phrase appeared to be an attempt to give rights to the Richtersveld Community that would approximate aboriginal title, which is a communal right vested in an aboriginal people based on their laws prior to and at the time of colonization.[54]

Another sign of the tension can be seen in the manner in which the SCA used the aboriginal title paradigm to prove a "customary law interest". Aboriginal title looks to whether a right in land existed at the time of colonization under the indigenous law, without regard to the state's, court's or Crown's acknowledgment.[55] This is a similar approach taken by the SCA when it accepted that the Richtersveld Community had "a customary law interest under *their* indigenous customary law" at the time of annexation.[56] Even methods of examining traditional laws and customs to prove aboriginal rights track those set forth for proving "customary law interest".[57] The court itself noted that "[l]ike the customary law interest that [the court had] found was held by the Richtersveld Community, aboriginal title is rooted in and is the 'creature of traditional laws and customs'".[58]

Additionally, the SCA actually cited aboriginal title articles and cases, pointing to the elements of aboriginal title as precedents for proving elements for a claim of a "customary law interest".[59] The SCA then proceeded to prove each of the elements of an aboriginal title claim: that the indigenous Richtersveld Community was a "discrete" ethnic group,[60] who "occupied" the land for a "long time"[61] prior to and at the time of annexation;[62] they enjoyed the "exclusive beneficial occupation" of the land;[63] and they had a "social and political structure"[64] that included laws governing the land[65] which they enforced.[66] But instead of finding a right under aboriginal title, the SCA concluded that such facts supported a "customary law interest". The SCA did not explain its dependency on the doctrine of aboriginal title or the difference between that doctrine and a "customary law interest".[67]

Another aspect of the opinion that seemed to underscore a tension between the SCA's impulse towards granting a right under aboriginal title and the SCA's decision to choose a more cautious approach can be seen in the court's discourses on law, several of which supported a claim under aboriginal title but served little or no purpose in relation to a "customary law interest". For example, the SCA widened the scope of the definition of a "right in land" to include rights not enumerated in the act as well as rights not even contemplated by law. The scope was widened enough to include a non-statutory, non-common law property right such as aboriginal title. Yet, the SCA did not use its broadened interpretation in its conclusion. Instead, the SCA found a right in land based on one of the rights already enumerated in the *Restitution Act*.

An even more intriguing example was the inclusion of a lucid and lengthy description of the doctrine of aboriginal title in the middle of the opinion.[68] This description, while an accurate summary, served no purpose in the SCA's final conclusion. The court did refer to aboriginal title to obviate the LCC's holding that it could not develop the common law to include aboriginal title. But the effort to reverse the LCC hardly called for the elaborate and detailed review of aboriginal title that the SCA presented.

After the lengthy discourse on aboriginal title, the court itself noted that its discussion of aboriginal title was unnecessary to pursue in the context of the court's conclusion. The court had already determined a "right in land" through a "customary law interest" and therefore did not need to address aboriginal title.[69] What seems to be a gap in the opinion is that the SCA made no effort to integrate its discourse on aboriginal title with, or to distinguish between a right in land based on the doctrine of aboriginal title as compared to, a "customary law interest".

Taken as a whole, in light of the forced fit of the SCA's conclusion of a customary law interest, the application of the aboriginal title paradigm in proving the SCA's conclusion and the unexplained and peripheral discourses of law, it can be concluded that the SCA opinion exhibited a tension between an intent to acknowledge a "right in land" based on aboriginal title and a judicial caution to stay within a safer application of the law by finding a "customary law interest" as an enumerated basis for restitution under the *Restitution Act*. Because of this tension, the SCA's opinion provided a useful recitation of facts and law in its parts but remains confusing with respect to aboriginal title and with respect to the nature and content of the "rights in land" set forth by the SCA. The SCA opinion set the stage for the Constitutional Court to clarify the law in favor of adopting aboriginal title as a "right in land" and to relieve the tension created by the SCA opinion.

Constitutional Court: Case Summary

Alexkor and the government appealed the holding of the SCA to the Constitutional Court of South Africa, the highest court of the land on constitutional matters (CCT). On appeal, Alexkor contended that the SCA erred in holding that the Richtersveld Community held a customary law interest in the land that was akin to ownership under common law and that this right included the ownership of minerals and precious stones.[70] Although the CCT noted that Alexkor and the government conceded this point in the lower court, the CCT allowed the appeal on the issue because the court felt "the proper characterization of the title is crucial to any order that the LCC may ultimately make".[71]

In response to Alexkor and the government's appeal with respect to a "right in land", the Richtersveld Community, as respondents, set forth the same positions they took in the SCA appeal. They contended that in addition to the right to beneficial occupation found by the LCC, the indigenous Richtersveld Community "held rights in the subject land under their indigenous law". [72] They introduced these rights as a form of indigenous title called "indigenous law ownership", which comprised communal ownership of the land and a right to exclusive beneficial occupation and use of the subject land and all its natural resources.[73] They further contended indigenous law ownership constituted a real right in land or at the very least "a customary law interest" within the definition of a right in land under the *Restitution Act*.

On appeal, the CCT adopted the facts as set forth by the LCC and by the SCA. The CCT also adopted a number of the SCA positions but overturned the SCA's finding of a "customary law interest" as the basis for "rights in land".

The CCT initiated its analysis by determining that the rights of the Richtersveld Community under the *Restitution Act* should turn on whether the community held rights under their own indigenous law at the time of annexation.[74] This position mirrored the SCA's approach that rights under indigenous law should be a basis for finding a "customary law interest".[75] The CCT eschewed limiting rights under indigenous law to only those recognized or acknowledged by the state, the courts or the Crown. The CCT emphasized that the South African Constitution expressly recognized and validated indigenous law to the extent the law comported with the purposes and values set forth in the Constitution.[76]

The CCT also made efforts to distinguish rights under indigenous law from the rights measured against and available under traditional conceptions of common law property law.[77] The court then noted that the nature of indigenous law as a normative evolving pattern, often not written or otherwise recorded, could be determined through evidence.[78] This emphasis on evidence diverged slightly from the SCA analysis but significantly in result. The CCT declined to affirm the "custom" test applied in the SCA opinion as proof of the content of indigenous law.[79] Instead, the CCT determined that, in the present case, it need look only to the evidence of the indigenous law of the Richtersveld Community to make its final determination of the type of rights the indigenous community held and the type of rights the court should recognize and protect.[80] Citing approvingly a case which held that native title required a determination based on the evidence of indigenous law, the CCT concluded that "[t]he determination of the real character of *indigenous title* to land therefore 'involves the study of the history of a particular community and its usages'. So does its determination of content".[81]

The court then applied the standard of proof of indigenous title to the Richtersveld Community. The court examined the evidence of indigenous law of the Richtersveld Community and their relationship to the subject land prior to and at the time of annexation. Adopting the factual findings of the SCA, the CCT determined that the land was owned communally by the community.[82] They had a right to exclude others, they regulated the land and they believed they owned the land. Other communities recognized the Richtersveld Community's ownership rights. The rights included prospecting, mining and using minerals.[83] In light of the evidence, the court concluded that "the real character of the title that the Richtersveld Community possessed in the subject land [at the time of annexation] was a right of communal ownership under indigenous law".[84] Adopting the term from the Richtersveld brief, the court referred to this "right in land" as "indigenous law ownership".[85]

After the finding of a right in land, the CCT turned to whether the right had survived extinguishment prior to 1913 and whether extinguishment was a result of "past racially discriminatory laws or practices" as set forth under the *Restitution Act*. After extensive analysis, the court determined that the Richtersveld Community had maintained their rights past 1913 and that their rights were extinguished in the 1920's by government conduct that could only be characterized as racially discriminatory.[86] Accordingly, the CCT concluded the Richtersveld Community was entitled to restitution under the *Restitution Act*.

Constitutional Court: Analysis

The holding of the CCT was a victory for the Richtersveld Community. But it was also a significant legal advancement with respect to the adoption of a form of aboriginal title in South Africa. In the lower court, the SCA had granted a right in land based on the principles of aboriginal title but enigmatically eschewed the adoption of aboriginal title in South African law. Instead, the SCA forced the "right in land" of the Richtersveld Community to fit into a "customary law interest".[87] The tensions created by the SCA's approach were resolved by the CCT which adopted the facts and much of the analysis and conclusions of the SCA but ultimately found that the right in question was an "indigenous law ownership". "Indigenous law ownership" is substantively identical to aboriginal title as developed under comparative jurisprudence and is thus a form of aboriginal title within South African law.

For example, the very purpose of the doctrine of "indigenous law ownership" mirrors that of the doctrine of aboriginal title as developed in comparative jurisprudence. Like that of aboriginal title, the purpose of "indigenous law ownership" is to acknowledge a right outside the paradigm of statutory or common law property rights.[88] Again, like aboriginal title, the CCT's "indigenous law ownership" created a right in an indigenous community who occupied land prior to and at the time of annexation.[89] The right, manifest from principles of justice and equality, survives colonization and other regime changes to the extent the rights have not been clearly extinguished by law or act of state, courts or the Crown. Under both doctrines, the title pertains to communal ownership of the land.[90]

Even the evidentiary requirements under the doctrine of aboriginal title track those set forth for "indigenous law ownership". One test for rights under aboriginal title is whether the right existed under "indigenous law" at the time of annexation.[91] The general principle is to look at the history and usages of the community at that time.[92] This is the same standard the CCT adopted for "indigenous law ownership". The CCT also quoted approvingly a passage of an aboriginal title case setting out this approach[93] and the CCT actually referred to "indigenous title" as the title it wished to prove before proceeding to examine the history and usages of the Richtersveld Community.[94]

In addition, other key characteristics of aboriginal title include evidence of a distinct community occupying the land at the time of colonization, a period of occupation resulting in communal ownership and exclusivity.[95] The CCT relied on these same characteristics for purposes of proving "indigenous law ownership". Citing approvingly the SCA's recitation of the facts covering the key characteristics,[96] the CCT then concluded "[i]n light of the evidence and of the findings by the SCA and the LCC", the Richtersveld Community had a right of indigenous law ownership.[97]

For all meaningful purposes with respect to finding a right in land, the two doctrines, aboriginal title and indigenous law ownership, are identical. Like aboriginal title, indigenous law ownership recognizes an indigenous right in land existing prior to and at the time of annexation. The CCT used the paradigm of aboriginal title to prove and define "indigenous law ownership" and the court made no effort to distinguish between, nor disaffirm that, the latter is a formulation of the former for purposes of South African law. It is clear that the CCT meant to formulate "indigenous law ownership" as a South African version of aboriginal title. Along with native title, indigenous title, Indian title and aboriginal title, the CCT has added "indigenous law ownership" as the South African contribution to the pantheon of names representing this most important aboriginal right to land.

Conclusion

Prior to the Richtersveld challenge, no country in sub-Saharan Africa had adopted aboriginal title into their laws.[98] Despite the widespread and notorious colonization of the region, the former colonies had not yet acknowledged the principle, based on equity, that certain land rights of the indigenous people occupying the land at the time of colonization should be legally recognized. After the South African transformation from an apartheid state into a constitutional democracy, a hope emerged that the new South Africa would lead the way in recognizing indigenous peoples´ land rights under the laws. In two parts, the questions were asked whether aboriginal title to land would be acknowledged under the new South African jurisprudence and, if so, whether any rights would really be granted for practical purposes under the doctrine. In the Richtersveld case, after challenges in the LCC and the SCA, the Constitutional Court answered both questions with a resounding "yes". Within the paradigm of the *Restitution Act*, the CCT found that the Richtersveld Community had a "right in land", the nature of which was "indigenous law ownership". "Indigenous law ownership" had the same purpose, nature and characteristics as aboriginal title as developed in comparative jurisdictions. There was no mistaking that the CCT had formally acknowledged a form of aboriginal title under South African law. Moreover, based on this indigenous "right in land", the court awarded restitution to the Richtersveld Community. In broad strokes, the CCT met the challenge of giving substance to the ideals of the new South African state by recognizing the land rights of aboriginal communities under the laws and granting restitution based on these rights.

At the same time, however, a closer look at the opinion underscores the limitations to the current reach of the CCT holding. First, the holding was narrowly developed within the precepts of the *Restitution Act*. A finding of a "right in land" based on "indigenous law ownership" only has beneficial consequences under the current holding if the claimant community can meet the other requirements under the *Restitution Act*. For practical purposes, under the act, dispossession of a right in land can only be redressed if the right was extinguished after 1913 as a result of past racially discriminatory laws or practices and if the claim had been filed prior to 1998.[99] In addition, the "right in land" was a statutory creation and it is unclear how a finding of such a right under the *Restitution Act* can be transposed into other contexts in the future. Moreover, under both aboriginal title and the *Restitution Act*, the state or the Crown can extinguish a right in land under certain circumstances. Extinguishment was not addressed in this paper but it should be noted that the practical implications of the CCT opinion may ultimately be circumscribed by the legal parameters of extinguishment.

In an attempt to cautiously develop the doctrine of aboriginal title under South African law, the CCT left the door open as to the application of indigenous law ownership outside the parameters of the *Restitution Act*. The full extent of the impact of the Richtersveld holding in South Africa and as a precedent in other sub-Saharan African countries remains to be seen. On balance, however, taking into consideration the limitations of the CCT's conclusions, it remains clear that the CCT's formal recognition of a form of aboriginal title under South African law significantly changes the legal landscape, improving the chances that avenues of recourse for dispossessed indigenous communities in South Africa will expand. It is indisputable that the CCT opinion and the restitution of land rights to the Richtersveld Community on the grounds of "indigenous law ownership" are victories for indigenous communities in South Africa and victories for all those who believe in the principles of justice and equality, which have always been the cornerstones of the doctrine of aboriginal title. ❑

Acknowledgements

The author would like to thank Henk Smith and Peter Hathorn from the Legal Resources Centre, South Africa, for their comments.

Notes

1   See *Alexkor v. Richtersveld Community*, 2003 (12) BCLR 1301 (CC) at para 38.
2   S. Afr. Const. (Constitution Act 108, 1996) § 25(7); see also the interim constitution, S. Afr. Const. (Constitution Act 200, 1993) § 121(2).
3   No. 22, § 2(1) (1994).
4   See Bennett & Powell, Aboriginal Title in South Africa Revisited, *South African Journal of Human Rights* Vol. 15: 449, 450 (1999).
5   See Hoq, Note, "Land Restitution and the Doctrine of Aboriginal Title: *Richtersveld Community v Alexkor Ltd and Another*", *South African Journal of Human Rights* Vol.18 (2002):421.
6   See Hoq, 2002:434.
7   See Bennett & Powell, 1999: 449-50 (noting that aboriginal title has not been adopted in Africa except for intimations by Namibia and Botswana that they may in the future invoke).
8   See Hoq, 2002: 421; see also Bennett & Powell, 1999:451 (noting Anglo-American precedent based on "principle and equity").
9   See Bennett & Powell, 1999:449.
10 See id. at 449; Hoq, 2002:421.
11 Compare generally Bennett & Powell, 1999 (arguing that the time was right to assert an aboriginal title claim in South Africa) with generally Lehmann, Aboriginal Title, Indigenous Rights and the Right to Culture, *South African Journal of Human Rights* Vol. 20 (2004):86 (arguing against the application of aboriginal title in South Africa). See Hoq, 2002:435 (discussing arguments against aboriginal title in South Africa and counter-arguments).
12 The following facts are a summary from *Richtersveld Community v. Alexkor*, 2001 (3) SA 1293 (LCC) at para 23-32 and *Richtersveld Community v. Alexkor*, 2003 (6) SA 104 (SCA) at para 2. The summary of facts by the Land Claims Court and the Supreme Court of Appeal was adopted by the Constitutional Court. See *Alexkor v. Richtersveld Community*, 2003 (12) BCLR 1301 (CC) at para 3. Also note, Alexkor is a public company established in terms of the Alexkor Limited Act 116 of 1992.
13 For example, the Constitutional Court has recognized that the Bill of Rights embodies socio-economic rights in *Government of the Republic of South Africa v Grootboom*, 2001 (1) SA 46 (CC); 2001 (11) BCLR 1169 (CC) at para 20 ("Socio-economic rights are expressly included in the Bill of Rights"). For examples of several of the basic rights included in the Constitution, see S. Afr. Const. (Constitution Act 108, 1996) §§ 29 (education), 23(1) (fair labor practices), 25(5) (access to land), 26

(access to housing), 27(1)(a) (healthcare), 27(1)(b) (food and water) and 27(1)(c) (social security).

14 See, e.g., *Soobramoney v Minister of Health, KwaZulu-Natal*, 1998 (1) SA 938 (CC); 1997 (12) BCLR 995 (CC) (constitutional challenge for socio-economic rights to healthcare); *Grootboom*, 2001 (1) SA 46 (CC) (constitutional challenge for socio-economic rights to housing).

15 See Bennett & Powell, 1999: 450.

16 S. Afr. Const. (Constitution Act 108, 1996) § 25(7).

17 Restitution of Land Rights Act, No. 22, § 2(1) (1994).

18 Restitution of Land Rights Act § 1.

19 See Bennett & Powell, 1999: 449, 450; Hoq, 2002:421, 434; Lehmann, 2004:86, 87.

20 Bennett & Powell, 1999:450.

21 See id. at 450; see also *Richtersveld Community v. Alexkor*, 2001 (3) SA 1293 (LCC) at para 48 ("[The doctrine of indigenous title] is an alternative remedy to restitution under the Restitution Act and falls outside this Court's jurisdiction".) and 53 ("The realisation of such a title will be a remedy that diverges from the remedy of restitution under the Restitution Act... ").

22 See *Richtersveld*, 2001 (3) SA 1293 (LCC) at para 44 (aboriginal title, Indian title, indigenous title and native title interchangeable); Bennett & Powell, 1999: 449 (native title); Lehmann, 2004:91 (aboriginal title, Indian title, indigenous title and native title interchangeable in legal parlance).

23 See Can. Const. (Constitution Act, 1985) § 35(1); see also Bennett & Powell, 1999: 453 (noting constitutions that expressly protect indigenous rights: Canada, Colombia, Brazil, Panama, Guatemala, Peru and the Philippines).

24 See Bennett & Powell, 1999:461.

25 See *Richtersveld Community v. Alexkor*, 2003 (6) SA 104 (SCA) at para 38-41; Bennett & Powell, 1999:449.

26 See Bennett & Powell, 1999:461-62; Hoq, 2002:437.

27 See Bennett & Powell, 1999:462; Hoq, 2002:437.

28 See Bennett & Powell, 1999:463-69.

29 See id. at 471.

30 *Richtersveld Community v. Alexkor*, 2001 (3) SA 1293 (LCC) at para 6.

31 Id. at para 37, 41-43, 107(a).

32 See id. at para 44-53.

33 See id. at para 48-53, 117.

34 Id. at para 94.

35 Id. at para 90.

36 See id. at para 48.

37 See id. at para 48.

38 See id. at para 65, 107(c).

39 See id. at para 93, 106, 108, 110, 112.

40 See id. at para 93.

41 See id. at para 120.

42 See *Richtersveld Community v. Alexkor*, 2003 (6) SA 104 (SCA) at para 11.

43 Restitution of Land Rights Act, No. 22, § 1 (1994).

44 See *Richtersveld*, 2003 (6) SA 104 (SCA) at para 9.

45 See *Richtersveld*, 2001 (3) SA 1293 (LCC) at para 48.

46 See *Richtersveld*, 2003 (6) SA 104 (SCA) at para 26.

47 Id. at para 28.

48 See id. at para 27.

49 See id. at para 26 (concession), 28 (facts).

50 See id. at para 29.

51 See id. at para 67.

52 See id. at para 109-10. For the full discussion of dispossession as a result of past racially discriminatory laws or practices, see id. 90-110.

53 Id. at para 111.

54 See Bennett & Powell, 1999: 449, 462 (describing aboriginal title and citing the seminal Australian case, *Mabo v. Queensland* (No.2) (1992) 175 CLR 1).

55 See Bennett & Powell, 1999: 468.

56 See *Richtersveld*, 2003 (6) SA 104 (SCA) at para 25, 26 (emphasis added).

57 Compare id. at para 28 (looking to traditional laws and customs to prove customary law interest) with Bennett & Powell 1999: 467-68 (looking to traditional laws and customs to prove aboriginal title).

58 *Richtersveld*, 2003 (6) SA 104 (SCA) at para 37.

59 See id. at para 23, 24.

60 See id. at para 15, 18.

61 See id. at para 14, 22.

62 See id. at para 14.

63 See id. at para 18, 22, 24.

64 See id. at para 15, 18, 19.

65 See id. at para 18, 19.

66 See id. at para 18, 21.

67 See id. at para 29.

68 See id. at para 36-43 (lengthy analysis of aboriginal title).

69 See id. at para 43.

70 See *Alexkor v. Richtersveld Community*, 2003 (12) BCLR 1301 (CC) at para 42.

71 See *Richtersveld*, 2003 (12) BCLR 1301 (CC) at para 45. The LCC is charged with sorting out the practical realities of an order from the CCT granting restitution to the Richtersveld Community.

72 Brief for Respondents at para 11, *Richtersveld*, 2003 (12) BCLR 1301 (CC).

73 See id. at para 11.

74 See *Richtersveld*, 2003 (12) BCLR 1301 (CC) at para 50 (beginning of "right in land" analysis).

75 See *supra* text accompanying note 56.

76 See *Richtersveld*, 2003 (12) BCLR 1301 (CC) at para 51 (referring to customary law). *See also id.* at para 7 n.8 (stating that "customary law" is synonymous with "indigenous law").

77 See id. at para 50.

78 See id. at para 52 (evidence), 53 (normative, unrecorded law).

79 See id. at para 54 n.56, 62 n.65 (declining to affirm SCA "custom" test). The SCA looked to evidence of indigenous law but used the evidence to meet an English and Roman-Dutch standard of "custom" to prove there was a "customary law interest". See *Alexkor v. Richtersveld Community*, 2003 (6) SA 104 (SCA) at para 27; see also *supra* text accompanying note 48.

80 See *Richtersveld*, 2003 (12) BCLR 1301 (CC) at para 55, 62.

81 See id. at para 56-57 (emphasis added).

82 See id. at para 62.

83 See id. at para 62.

84 See id. at para 62.

85 The CCT refers to the right in land as "indigenous law ownership" throughout the opinion. See *Richtersveld*, 2003 (12) BCLR 1301 (CC) at para 70, 81, 86, 87, 92, 96, 99. This term was initially introduced in the Richtersveld briefs. See *supra* text accompanying note 73.

86 See *Richtersveld*, 2003 (12) BCLR 1301 (CC) at para 99 (holding that the Precious Stones Act 44 of 1927 was a racially discriminatory law depriving the Richtersveld Community of its land rights).

87 See discussion *infra* Supreme Court of Appeal: Summary of the Case.

88 Compare *Richtersveld*, 2003 (12) BCLR 1301 (CC) at para 50, 53 (differentiating indigenous law ownership from written law and English conceptions of property rights) with Bennett & Powell, 1999:462 (differentiating aboriginal title from common law property rights), 463 (differentiating aboriginal title from written law).

89 See *Richtersveld*, 2003 (12) BCLR 1301 (CC) at para 3 (adopting uncontested SCA facts such as the fact that the Richtersveld inhabitants make up an indigenous community), 62 (recognizing a right prior to annexation), 69, 82 (agreeing that rights survived annexation).

90 Compare *Richtersveld*, 2003 (12) BCLR 1301 (CC) at para 62 (communal nature of indigenous law ownership) with Bennett & Powell, 1999:462 (communal nature of aboriginal title).

91 See Bennett & Powell, 1999:462, 468.

92 See Bennett & Powell, 1999:468.

93 See *Richtersveld*, 2003 (12) BCLR 1301 (CC) at para 56, 57 n.59.

94 Id. at para 57 (referring to "indigenous title"); 58-62 (examining history and usages).

95 See Bennett & Powell, 1999:463-69.

96 See *Richtersveld*, 2003 (12) BCLR 1301 (CC) at para 58-59, 61.

97 Id. at para 62; see also *supra* text accompanying nn.84-85.

98 See *supra* note 7 and accompanying text.

99 See *supra* note 17 and accompanying text.

EQUALITY AND ETHNICITY: HOW EQUAL ARE SAN IN BOTSWANA?

Isaac Mazonde

Studies of the San (also known as Basarwa in Botswana) have taken the ethnicity issue as a given, without problematizing it to understand the reason for the deep-seated prejudice surrounding the San and the San question. In this chapter, an attempt is made to interrogate the ethnicity issue by trying to explain the persistent contempt with which the San are held in Botswana. The chapter recognises that the negative attitude towards the San is a complex issue, and that many issues are at play, yet it locates the ethnicity factor at the core of these complexities.

Botswana has come a long way from the stance it cherished three decades back at independence when Setswana language was the only official vernacular, much to the dismay of many citizens to whom it was as alien as English. Recently, the thinking among the most senior policy makers in the country is that the time has come to officially recognise the languages of the so-called minority tribes. But the matter does not begin and end with language; it is wider. Included within its ambit is freedom of expression of the different cultures that make up Botswana.

Botswana has not just matured into this tolerance of its diverse cultural groups without pressure from outside. Pressure has been brought to bear from surrounding countries such as Zimbabwe and South Africa, which gained their independence much later but have nonetheless upheld multiculturalism within their communities. The race relations between peoples of these countries may not necessarily be perfect but the recognition of cultural diversity and tolerance of differences in ethnicities is commendable in these countries.

While Botswana is clearly moving towards accommodating the various cultures of its different peoples, its policy towards the San is different and seeks to integrate them into the culture(s) of mainstream Batswana.

Whereas there are differences between the cultures of the various ethnic groups in the country, cultural differences are perceived as being greatest between the San on the one hand, and the rest of Batswana on the other. Perceptions are one of the most important aspects of social or human-centred development, particularly with respect to indigenous peoples. Perceptions are a crucial aspect of the life of the San because their plight is, to a large extent, attitudinal in nature; it hinges on the way they are perceived and treated by the

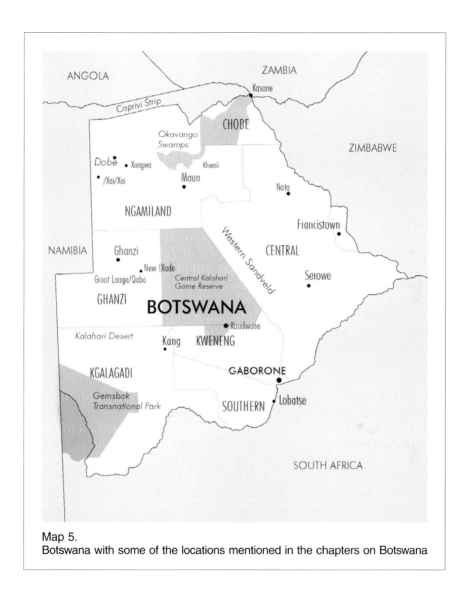

Map 5.
Botswana with some of the locations mentioned in the chapters on Botswana

mainstream or dominant non-San communities, most of whom are the so called "blacks".[1]

The way the San perceive themselves is also important but it is, to a large extent, a direct result of the manner in which they are regarded and dealt with by non-San. In view of that, any viable change of attitude in favour of the San must originate with and be initiated by the dominant non-San peoples, who deny the San the central credos of democracy, namely freedom, autonomy and the right to be different. As I shall demonstrate later, the last credo, the right to be different, is denied the San mainly by the state. The aim of this chapter is to expose some of the processes that construct such denials.

Another purpose is to look at the way the government has dealt with the San within this complex social set-up. Some have interpreted this government policy as a reactionary move. My aim is to demonstrate how this move is simultaneously reactionary and progressive and, furthermore, to show how this paradox epitomizes the complexity of the concept of social development.

However, to lay the foundation for these arguments, it is first necessary to provide an overview of the situation of Basarwa with respect to the law and human rights in the country.

The 1993 Regional Conference

Whereas San have generally been seen as helpless, the situation has recently been changing. They have come a long way from being the "docile people" they used to be. They have become more united and more forceful in claiming their rights.

A watershed was provided by the Conference on Development Programmes for Africa's San/Basarwa Populations convened in Gaborone, 11-13 September 1993 by the governments of Botswana and Namibia. It followed another conference held in Namibia the previous year, both conferences being funded by the governments of Norway and Sweden.

The 1992 conference was regarded as rather unsuccessful because the delegation from Botswana did not include any San. The officials representing the Botswana government appeared too defensive of their government's position on the San issue. Things changed during the 1993 conference. Preparatory meetings were held among the various San communities in Botswana, with the help of NGOs. The San themselves decided what issues they wanted discussed at the conference and who their representatives would be. Consequently, the 1993 conference can be taken as a critical turning point for the San in Botswana in that they spoke their minds freely without any restraint from the government. The views they expressed at this conference must therefore be taken seriously, as should the resolutions reached at this conference.

The San expressed their views on a number of issues. For reasons of space, only a few will be highlighted here. Land was one issue of contention. They wanted to be given an area in which they could live as they chose, in line with their culture, headed by a San chief who would also be a member of the House of Chiefs.[2] With respect to communication, they complained that they never met on any issue, because they did not know each other. San from Namibia explained that their problem was compounded by the fact that they were scattered over many farms, lying far apart. San from both Botswana and Namibia said that the reason why non-San did not consult them was because of the contempt in which they were held by such people. In summary, the San called for a right to self-determination and respect for their human rights.

Many resolutions were passed. Again, through lack of space, only a few of those that are relevant to this discussion will be mentioned. One of them relates to land. Resolution No.7 states, "All communities (Basarwa/San included) need ownership, control over and access to land to preserve cultural identity and foster survival through agriculture, hunting and gathering". The following resolution (No.8c) states that Basarwa/San people should be adequately represented in land allocation bodies (Land Boards). The final one mentioned refers to education. Resolution No. 4 states that mother tongue teaching be encouraged or introduced for the first three primary school grades.

Today, a decade later, none of the resolutions raised above have been implemented. Only now is UNICEF sponsoring a study by the University of Botswana (Directorate of Research and Development) to look into an educational curriculum that is appropriate for the San in remote areas.

Continued Denial of Rights

There is evidence that the Botswana government treats the San as secondclass citizens or as if they were not citizens at all. In this context, Saugestad (1998:33) talks of the mother country becoming a stepmother to its minorities. The San themselves perceive that they are being discriminated against by the dominant non-San people, including the state.

The San have been denied the constitutional rights to which every other Motswana has claim. The San are not mentioned in the country's first constitution (1966), which only names the eight principle tribes (Sections 77, 78 and 79 of the Constitution)[3] and leaves out the minority tribes. In July 2000, a commission known as the Balopi Commission was set up to investigate any discriminatory clauses in the Botswana constitution. Following the Commission's study, in December 2001, the Government released a policy paper recommending constitutional amendments to make the House of Chiefs more inclusive and ethnically neutral. Parliament adopted its recommendation; however, no date has been set for implementation. But while these recommendations may benefit small tribes such as the Bayei, it will not assist Basarwa in any way, as the Commission did not even make any reference to them.

However, in 2000, the House of Chiefs welcomed its first San and first woman member, Chief Rebecca Banika. She is a lesser Chief from Chobe but had, until 2003, had little contact with other San groups and does therefore not constitute a strong "San" representation in the House.

Unlike every other Motswana, the San have no recognised paramount chief, and there are only few Basarwa traditional leaders and political leaders in Botswana, apart from the recently appointed headmen at settlement level. Rivers (1999) reports that all RAD settlements in the Ghanzi District now have a headman (in one case, the head of a settlement is female). But an important feature of these recently elected headmen is their ineffectiveness. San headmen must either toe the line or face removal from office. The San acknowledge that the election of local leaders has not brought about any changes for them and, although they express the desire to have Basarwa leaders and representatives, they end up electing non-Basarwa[4] who are able to buy votes with food and other cheap commodities that Basarwa candidates cannot provide.

The San generally also find themselves as a social grouping that falls outside the law in terms of the *Tribal Land Act of 1968*, which divided residents into territories that were recognized by the country's constitution. With the exception of the urban areas, state lands and freehold farms, the country is divided into territories over which the eight principle tribes have control. Basarwa do not have any specific territory that they can call their own. Like aliens who come from outside the country, they have to be incorporated into the eight major tribes.

Given all this, it is no wonder that the San have not enjoyed the socio-economic development that Botswana has achieved over the past two decades of high economic growth. Actually, the San have fared worse than any other community in Botswana. They have become poorer economically and more so socially, through the state's relocation policies (Panos Oral Testimony Programme, 1998). Elaborating on this point, Good (1999) puts the blame for the hard circumstances of the San entirely on the Botswana Government. He notes that "necessary improvements (of the lives of the San) depended on the political and administrative will of government and Councils and this had been distinctly lacking". What this means is that the San have not enjoyed any social development that might have resulted in the realisation of self-worth, the one ingredient that is expedient in determining attitudes.

Land Dispossession

Land is a major concern for the Basarwa. Throughout history, they have been dispossessed of their ancestral territories and their land zoned into cattle ranching for others, wildlife conservation, arable farming and cattle posts, all for tribes other than themselves. Hunting and gathering, as a lifestyle of the Basarwa, is not enshrined in the laws of Botswana. Consequently, Basarwa easily lose their land because they do not have any legal protection. The position of the government is that all citizens have land rights. The government fails to recognize that land rights are invoked through belonging to a designated territory. Basarwa, not having a designated territory, are unable to claim any land rights in the way that members of the tribes mentioned in the constitution are able to do.

Despite the resolution made in 1993 to provide them with land to live according to their culture, the San virtually still have no rights to land outside the recently created settlements where the people from the Central Kalahari Game Reserve have been re-settled. Here, the San are given small and inadequate pieces of land, on average 2 acres. Collective land rights, such as grazing areas, are not available to them in amounts that are adequate for cattle raising. The land plots designated for their use are therefore too small to enable Basarwa to live a traditional Tswana life of pastoral and arable farming. Furthermore, such plots are often invaded by the mainstream non-Basarwa Tswana, who quietly take over grazing meant for Basarwa.

The government has recently adopted a new policy that encourages the fencing of grazing areas. This policy will lead to further displacement of Basarwa as they are the ones who live in the areas to be fenced (see Taylor, this volume). They do not have a voice, so their resentment is usually ignored.

Language and Formal Education

A second concern is the issue of language. Not all Basarwa are able to speak Setswana, and whereas the 1993 conference resolved to encourage the use of mother tongue in the first years of primary education among remote area children, so far nothing has been done in this regard. This is due to several factors. With a few exceptions, such as Naro and Khwedam, most of the Basarwa languages have not yet developed an orthography. This development, however, is vital for Basarwa children so they can learn to read and write, as a way of self-development. This would boost also their identity, and enhance their self-esteem as well as secure the survival and further development of the San languages. Another factor is the lack of San teachers. The vast majority of teachers in RAD settlements are from the "black" community. For example, in New !Xade, the largest re-settlement centre for people from the Central Kalahari Game Reserve, there is only one San teacher within a staff complement of 11.

The formal education system is thus dominated by mainstream Tswana groups who force Basarwa children to learn in Setswana (and English from Grade 4). This discourages Basarwa children, who end up dropping out of school before they complete their studies.

Much can be said about formal education. In many ways formal education has today substituted land and cattle, the main factors of socio-economic control in earlier times when the San were dispossessed of their influence and dignity by the Batswana. Equipped with formal education, most people would usually be able to provide respectable service and achieve recognition.

Another important reason for focusing on formal education for San is the fact that the last few decades have witnessed a substantial move away from foraging among the San. The expanding cattle industry has reduced the San's access to and control over lands that previously provided a sustainable livelihood (Saugestad 1998:89), and increased their reliance on domestic food production, occasional wage earning and welfare. These developments will require the San to have formal education in order to fit into the world they are now living in. In fact, 88 per cent of the so-called "missing" children live in rural areas. Within this sub-group, non-enrolment, drop-out, repetition and sub-standard academic performance rates are highest among the RAD dwellers, "especially among the non-Setswana speaking ethnic RADs of the western (Kgalagadi and Ghanzi) and North West Districts for whom access to basic education has been limited due to poverty, distance from schools, cultural values and negative public attitudes" (Botswana 1994:76). In a related study, Good (1999) has indicated that with a 77 per cent illiteracy rate, the San rank highest among all RAD people.[5]

Against this background, this chapter will look at the acquisition of formal education by San children living in RAD settlements, taking Dobe and Xangwa, in Ngamiland (part of North West District) as an example.

Usually, at the beginning of the school term, San children are collected by the Remote Area Development Officers (RADOs) from various nearby settlements where there is no school and ferried by District Council trucks, usually against their will, to settlements where there are schools. Dobe is one such settlement where there is no school and, as of January 1999, there was no San on either the Parent Teacher Association (PTA) committee or the Village Development Committee (VDC) of Dobe, the two organisations that deal with formal education at the village or settlement level. Both these social structures seemed to reinforce the prejudices that non-San, or the "blacks", had with regard to the San children and their parents. The nearest school is in another settlement, some 20 kms away. In that settlement, San children, along with the rest of the RAD children, live in very low-quality hostels, usually sleeping on the ground. There have been reports of sexual harassment of female RAD pupils in these hostels, by males who come from outside the school. In 1994, the National Development Plan 7 document noted that "prevailing hostel conditions and modes of operation often make RAD parents reluctant to enrol their children in primary school and often contribute to student drop-out. With appropriate intervention, these facilities can be changed from sub-standard boarding facilities into active learning, cultural and recreation centres" (Botswana 1994).

In interviews (see e.g. Reynolds 1999) San children complained that they were ill-treated at school and in the hostels. They reported that they were sometimes beaten up and berated for not learning by the non-San teachers. Sometimes learning is made difficult by the non-San teachers, apparently in the hope that the San children will discontinue their formal education and go back to join their parents in their settlements of origin. But it must be noted too that the San's learning problems are not caused only by the non-San teachers. There are different social groups among the San and, occasionally, there are clashes at school between them. For example, in one school, Ju|'hoan pupils from one San group complained that the ‖Anikhwe, another San group, urinated on their blankets deliberately, just to provoke them into a fight.

At Xangwa, parents of San children complained that their children were taught by non-San teachers who did not know any of the San languages. San parents reported that their children suffered a great deal of discouragement from the non-San structures in their efforts to acquire a formal education. The school-going RAD children in Xangwa include the Herero, the Bayei and the San. The highest drop-out rate is among the San children. This is really unfortunate, given that non-San teachers admit that San children are generally more intelligent than other children in RAD settlements (Reynolds 1999). This high rate of intelligence is acknowledged, despite the fact that other RAD children like the Bayei and the Herero know both their own mother tongues and the languages of the San among whom they live. In fact, the situation at Xangwa was that Bayei and Herero children often translated for the San children, when a teacher used the Setswana language as a medium of instruction. San children usually cope very well with Setswana within a year.

In Xangwa, non-San teachers were more sympathetic to the plight of the San children. They encouraged San pupils to do their traditional dancing at school and, in general, viewed all pupils at school as belonging to what should be seen as a big family. Unfortunately, in spite of their sympathy for the San children, the non-San teachers in Xangwa failed to recognise the validity of San cultures, beyond merely encouraging the children to do their dances. For example, the big family image of the non-San teachers was one in which the San children would be invited into Tswana culture. In other words, it was to be a form of assimilation. In actual fact, this is the Botswana Government's view with regard to addressing the San problem in general. In spite of the government's state d position that "the curriculum will be made flexible enough to take into account cultural and linguistic diversities of the different ethnic groups and teacher training will sensitise teachers to cultural differences" (Botswana 1994:78), its overall approach is to integrate the San into mainstream Tswana society.

It has been observed that the very few San who manage to obtain a formal education become dislocated from their San culture and even appear to be alienated from their parents, who were never exposed to education. In Xangwa, the San children who lived in the hostels began to lose interest in their traditional food, such as the *veld* (bush) products, instead developing an interest in modern dishes. Yet, unfortunately, formal education does not result in the San gaining as much recognition as is normally gained by educated members of the mainstream Batswana. However, my own observation is that while the few Basarwa who have received a formal education have adopted Western dress values and comfortable lifestyles, they have also become sterling advocates for the rights of their less fortunate group members. The two Basarwa students who were able to gain a university education through the support of NUFU - the Norwegian Council for Higher Education - have joined NGOs and are now eloquent spokespeople for San rights.

Identity

Basarwa do not find it easy to maintain their ethnic identity. In schools, Basarwa children are sometimes given Setswana names because the teachers claim that San names are too difficult for them to pronounce. For the same reason, some Basarwa elders were also given Setswana names during registration for national identity cards. Public officials organising the registrations claimed that it was difficult to write San names. Basarwa view this as contempt by mainstream Batswana because Asians and Afrikaners are not asked to change their names during such registrations (Nkelekang 2003).

Furthermore, I have noted above that Basarwa are refused the right to be different by the state, in a bid to try to "develop them" through integrating them with the mainstream Batswana. This issue is really a hard choice for the state because it feels that, if Basarwa are left to decide their own future, they may choose to remain on the margins of development. Yet the way government "develops" them does not seem

San children at boarding school, D'kar. Photo: Chris Erni

to work in the interests of Basarwa: Basarwa remain marginalized despite these well-meaning efforts on the part of the state. Above all they lose their identity, which has been their strength.

These are some of the basic facts on the problems faced by the San. What follows is an analysis of the root problem, which is the ethnicity factor.

Perception and the Ethnicity Factor

One of the recommendations of the 1993 San Conference was that the way to reverse the negative stigma of the San was to empower them economically. On the basis of available evidence, this approach may not work as easily as it was assumed. Good (1999) has indicated that, in a few cases, the San once owned livestock and tilled fields, but were dispossessed of their livestock by the dominant non-San Tswana communities, who subsequently subjugated them. My point is that efforts to empower the San are bound to fail as long as the stigma and powerlessness that is responsible for the contempt in which they are held by the dominant groups remains. Thus, the first thing to address in all genuine efforts aimed at assisting the San is the ethnicity issue, which underlies the negativity towards the San. In this regard, it is essential to keep in mind the covert but fundamental difference between the San and non-San in reference to Botswana's remote area dwellers. Being a remote area dweller has its own perception problem, apart from the ethnicity issue of the San. Remote areas are very under-developed. They lack basic facilities and, as a result, public officials are very reluctant to work in these areas. The public officials who seem comfortable in the remote areas are the unskilled, or those generally considered failures elsewhere. In other words, remote areas even get the worse human resources for their development programmes. Consequently, the turnover of public servants is high in the remote areas. This means that whatever small developments these places might have are never forthcoming due to high staff turnover. Overall, this situation enhances the stigma of the residents of the remote areas, and increases the negativity towards the San, in particular.

The ethnicity issue is closely related to that of being "indigenous". Although the Botswana government takes the view that all Batswana are indigenous, the San are widely regarded as an "indigenous people" wherever they are found. The International Labour Organisation in its Convention No.169 refers to indigenous peoples as "tribal peoples in independent countries whose social, cultural and economic conditions distinguish them from other sections of the national community, and whose status is regulated wholly or partially by their own customs or traditions or by special laws or regulations"(Kipuri 1999:19). Across the world, indigenous peoples have a special attachment to land. They have their own language or languages, their own social institutions, consensual decision-making processes, community life and collective sharing.

The problems experienced by the San are typical "indigenous peoples' problems" (Saugestad 1998:17). In view of that, it is expedient to consider the term "indigenous" vis-à-vis "ethnicity". According to Saugestad, "ethnicity is a cultural construct assigning social meaning to some diacritical signs, while ignoring others. In its most elementary sense, ethnicity refers to social relationships where basic classificatory differences between categories of people are perceived to be important, and made relevant in interaction. Ethnicity is created and re-created in social situations and encounters" (Saugestad 1998:45).

Saugestad goes further, and makes some link between ethnicity and class: "Ethnicity is not synonymous with class but the two often coincide. Marxian theory stresses the relationship to property in class ranking while the Weberian theory of social stratification combines criteria such as income, education and political influence to delineate classes" (Saugestad 1998:50). Suffice to note, for now, that the two concepts of indigenous and ethnicity complement each other, as the situation of indigenous peoples must be understood as the outcome of a process of interaction between ethnic groups.

Thus, for the San, the situation of being indigenous, which confers an inferior social status, combines with the negative aspects of ethnicity to bring about a stigma that is aggravated by the additional fact that the San are a people of the past that "in school textbooks are generally dealt with in a chapter between the Stone Age and the Iron Age" (Saugestad 1998:60).

It is within this context that many people have asserted that the main problem for the San is that they are too far outside society, with too little influence over the decisions made by society and the state. In her assessment of the inconvenience that the San pose to the apparent unity of the tribes in Botswana, Saugestad, referring to the word "inconvenient" in the title of her book, notes that "inconvenient" indicates an attitude that is rather dismissive, often condescending, ambivalent, but not overtly hostile. The term is not a description of a group, it denotes an attitude towards the group (Saugestad 1998:3).

But, as indicated earlier, this is not a situation created by the laws of the land; rather, it is created by the interaction that has structured the relationship between the San and non-San.

The Ethnicity Question Within The RAD Settlements

The issue of negative attitudes towards the San is a difficult subject. The account given so far regarding the nature of the contempt in which San are held does not claim to be exhaustive. The issue of the sense of community as applied to the remote area dwellers, a collective term for the San and others who live in the margins away from large settlements, merely adds to the complexity of the problem under discussion. The remote area dwellers (RADs) are made up of different peoples with varying ethnicities. In Zutshwa, for instance, and as in many other RAD settlements of western Botswana, there are the San, different classes of the Bakgalagadi, and "Batswana". "Batswana" come from the dominant major tribal groups. They are the group that is normally referred to as the "blacks" by the San. The San almost always constitute the largest proportion of the RADs, yet they are hierarchically the lowest ethnic group in terms of resources, power and influence. All these diverse groups of people have very different incentives and motivations for resource use and employ differing livelihood strategies. Furthermore, the notions of community and community consensus mask the complexity and diversity of interests within such groups (Twyman 1998:764). The San are the most vulnerable to abuse by any other social group. This is a factor that is responsible for their perpetual poverty and low status. As a result of this condition, development packages that sometimes work successfully to empower non-San RADs never work for the San, even within the same community. The Wildlife Management Area programme, which is discussed elsewhere in this section, is a case in point.

Actually, the existence of the First People of the Kalahari (FPK) movement, which is made up of San and seeks redress against the injustices being committed against San, is a clear indication of the important ethnic differences among RADs. It also shows a clear lack of sense of community between the San and other RADs with whom they live.

An attempt will now be made to expand and contextualise the general observations thus far made on San perceptions. The negative attitude towards the San is so deep-rooted and widespread that it is evident not only at a personal and community level but at the state or government level as well. This simply means that the raw deal and lack of recognition that the San receive in their interactions with the dominant social groups at individual level is sanctioned by communities and upheld by the state through the national institutions of the courts and governance. This is understandable when one adopts Saugestad's view, which sees government both in its constitutional role as defining the policies of a sovereign state, and more loosely as representing the views of the majority of its people (Saugestad 1998:3).

For example, at an individual level, the non-San cattle owners for whom the San work underpay them, ill-treat them and sometimes sexually abuse San women, all with impunity. At a community level, the picture is no different. The mainstream Tswana tribes have amassed wealth through the exploitation of San labour. Ngwato[6] wealth depended on the San (Wylie 1990:138) and the San suffered continued exclusion from the Ngwato family. Among the Ngwato and the Tawana, all San living in a headman's hunting and grazing area came under the control of the headman. Their duties were gradually extended to include hunting, herding cattle, ploughing and other domestic work for their masters (Saugestad 1998:110).

Today, the San may not necessarily be ploughing for their masters but they still herd for them and their situation has changed very little in other respects, even in the course of the implementation of the RAD programme, which seeks to reduce their exploitation by putting them in new settlements.

The Ethnicity Question and Natural Resource Management

One of the 1993 conference resolutions that was taken up by the Botswana Government was that regarding the management of natural resources, and much effort has been put into this. The Community Based Natural Resources Management programme (CBNRMP) has been de-

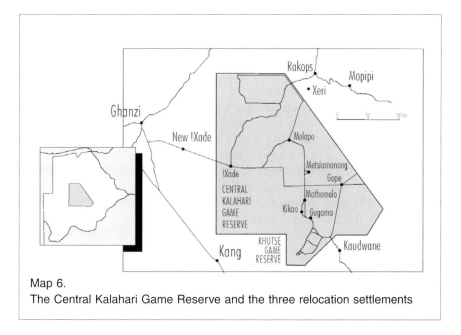

Map 6.
The Central Kalahari Game Reserve and the three relocation settlements

signed to assist San earn income from wildlife in the remote areas (see Rivers 1999) and the San have been able to achieve some economic success with projects under this programme, albeit on a very limited scale (see Hitchcock, this volume).

As part of the CBNRMP, the government also has two land-use systems, the wildlife management areas (WMA) and the controlled hunting areas (CHA). Within the WMA the primary form of land use is wildlife management. In theory, this land-use designation would appear to favour the San, who rely far more on hunting and gathering than the Bakgalagadi, who keep livestock. In Zutshwa, however, it is the Bakgalagadi who actually benefit from the WMA programme at the expense of the San. This is because the WMA concept has the effect of taking away from the individual and the family the direct access to wildlife meat and wildlife products, as well as the flexibility of hunting according to the needs of individuals and families. In the WMA concept, the right to determine hunting and natural resource use is ceded to the community. In the course of this process, the benefits of the regulation pooling these resources are enjoyed by the most influential members of the community, to the disadvantage of the weak. Thus, the San, who are on the bottom wrung of the social ladder among RADs, end up losing even when they should have been the chief beneficiaries of the WMA by virtue of their hunter lifestyle. This lowest social position translates into the lowest influence as well as the lowest self-worth. Underlying the weak position of the San is what has been underscored by Good in his discussion of the RAD settlements: although such settlements were created for occupation by San and other remote people, the government still has no specific policies as to who should be allocated land for residence or allowed to graze and water cattle there (Good 1999).

The fact that outside owners of large cattle herds can move on to West Hanahai (a settlement created specifically for the San in Ghanzi District), causing "numerous problems for its Basarwa (San) residents including overtaxing the low yielding water supply and denuding the surrounding *veld* area" suggests that the problem of encroachment of the "blacks" into settlement created for the San is widespread. Actually, Good has maintained that this is a general phenomenon: "Where grazing and water existed, these are usually appropriated by outside cattle-men with the tacit or explicit consent of government, under the rubric of a citizen's freedom of movement in Botswana". It is for this reason that "domestic water sources have been turned into cattle watering points, and settlements into the equivalent of cattle posts", to borrow from Good (1999).

In a discussion of the CBNRM programme, Rivers states that the Khwai constitution of CBNRM is different from others in that it ties membership to ethnicity. It is essentially for the San. Non-San can only become members if they apply to the board and are accepted by it. When non-San argued that this arrangement was discriminatory, a San retorted: "How can this (deed) be discriminatory when the constitution itself is discriminatory against Basarwa (the San) by saying we don't exist?" (Rivers 1999:21). In other words, this particular San is aware that San are not recognised by the country's constitution. In this context, it should be stated that Botswana's position, which takes a non-ethnic approach in all its policies, should not be an excuse for the country to ignore the special circumstances of the San, since this approach has the effect of denying the San their political rights.

The forced removal of the San from the Central Kalahari Game Reserve CKGR) is another example of the base manner in which San are treated by the state. (see Taylor, this volume). What needs to be emphasised here is that this is a common experience among marginalised peoples generally (see e.g. Kipuri 1999).

There are several reasons why the government may continue with this policy. The government has maintained that any policy that treats different ethnic groups separately would be akin to the apartheid policies practised in the former racist South Africa. At independence, the government deliberately turned a blind eye to ethnic differences within Botswana in a bid to create a unified nation. The ethnic diversity of the nation was under-communicated in the name of national unity during the formative years of the new state. The flaws in this reasoning have manifested themselves with time, especially over the past decade when state policies clearly had the effect of disadvantaging the San. Nor would the all-consuming idea of globalisation, which is the buzzword of our times, appear to justify efforts to assimilate the San within the mainstream Tswana community. While globalisation attempts to make all fit into one global village, it must leave room for differences. It was never meant to be a homogenising concept (Werbner 1999).

Actually, Botswana has come to acknowledge the wisdom of cultural diversity (Botswana 1999). However, such acknowledgement has not yet resulted in any tangible action and the feeling that the state does not recognise the San in the way it recognises other Batswana has made them feel that they could receive better assistance from people outside Botswana, given that foreign organisations have shown to take a greater interest in their welfare than their own government. For example, the San, through the late leader of the First People of the Kalahari (FPK), have been allowed a voice in the UN, and they continue to have a voice even after his death. Consequently, they regard current efforts around the UN Draft Declaration on the Rights of Indigenous Peoples to be a sign that they have more support from the international community than from Botswana. Hence San perceive that it is only with assistance from outside Botswana that they can succeed in their fight for self-recognition and their constitutional as well as human rights.

Conclusion

This chapter has been concerned with identifying and discussing the phenomenon of perceptions. Proceeding from an explanation of what perceptions are and how they are linked to attitudes, the paper has emphasised the need to realise that the perceptions that really matter in the emancipation of the San are not merely those of the San themselves. Rather, the paper has argued that, in view of the power relations that form the bedrock on which the San disadvantage lies, it is expedient to focus at length on the perceptions of the dominant non-San Batswana, the so-called "blacks", since it is they who - to a large extent - determine the fate of the welfare of the San in Botswana.

It has been recognised that the mainstream Batswana dominate the San and deal with them injudiciously and with impunity at the three levels of the individual, the community and the state.

Good (1999) has posited that the San were dispossessed of their land, cattle and labour power and skills by the rising Tswana elites. At the time in question and for the generation concerned, land, cattle and labour constituted the crucial factors of production and self-determination. In the present era, acquisition of formal education has become a paramount source of livelihood. In this present chapter, I have attempted to demonstrate how the same process, this time not of dispossession but of deprivation, is being extended into the critical arena of formal education in a bid to maintain the status quo in terms of social relationships between the San and the "blacks". Once again, the dominant non-San "blacks" are perpetuating the subjugation of the San by significantly reducing their chances of receiving a formal education, currently the most crucial tool in connecting any people with economic opportunities. More than three decades on from Botswana's independence, formal schooling has not placed any San in a position of influence. The San remain stigmatised, despised and without any clout. Because they are dehumanised, they continue to be as vulnerable as ever to abuse from the "blacks". To all intents and purposes, their perception that they may not achieve any significant self-determination or recognition through their own efforts, unless they receive external assistance, appears completely valid.

It would appear that the greatest mistake government has made is to pursue a non-ethnic approach to the development of the remote area dwellers. The government might have been correct in avoiding an approach that showed any semblance to the policy of apartheid practised by the former South African regime. However, the San in Botswana have come to realise that being grouped together with ethnically different RADs has not assisted their cause at all. The other RADs do not share the stigma, nor do they share the San culture, which is responsible for the stigma and the perception the "blacks" have of the San. More importantly, for the San, life among the RADs means total assimilation into a completely different culture, the culture of the "blacks", while that is not by any means the case for other RADs. As the CBNRM programme has indicated for Zutshwa, other RADs not only subordinate the San but they exclude them from development programmes and projects that were meant for all RADs in a community.

The way forward will be for the Botswana Government to realise the significance of differences among the RADs, even though they may live in the same communities. It is now clear that the empowerment of the San requires a different approach from that of other non-San RADs within the same community. This means that the Remote Area Development Programme (RADP) needs to re-focus, taking cognisance of the special circumstances of the San vis-à-vis other RADs. However, over and above all else, a change in attitude needs to be initiated among the "blacks". ❑

Notes

1. "Blacks" is what the San call the mainstream Batswana.
2. The Botswana House of Chiefs is an advisory body to the government on matters pertaining to customary law and practises. It consists of eight ex-oficio members (the chiefs from the eight major tribes), four elected members (elected by the sub-chiefs in North East, Chobe, Kgalagadi and Gantzi Districts) and three specially elected members (elected by the ex-oficio members and the four elected members from among persons who have not, within the preceding five years, actively engaged in politics). –Ed.
3. The eight major tribes are the BaKgatla, BaKwena, BaMalete, BaMangwato, BaNgwaketse, BaRolong, BaTawana and BaTlokwa tribes. –Ed.
4. It could be for this reason that, in two instances, the San chose a "black" to head their settlement, deliberately avoiding one of their own.
5. It is unfortunate that figures are not available to show the magnitude of the problems being discussed.
6. The Ngwato constitute the largest of the eight Tswana tribes, BaMangwato. –Ed.

THE PAST AND FUTURE OF SAN LAND RIGHTS IN BOTSWANA

Michael Taylor

In February 2002, the government of Botswana, in the face of domestic and international criticism, cut all services to the residents of the Central Kalahari Game Reserve, most of whom were San. Claiming it was not "forcing" residents to leave, the government Minister responsible for overseeing their removal explained that those who wanted to stay could do so, but that they would receive no social services or water. These services would instead be made available in three government-created settlements outside the Reserve – New !Xade, Kaudwane and Xeri. With these conditions, only a handful of the remaining 700 residents inside the reserve expressed their resolve to stay in their ancestral homeland, a vast area that contains no permanent surface water.

Central Kalahari Game Reserve was a creation of the British colonial government in 1963. It was unique in southern Africa, in that it was created with the aim not only of nature conservation but also of protecting the rights of the 5,000 or so people (mostly San) living within its 52,347 square kilometre area who wanted to maintain hunting and gathering as part of their lifestyle. Nonetheless, in 1986, the government began requesting that the residents move to locations outside the reserve. Few people actually moved, however, until 1997 when the government began bringing in trucks to remove residents. The removals culminated in 2002 with the complete cessation of all services to remaining residents of the reserve (see Map 6).

Various reasons have been proposed as to why the government of Botswana has so determinedly attempted to empty the reserve of its residents, despite its initial design as a haven for hunter-gatherers. Some point to the favoured model of conservation that regards the presence of people as necessarily detrimental to the interests of nature conservation. Speculation has also arisen after the discovery of diamonds within the Reserve. Guessing at the motives of bureaucrats, nonetheless, distracts one from the deeper commentary that these removals provide on the relationship between San in Botswana, their government and their land.

This chapter focuses on the situation of San land rights in Botswana. It is a situation that must be understood in the light of the place that San generally occupy in the worldviews of policy makers in Botswana, described in the first section of this chapter. To many, San represent a form of primitivity that can be most effectively overcome by assimilation and, as such, no special dispensation is made in land policy for the distinct needs of San as part-time hunter-gatherers. The second section of this chapter examines the central importance of land in considering livelihood options now and in the future. The third section discusses the legal framework that governs land rights in Botswana, before going on to the final two sections that look at two specific policies that have impacted on the possibilities for San land rights in Botswana: the Tribal Lands Grazing Policy, and Community-Based Natural Resource Management.

San in Botswana

San in Botswana comprise a distinct minority of about 50,000 out of a total population of 1.6 million, or roughly 3% of the population. The non-San population of Botswana is about 50% ethnically Batswana, with the other 47% of the non-San population comprising around 17 other ethnic groups. Nonetheless, San are a distinct minority among minorities, in that they are the first peoples of the subcontinent, and have an identity based on hunting and gathering rather than agriculture or pastoralism. Understanding the implications of how the majority population views a lifestyle based on hunting and gathering is key to comprehending the position of San (or Basarwa as they are often called) in contemporary Botswana, and thus their struggles for land rights.

Botswana is a country that has enjoyed tremendous economic growth over the last three decades, achieving for many of these years, thanks to diamonds, among the highest national economic growth rates in the world. This growth has prompted massive social change, as an almost wholly rural population at independence in 1966 has become rapidly urbanised and integrated into the global economy. In this economy, the persistence of people who hunt and gather for part of their subsistence is seen not in a romantic sense, as by many Western observers, but as an embarrassment. They are, in the eyes of many Batswana, an indication of the failure of the country's prosperity to reach its poorest citizens. Hunting and gathering, and the lack of personal property that this indicates, is strongly associated with poverty. Moreover, this is a form of poverty many other citizens of Botswana themselves relate to. In the generations before the wealth of the mineral boom, even many non-San relied in part on hunting and gathering, especially when drought or war temporarily destroyed their other forms of livelihood. As expressed by a retired civil servant at a recent workshop on poverty in Botswana:

Our grandparents lived like Basarwa - all Batswana lived like Basarwa. But we left that lifestyle behind and moved on. It is a tedious life and they must be brought out of it to live like us.

From this point of view, widely shared among non-San in Botswana, the solution to the poverty many San face is clearly assimilation into the practices, norms and values of dominant society (see Taylor 2003).

Although several different factors have undoubtedly motivated the removals from Central Kalahari Game Reserve, they can be understood primarily as the actions of a paternalistic government attempting to integrate and assimilate a people whose poverty they regard as being a product of a lifestyle associated with hunting and gathering. This has been the mainstay of the Botswana government's implicit and explicit policy towards San.

Considering the general conception among policymakers in Botswana that a hunting and gathering lifestyle is "backward", it was perhaps inevitable that an anathema created by the colonial government - that of a Reserve protecting the rights of "hunter-gatherers" - would eventually be ended.

The removal of San from CKGR can essentially be understood as a civilising project towards the segment of Botswana's population considered to be the most "backward". This also explains the phenomenal investment that the Botswana government has placed in New !Xade, the largest relocation centre. As of June 2002, the Ghanzi District Council had reportedly spent P9,441,448.65 (US$1 = approx 4.5 Pula) on buildings alone in New !Xade, in addition to buildings constructed under the Drought Relief Programme, water provision from 40km away, the access road, compensation and relief programmes. Residents were paid amounts up to P24,000 per family in 1997, and P93,000 in 2002 as compensation for rebuilding their houses. Since 1997, every family in New !Xade has been given monthly food rations, and each family can claim 5 cattle or 15 goats. Although it is impossible to accurately calculate total government expenditure on New !Xade in the first five years of its existence, over and above recurrent expenditure had the removals not taken place, it can reasonably be estimated to be well in excess of P80 million. This is an expenditure of over P50,000 per resident, at the April 2002 population estimate of 1,598 people. The Ghanzi District Council has proposed that the road to New !Xade be tarred under National Development Plan 9 (2003-9).

Land, Livelihoods and Identity

Although San have a strong heritage of hunting and gathering, most San today would probably express a preference not to live primarily from subsistence hunting and gathering. San themselves admit it was a difficult lifestyle, with periods of hunger as frequent as times of plenty. Nonetheless, hunting and gathering remains a very important el-

San farm hand at cattle show in Ghanzi. Photo: Chris Erni

ement of the identity of most San, who would like to integrate some hunting and gathering with other forms of gaining a livelihood (see Taylor 2001, Barnard and Taylor 2002). Most of all, San, as any other people the world over, would like to be able to control their own destiny, rather than have it overwhelmingly dictated by a government from which they feel alienated.

In negotiating livelihood options for the future, whether they include hunting and gathering, livestock raising, or tourism enterprises, control over land is an absolutely central issue. As a Ju|'hoan delegate to an historic regional conference on "San and Development" held in Gaborone in 1993 explained:

> *We have so many plans and things to do, but without the right to land, we cannot do any of them. We first need land to call our own, then we can move forward.*

Unfortunately, over ten years later, many San in Botswana consider themselves further from this goal than when it was expressed in 1993. Expressing a similar sentiment, Roy Sesana, Chairman of First People of the Kalahari, told a visiting group of San delegates from northern Botswana in 1998: "Our human rights are our land. They cannot do anything for us if they take us off our land". Sticking to his conviction, Roy Sesana was one of the few stalwarts in Central Kalahari Game Reserve to have ostensibly resisted the removals of February 2002.

Having land to call one's own provides more than just expanded options for the future. As the primary productive asset, it also gives a sense of standing in the wider social economy that landless San cannot achieve. This principle is confirmed by Wily (1976:16), who observed that relations between San and non-San at Bere, a settlement south of Central Kalahari Game Reserve, improved after they were officially allocated a small tract of land, as it gave them a standing by being able to declare, "we have a place". Woodburn (1997) also observed higher levels of discrimination against landless Hadzabe in Tanzania than against those who were still able to assert a measure of control over land. For a society founded on a land-based socio-economy and culture such as that of San, preventing social disintegration is also largely dependent on retaining access to land.

Rights over land – and thus the resources on it – are probably the primary issue in considering the future of San in Botswana. In a basic sense, having access to productive land enables survival. Furthermore, rights to land allow different development options for the future to be considered. On a political level, having land to call one's own commands a sense of dignity and respect and, on a cultural level, secure rights to land help maintain social and cultural cohesion.

The fundamental disjuncture between dominant values over land and those predominant among San is evident in the official insistence that the land requirements of resettled San are met by the allocation of residential and arable plots. This ignores the extensive nature of land use that hunting and gathering subsistence practices demand.

Apart from the removals from Central Kalahari Game Reserve, what then is the status of San land rights more generally in Botswana? The following section will consider the legal framework in which land rights operate in Botswana, followed by an analysis of two government policies (and resultant programmes) that particularly affect San land rights in Botswana. In each of these sections, the main principle established so far remains central to understanding the status of San land rights in Botswana: that government policy does not recognise the particular needs of "hunter-gatherers" with respect to land but is instead directed at actively assimilating such people into the patterns of living followed by the majority.

Land Tenure and San

Customary land rights in Botswana, like in many parts of Africa, have operated by default. In other words, they have continued only to the extent that no other interests present have been sufficiently important to contest their validity. In a large and sparsely populated country like

Botswana (average population density: 2.2 people per square kilometre) this has in the past worked to the benefit of politically weak people, like the San. Hunting and gathering, which requires large tracts of land, remained feasible for as long as these areas were not claimed by more powerful groups. Ambiguities inherent in land tenure systems thus functioned to allow San continued access to land and the resources on it. As noted by Behnke (1994:15, quoted in Scoones 1995) on resource rights in an African context: "certain critical ambiguities as to who owns what and can go where provide a degree of fluidity which suits everyone's purpose".

Such fluidity began to be broken down during the colonial period in Botswana, which began in 1885. The first territorial concern of the colonisers was to identify and demarcate the territories of chiefdoms as "Tribal Reserves". These were drawn up according to the claims of the eight dominant Tswana tribes, under which San and other minorities were subsumed. The second concern of the colonisers was to validate land acquisitions by white settlers and companies, which became freehold land. Remaining lands became "Crown Lands", which were appropriated by the Crown by virtue of it being the protecting power (Ng'ong'ola 1993). The territories of San and other minorities were henceforth submerged under these new land categories. The rights of those who had lived on freehold lands were obliterated, which particularly affected San on the Ghanzi Ridge, whose land was ceded to Cecil John Rhodes at the end of the 19th century. Those who continued to live on Crown lands were tolerated, but their position was precarious as they were, in theory, tenants at the will of the Crown. The remainder of minorities in the tribal reserves, of whom San were at the bottom of the ladder were, as subjects of their Tswana masters, given no distinct tribal rights of their own (ibid.)

Despite the *de jure* changes to land tenure in this period, the actual claims that they represented remained generally weak, apart from claims over land that had become freehold. *De facto* systems of resource tenure throughout much of the colonial period continued to contain enough ambiguities that those with few formal land titles, like San, were able to continue gaining access to land, even if not as extensively as before.

With independence in 1966, the colonial division of land carried over. Freehold land remained freehold, comprising 5.7% of Botswana's land. Crown Land became State Land, comprising 23% of Botswana's land. Tribal Reserves became Tribal Land, covering 71.3% of Botswana's land. Land tenure in Botswana today represents a profoundly political dilemma of competing claims among different social groups and interest bodies. International conservation concerns consider much of Botswana's landscape as part of a global heritage in need of "preservation". Allied with them are tourism interests, which fuel Botswana's fastest growing industry, generating ever increasing revenues and providing hope for employment. Added to these are the claims of large cattle owners wanting to make use of the extensive grazing areas opened up by boreholes and Botswana's expanding road network. The ambiguities inherent in resource tenure are becoming increasingly restricted, as these more powerful interests have provoked the clear demarcation of rights of access to land and other natural resources. The original inhabitants of the land are increasingly vulnerable to having the remaining ambiguities in resource tenure exploited by those more powerful than themselves. The struggle to legitimate and realise claims to land is one in which certain groups lose out and, so far, San have consistently lost the most.

At the heart of these struggles are debates as to how "ownership" of land is constituted and legitimated; what constitutes legitimate land use, and thus how can land be legitimately "owned". Freehold rights are absolute, and are available to those with the capital to purchase them, which excludes virtually all San. State land remains in the hands of the State and cannot be individually owned. Most State Land is now National Parks or Wildlife Management Areas (See Map 7). Tribal land was customarily held by chiefs who allocated it at the request of individuals or groups of their tribe. As San had no recognised chiefs, they were excluded from allocating land themselves, remaining subject to dominant tribes for land allocations.

The 1969 Tribal Land Act transferred the powers of allocating tribal land to Land Boards, set up for each Tribal Authority. The Tribal Land Act recognises land ownership arising from residential, commercial, agricultural or pastoral use, but not hunting and gathering (which requires much more extensive areas). Hunting and gathering is not regarded as "productive" use of the land, despite its enormous importance to the subsistence of many San, particularly the poorest. Small parcels of land can thus be allocated to any citizen for the first four purposes but not for hunting and gathering. In this sense, all Botswana citizens have *de jure* equal access to land but, in practice, San lose out in two respects. Firstly, few San own significant herds of livestock or have the capital to sink a borehole, and so have difficulty in being allocated land for grazing - the most extensive form of allocation, often 64 square kilometres. Secondly, many San - who are generally not represented on Land Boards - claim that, because of their depressed status, their applications for land in competition with Tswana often receive low priority (e.g. Moeletsi 1993). A current example of this is a community of San living at Jamakata in North-East District, who claim to have been living there since the 1930s. Nonetheless, the land on which they live was, in the late 1990s, allocated by the Land Board to a cattle owner who then attempted to evict the residents. The residents have refused to move, and have appealed to DITSHWANELO, the Botswana Centre for Human Rights, for assistance against removal. As of 2004, the case remained unresolved.

San in Botswana therefore find themselves facing legislation over land that makes no special provisions for their particular needs, and that takes no account of their particular historical circumstances as a category of people that have been progressively marginalised from control over land. Moreover, active attempts have been made to remove anomalies in official policy that fail to recognise the implications of ethnic difference, such as the anomaly of the Central Kalahari Game Reserve, which gave special rights to "hunter-gatherers". San in Botswana are therefore constrained to seek land rights within the national frameworks applicable to all citizens, despite the disadvantages they face.

This chapter finishes with a look at two national policies that have had particular impact on San opportunities for land rights. The first is the Tribal Lands Grazing Policy, and its successor, the National Fencing Policy, which promote the effective privatisation of extensive tracts of Tribal Land at the expense of residents who may have used this land in the past, usually as part-time hunter-gatherers. The second is the Community-Based Natural Resource Management Programme, which provides a means for some communities, including San, to gain a limited form of control over significant tracts of land.

Fencing of Grazing Lands

The Tribal Grazing Lands Policy (TGLP) was adopted in 1975 with the specific objective of privatising communal rangelands on Tribal Land. Based on the assumption that the communal land tenure system was a major factor in poor production in the livestock industry, it promoted the creation of large (6,400ha) ranches on communal land that would then be allocated, at a nominal lease rental, to individual farmers. Approximately 335,000ha of communal land was made into leasehold ranches under TGLP. Although the TGLP ranches were generally demarcated some distance from established villages, this was not empty land. A number of studies, the most well known of which was Hitchcock's 1978 "Kalahari Cattle Posts", showed that the proposed TGLP areas were lived in and widely used, particularly by San.

The TGLP White Paper stated its intent to protect "the interests of those who only own a few cattle or none at all" by setting aside "reserve areas... to safeguard the poorer members of the population" (Botswana 1975:6, 7). However, the subsequent land-use zoning process completely left out such reserve areas. The new owners of the ranches were given exclusive rights to not only the land but also all the wild-life and plant resources within their ranches. Hunting and gathering became impossible in these areas, and an estimated 28,000-31,000 people were displaced from the TGLP ranch areas, according to a World Bank report commissioned by the Ministry of Agriculture.

Neatly dovetailing with the removal of scattered populations in TGLP areas was the creation of "settlements" for San, to encourage their congregation in centres where services such as schools, clinics and water could be provided. Although the provision of such services has been beneficial, the ultimate effect of sedenterisation in this manner has been that, having lost access to the land they used to live on, residents remain vulnerable to further dispossession in their new settlements. In keeping with the national policy of giving all citizens equal treatment, the settlements are open to all who wish to live in them. In many settlements, non-San cattle owners have moved in to take advantage of free water and cheap labour for their cattle and, once again, the San have been squeezed out. The communal areas allocated to each settlement, usually in the region of 10,000-15,000ha, are too small to support hunting and gathering, and yet often become overgrazed by the livestock of newer immigrants. While the 27 settlements that had been created by 1992 had thus been allocated a total of 352,300ha (Hitchcock 1996:15), their San residents had, in effect, very little meaningful control over this land or the resources on it.

Despite the enormous human cost in creating the TGLP ranches, much research over the two decades since its implementation has suggested that such ranches actually have no higher productivity - and in fact often lower - than open commonage (Perkins 1991:90, White 1994:5, Selolwane 1995). Nonetheless, the effective privatisation of large tracts of communal land that it promoted benefits a cattle-owning elite, many of whom are also senior policy makers.

The process begun by TGLP is now being continued in the Fencing Component of the 1991 National Agricultural Development Policy. Under this successor to TGLP, pre-fenced ranches are no longer allocated but owners of boreholes on communal land are allowed to fence the grazing lands around their borehole (typically about 6,400ha), gaining exclusive rights to the fenced land and plant and animal resources on it. There are no known San owners of such boreholes on communal land in Botswana. Although this policy framework has been in place for over a decade, implementation has been delayed, indicating some recognition of its potential to further dispossess poor residents of natural resources. Nonetheless, implementation of the fencing policy began in earnest in 1996. As of April 2003, 539 ranches had been demarcated and approved for fencing, covering an area of two million hectares.[1] The Ministry of Agriculture intends to approve a further 250 ranches by March 2006.

Khwai village, 1996. Photo: Diana Vinding

The current and ongoing implementation of the Fencing Component of the 1991 National Agricultural Development Programme threatens to dispossess many more rural residents, many of whom are San, of access to land and other natural resources than those affected by the CKGR removals.[2]

Conservation

Alongside cattle, conservation has created the other great demand for land in Botswana's remote areas. National Parks and Game Reserves created since the 1940s now make up 17.4% of Botswana's area (See Map 7). As with the creation of ranches under TGLP, the land on which these reserves were created was not empty, and people - more often than not San - who had used this land were excluded from it. This was particularly the case with - aside from Central Kalahari Game Reserve – Chobe National Park, Moremi Game Reserve and Khutse Game Reserve. In addition to land set aside as National Parks and Game Reserves, a further 20.9% of Botswana's land area is set aside as Wildlife Management Areas (WMA). These are areas in which wildlife is given priority but which – unlike National Parks and Game Reserves – do not exclude human habitation.

161

Despite their role in alienating some San from land they regard as their own, conservation initiatives have also indirectly assisted other San in maintaining access to land and the resources on it. Most of the settlements within Wildlife Management Areas are predominantly San. Although livestock is tolerated within a twenty-kilometre radius of settlements in Wildlife Management Areas, it is generally discouraged. For example, the government is not obliged to compensate for livestock killed by predators within these areas. Consequently, immigration by cattle owners into these areas has been limited, reducing competition for land and the resources on it. Nonetheless, although San retain access to land in these circumstances, they have no formalised *rights* over it, and their needs are often secondary to other interests (see Taylor 2002). Take, for example, the story of Two-Boy and his family, who lived in an area north of Moremi Game Reserve, which became a Wildlife Management Area. By the time he told his story, the area had been leased directly by the government to a safari operator, who employed Two-Boy as a tracker (Taylor 2000:88):

> *The Botswana Defence Force came to my house and asked for me, saying that the soldiers would end up shooting me, as they said I was harassing the animals. But I thought, "If I am harassing them, why are they still around?" Nonetheless, I broke my village and moved to Gudigwa [the nearest government-created San settlement].*
>
> *Today we give ourselves nothing, living instead at the hands of white people. I didn't want to fight with the soldiers because I am illiterate and don't know how to protect myself, or my younger brothers and children who were with me. If they had not harassed me, I would still be there.*

As is evident in the circumstances of people such as Two-Boy, despite being protected from the influx of cattle owners, San in Wildlife Management Areas remain vulnerable to interests more powerful than their own. The only possibility for residents to retain the last vestiges of resource rights is to find a way of formalising tenure rights to more solidly protect their own interests rather than primarily those of other interest groups. This is a possibility made real by a programme that has been implemented in Botswana over the past decade, which aims to decentralise management of natural resources to local communities. This is known as Community-Based Natural Resource Management (CBNRM).

CBNRM and Communal Land Rights

CBNRM began in Botswana in 1992. The programme allows eligible communities to be given management rights over a given section of

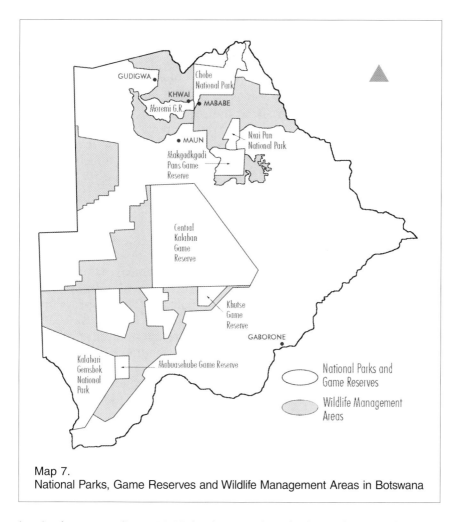

Map 7.
National Parks, Game Reserves and Wildlife Management Areas in Botswana

land, often exceeding 100,000ha (see Hitchcock, this volume). Although no ownership rights are transferred to the community, they are given the rights to manage, and benefit from, the resources within their area. CBNRM offers an unprecedented opportunity to formalise limited rights over a large tract of land on a communal level. It does this by providing the legislative and policy framework for residents to assert control over tracts of land beyond plots individually allocated for pastoralism or agriculture. As it is communities in remote areas that are most eligible for inclusion, where the natural resource to population ratio is relatively high, the majority of villages that have opted to take part in CBNRM are predominantly San villages.

CBNRM was initially designed as a programme to promote more effective local level conservation, under the assumption that allowing local people to more directly benefit from the natural resources in their vicinity would encourage them to more actively conserve them. However, in doing this, it has also provided the framework for local residents to gain at least a limited form of communal control over large tracts of land. A number of San communities, particularly those that have lost land to conservation in the past, have seen CBNRM as an opportunity to regain a form of land rights. In attempting to advocate for management rights over land under CBNRM, these communities have set up committees and legally registered trusts, which have enabled them to gain a political voice and thus advocate for rights beyond those related to land.

An example of one such village is Khwai, situated on the northern border of Moremi Game Reserve. Their village was moved to its present position in 1965 when Moremi Game Reserve was created, enclosing the land on which they used to live. In 1992 they were again threatened with removal, this time by their Minister who explained that the government wanted to develop the tourism potential of the area. This new threat coincided with the beginning of the CBNRM programme. They then formed a committee to oversee their entry into CBNRM. The first task of the committee was to secure the land, under the CBNRM programme, on which their village was situated, so as to avoid removal. The committee travelled to Gaborone to present their case to the government, which conceded to their demands. Having secured their land, they have since proceeded to set up their own community-based safari enterprise.

Although some other San communities have yet to achieve the success of Khwai in similar efforts, the opportunities afforded by CBNRM may be decisive in struggles by San to achieve a form of land rights. Despite a lack of support for the principles and practice of CBNRM in some sectors of the Botswana government, there is little likelihood of its official rejection in the foreseeable future. This is in no small part due to the strength and voice that Community-Based Organisations formed under the CBNRM Programme (most of which represent primarily San organisations) have achieved over the last decade of their formation.

Conclusion

San in Botswana have faced progressive dispossession from land they have called their own: in the face of immigrations of more politically organised people into the subcontinent over the last two millennia; and in the face of the expanding cattle, conservation and tourism interests of more recent history. This has not always been purposeful dispossession: they have lost land simply by being unable, or unwilling, to defend it against more powerful interests that have more clearly demarcated their claims to this land. Much of the land now encompassed by parks or cattle ranches is a tangible representation of the history and identity of many San who used to call this land their own. It is also a reminder of their alienation from not just their physical space but from many of the markers by which they have come to define themselves.

At the root of continued loss of access to land by San in Botswana today is a fundamental difference in values and perceptions as to what constitutes "progress" or "development". For many San, continued access to extensive tracts of land is a prerequisite to attempting to retain social cohesion, as well as preserving development options for the future. In contrast, many policy makers see the only way of ensuring San a viable future as promoting their assimilation into dominant values and ways of living. Part of this involves moving San off their land into situations where they are more likely to enter into "productive employment", as is evident in the recent removals of residents from the Central Kalahari Game Reserve.

Despite extensive loss of land in the past few decades, the prospects for San to retain the few vestiges of land rights they still have – and to regain more – are hopeful. The rise of national San representative organisations, alongside the growth of community-based organisations representing the interests of many San communities are giving San a political voice that – until a decade ago – was unheard. The challenge of gaining meaningful *rights* over land, rather than simply maintaining *access* to it is a daunting one, requiring in part a significant shift in the mindsets of many policy makers. San in Botswana have been faced with significant setbacks in their struggles for land rights, exemplified by the removals in 2002 of most of the remaining residents of Central Kalahari Game Reserve. Nonetheless, the successes of villages such as Khwai point to the potential of San community-level organisations to gain an albeit limited form of land rights. ❑

Notes

1   By area, these ranches are distributed as follows: Makopong (9), Ghanzi (2), Kaka (99), Kang (11), Western Sandveld (200), Area 4B (92), Lerolwane (28), Maun (56) and Matlhoaphuhudu (42).

2   It must be remembered that, despite the international focus on CKGR removals, the April 2002 population of New !Xade of 1598 people constitutes only 3% of the estimated population of 50,000 San in Botswana.

INDIGENOUS WOMEN IN BOTSWANA: CHANGING GENDER ROLES IN THE FACE OF DISPOSSESSION AND MODERNIZATION

Robert K. Hitchcock, Melvin Johnson
and Christine E. Haney

Modernization, development and globalization have, over the past few decades, resulted in dramatic changes in the roles, status and socio-economic well-being of women worldwide. This is true in Africa, where some of the continent's countries are in serious economic and political straits. A combination of war, economic depression, environmental degradation, health problems and poorly targeted development programs have left many people worse off (UNDP 2003).[1] The structural adjustment programs and privatization efforts of the International Monetary Fund and the World Bank have led to cutbacks in spending on health, education and welfare. These policies have had serious social impacts, and livelihood support systems have been eroded, along with social and physical infrastructure and civil society. All of this has also seriously affected the situations of women throughout most of Africa (Human Rights Watch 1995:196-340; Schoenberger 2000:14-17).

In many ways, the Republic of Botswana is seen as an exception to these generalizations.[2] Botswana, an independent nation-state since 1966, is Africa's oldest multiparty democracy and has held six open elections with a number of different parties participating. It has a very good human rights record, and there are no political prisoners in the country. Botswana has also had one of the highest economic growth rates of any country in the developing world, and poverty alleviation has been an important focus of government policy (Botswana 1997).

Botswana prides itself on its human rights and development records. Primary education has been made available to the majority of the country's people. The percentage of the population living below US$1 a day has been reduced through rural and urban economic development programs and the provision of a social safety net for people in the country. There have been efforts to promote gender equality and empower women both by the Botswana government and civil society.[3]

There has been a concerted effort by women to promote their rights in Botswana. Part of the reason for this situation is that, traditionally, Batswana women held an inferior position in society. They were not supposed to speak in public meetings, known as *kgotla* meetings, and they did not have the same rights to land, livestock or other property as men (Shapera 1938:28-29, 202-207, 218-221). Women in Botswana felt that they did not have the same rights as men in terms of public participation. They also felt that women were unequal to men when it came to provisions of the Botswana Constitution and some government legislation, notably the 1984 *Citizenship Amendment Act*. Women who are married under customary law in Botswana are considered legal minors. Women's rights within the family traditionally were not the same as those of men (Selolwane 1998: 400-401).

Today, the female share of non-agricultural wage employment in Botswana is 45 per cent and a great number of women work in the formal sector of the Botswana economy and in the civil service. The number of women in Parliament has increased from five in 1990 to 17. A growing number occupy senior posts such as judges, professors and government ministers.

The livelihood and roles of indigenous women have changed too. While in theory at least, San women were traditionally equal to men, took part in public discussions, controlled land and other resources and had rights over the goods that they produced (Draper 1975a; Lee 1979:146-156, 309-332), they today face a number of constraints. Although there have been some improvements, especially within health and education, their overall situation has in many ways deteriorated. This is the result of a set of processes that they share with their men that include land dispossession, resettlement, sedentarisation discrimination, and increased contact with non-San societies.

It is important to note that these processes have had different impacts on men and women. The constraints that indigenous women in Botswana have to cope with today include poverty, illiteracy, loss of decision-making power, violence – both structural and domestic - and health problems, constraints that have many gender specific aspects and which they therefore share with other ethnic minority women, including San women in other parts of southern Africa (Gaeses 1998; Felton and Becker 2001; Becker 2003; Sylvain 2004). Botswana is a signatory to the Convention on the Elimination of All Forms of Discrimination against Women (CEDAW), and the government and non-government organizations in Botswana have sponsored symposia and meetings on women and their rights.

While non-indigenous women in Botswana have for some time been demanding recognition of their rights, including the right to equitable treatment under Botswana's constitution, in line with international human rights law, indigenous groups as well as indigenous women themselves are only just beginning to concern themselves with gender issues. One reason may be that many indigenous organizations tend to be male-dominated. Another reason may be that thinking in gender specific terms was not as necessary in a society characterized by a high degree of gender equality.

Indigenous Women in Traditional San and Nama Society

For thousands of years, the San of southern Africa subsisted as hunters and gatherers. The Nama, who together with the San make up the Khoesan peoples, were primarily pastoralists who supplemented their subsistence with foraging and trading.[4] Both were totally dependent on the natural environments in which they lived.

During the 19th century, as the power and influence of the Tswana tribes grew, the San and the Nama experienced dramatic changes in their ways of life. Neither San nor Nama were considered to be members of Tswana tribes. They lacked tribal citizenship rights. Both San and Nama were classified by the Tswana as *bolata (malata)*, a term that is sometimes translated as serfs or indentured servants. Some San and Namba worked for other people as domestic servants, herders, or field hands. They were not usually paid for their work; instead, they were sometimes given clothing, food or, rarely, a goat or calf in exchange for their services. They did not have the right to take part in public meetings, and they were not allowed to speak for themselves in tribal court. It was not unheard of that they could be transferred from one "master" (*mong*) to another, something about which they had little say. It was considered inappropriate for Tswana to marry members of groups considered to be *bolata*, and San and Nama women were not usually considered as wives or co-wives but rather as concubines (*nyatsi*).

San and Nama also lacked property rights. Tswana and other groups could take livestock, pots, skin blankets or other goods away from them without paying anything in return. In a number of instances, San and Nama were required to pay tribute to the tribal authorities of the Tswana and they were also required to provide labor, for example, in ploughing, planting, weeding and harvesting the fields of chiefs.

However, up to the 1950s-60s, some San still lived as hunters and gatherers, and had only little – if any - interaction with non-San individuals. The status of San women in this context was characterized by a high degree of autonomy and equal gender relations. Patricia Draper (1975a:78), in her writings about the !Kung (Ju|'hoansi), pointed out that in many ways, women were the equals of men. Ju|'hoan society could be seen as non-sexist in its gender orientation. Among the most salient features that promoted egalitarianism, Draper notes, were women's substantial subsistence contribution and the control that they had over the foods they gathered; the fact that foraging in the Kalahari required a similar degree of mobility for both sexes; and the lack of rigidity in the sexual stereotyping of many adult activities, including domestic chores.

Adults of both sexes seemed surprisingly willing to do the work of the opposite sex. Building huts was predominantly women's work, but men might also do it. While gathering of wild plant foods, medicines and fire-

San woman with veld food, CKGR. Photo: Arthur Krasilnikoff

wood was often women's work, men also engaged in gathering. Domestic tasks frequently involved both women and men. Both parents took part in socializing their children, reprimanding them gently if they misbehaved or acted out of sorts. Ju|'hoan children were not trained to fear male authority. Authoritarian behavior was avoided by adults of both sexes.

Among the Ju|'hoansi there was an extremely low cultural tolerance for aggressive behavior by anyone, male or female. As Draper (1975a:78) points out, "Without question, women derive self-esteem from the regular daily contribution they make to the family's food…. And !Kung women impress one as self-contained people with a high sense of self-esteem… they are vivacious and self-confident".

The Ju|'hoansi traditionally did not have status hierarchies or institutionalized public authorities. Although a small number of men and women did function as leaders, their influence was derived primarily from having earned the respect of others, and was essentially informal. Women's status in the community was high and their influence considerable. They were often prominent in major family and band decisions, such as where and when to move and whom their children would marry. Many also shared core leadership in a band and ownership of water holes and foraging areas. There are a number of cases where women were *n!ore kxausi* – traditional Ju|'hoan land managers who had a say over the ways in which traditional Ju|'hoan territories (*n!oresi*) were used.

In the Kalahari Desert, as elsewhere in southern Africa, women did much of the collecting of natural resources to sustain their families, including the fetching of water and fuel wood, the gathering of timber products for construction and tool manufacturing purposes, the cutting of wild grasses for use as thatch for roofs of homes, and the exploitation of specialized resources such as medicinal plants and ochre for decorative purposes. Given their wide-ranging environmental knowledge and extensive practical experience, women were often able to predict the locations and yields of indigenous wild products and, by using a variety of species, promote sustainable utilization.

While men were primarily the hunters of large mammals, observers have often tended to overlook the important role women had in the sighting and tracking of large and small animals or in post-hunting processing of prey animals (Hunter, Hitchcock and Wyckoff-Baird 1990). Among the G|ui and G||ana of the Central Kalahari Game Reserve, for instance, women played a crucial role in the dissemination of information about the state of the environment and reported back to their homes or camps what they had seen in the way of animal tracks while on gathering trips. This information-gathering and dissemination was essential to the adaptive success of rural populations.

Women also captured animals and other fauna of all sizes, especially small mammals, birds and insects.[5] Insects, like the mopane worm, and insect products were used extensively by women in the Kalahari for subsistence and, in more recent times, cash income. For San women and men, subsistence was far more than simply a means of making a living. They saw it also as a complex system of obligation, distribution and exchange that was crucial to the well-being of people. Without these reciprocal exchange systems, people's quality of life would be much worse, and levels of social conflict would be higher.

A classic example of this situation was the manufacture and exchange of ostrich eggshell bead necklaces and bracelets that used to occur in the Kalahari Desert. The egg of the ostrich is an important wild resource that women exploit extensively in the central and western Kalahari. San women used to manufacture beads from broken pieces of ostrich eggshell, and both women and men would decorate whole ostrich eggs by carving designs in them with a pointed tool. The exchange of these items linked people together in a complex system of mutual reciprocity.

Land Dispossession, Sedentarization and Women

Today few, if any, San and Nama follow traditional foraging and pastoral lifestyles, and most of them live in permanent settlements of 300-500 people. They have access to certain facilities (e.g. water, health clinics, schools) and to social welfare projects provided by the Remote Area Development Program (RADP), a program that was established to cater for San and other rural people who lived in remote areas outside of recognized villages.

This is the result of a long process of land dispossession. Since the middle of the 19th century, much of the land traditionally occupied and used by the San and the Nama has been taken over by other Africans, including whites of European descent, and some of it has been turned into cattle ranches, farms, or national parks and game reserves. It was in the latter part of the 20th century, however, that this dispossession took a dramatic turn with the adoption in 1975 of the Tribal Grazing Lands Policy (TGLP), which transformed the land tenure system in Botswana and divided the country into a number of different land-use categories.[6] But contrary to the intentions expressed in the original documents,[7] virtually no land was set aside as "reserved land" to protect "the interests of those who own only a few cattle or none at all". On the contrary, it is estimated that as many as half of all San and two thirds of Nama were affected by the land reform. Of those who received land allocations under the Tribal Grazing Land Policy, none was either San or Nama, and only a small percentage were women.

The Bushmen Development Program (the predecessor to RADP) realized early on what the potential implications of the TGLP were going to be for people who depended largely on foraging for their existence. It therefore attempted to ensure that people in areas zoned as commercial were not deprived of access to land when ranches were established. However, the amount of land provided for people in these areas turned out to be insufficient for them to continue foraging, or grazing in the case of the Nama.

The RADP attempted to mitigate the impact of the TLGP on Remote Area dwellers by getting some land set aside as settlements, especially in western Botswana. In these areas, people had customary rights to water and land for subsistence production purposes. Over the years, at least 65 settlements have been established by the government of Botswana, with a total population of over 20,000 people.

Land dispossession however is not a thing of the past. A more recent case of dispossession has been the relocation of resident populations from the Central Kalahari Game Reserve (the CKGR). Between 1997 and 2002, almost 2,000 San and Bakgalagadi – or approximately 400 families – have been moved out of the CKGR. They too have been resettled in three new settlements – New !Xade, Kaudwane and Xeri (see Map 6). In the Central District, even more San and other poor rural residents are currently under threat of dispossession (see Taylor, this volume).

The change from a hunting and foraging way of life – or from pastoralism as the case may be - to sedentarization and crop production and small-scale rural enterprises has had a number of impacts on the situation of the San and the Nama in general and of the San and Nama women in particular.

The land and water schemes of the RADP proved to be a useful strategy for providing access to land but, as yet, rural poor people have not obtained secure tenure rights over these areas. This is especially true for San and Nama who have not been able to obtain grazing and water rights. San and Nama women and women from other groups (e.g. Bakgalagadi) have in particular had difficulties in getting the Land Boards to allocate land to them for arable and business purposes. While the Botswana government continues to claim that all Batswana have the right to land, clearly, that right is not as widely available for women or for members of indigenous and ethnic minority groups.

Another issue faced by the San and the Nama was that, over time, they came to live with people from other, dominant ethnic groups in the settlements. Soon after the first RAD settlements were established, the local authorities took the position that settlements were open to anyone. The argument that they gave was that citizens of Botswana have the right to live anywhere they choose. In practice, what this has meant is that fairly sizable numbers of people from other ethnic groups have moved into RAD settlements. In many cases, non-San individuals have taken over the water points and they use the domestic water sources for their livestock. They own most of the local stores, including the "shabeens" (beer halls), and they also often appropriate the leadership in the settlements. For San and Nama women, it means that they often feel they cannot easily take part in *kgotla* meetings. They also say that they find it difficult to play an active part in the Village Development Committees and other local institutions besides Parent-Teacher Associations, which tend to be headed by non-San.

Another effect of RAD resettlement schemes has been the social upheaval that follows the physical movement of people. It means that people lose the previous advantages of intimately knowing an area and its resources, and therefore have to abandon old ways. For subsistence, people in the settlements now depend on whatever crops and domestic animals they can raise themselves. There are few opportunities for employment and many San and Nama depend today on food and cash provided by the Botswana government through drought relief, cash-for work and poverty alleviation programs, including the Remote Area Development Program. Moving to settlements has made people become dependent on new alternatives being provided by the government. Villagisation has reinforced the process of clientisation.

San women building a new hut, Metsiamenong, CKGR. Photo: Chris Erni

Poverty, Drought and Alleviation Efforts

The process of clientisation was greatly accelerated as a result of the serious droughts that hit Botswana in the years 1961-62, 1965-66 and 1982-1985 causing serious difficulties for many people, in particular the people living in remote areas such as the Central Kalahari. In response, Botswana initiated relief efforts that included the provision of food, water and well-digging assistance. It should be noted that not a single life was lost to starvation during the severe droughts of 1982-1985 and the early 1990s, thanks to the effective nutritional and health surveillance and relief programs that were established by the Botswana government.

Since that time, Botswana has institutionalized its drought relief system into a system that includes not only the provision of food but also assistance to pregnant and lactating mothers, children under five and people categorized as destitute, that is, those persons who lack sufficient resources to sustain themselves.

In 1985, it was estimated that 90% of households in rural areas were receiving some kind of food ration, and 43% were receiving between 100 and 300 kg of food per annum.[8] In the 1980s the feeding program was oriented heavily toward feeding children. RADs were provided a full ration, which was intended to cover all their food requirements. The result was that food rations made up more or less 90-100% of the total food consumed in the settlements. It must be pointed out, however, that there were sometimes differences in well-being within households, with younger girls being worse off than boys. When asked why this was the case, the answer was that it was because boys were sometimes allowed to eat more of the rations since it was they who were doing the physical work (i.e. looking after livestock). This rationale was questioned when field workers noted that girls and young women would take care of their younger siblings, engage in domestic work and leave their homes to collect water and other goods for their families.

Coping Strategies in the Settlements

This high level of dependency on Botswana government welfare and assistance programs, however, must be seen in context. Currently, the various settlements offer limited opportunities for subsistence or income-generating activities.

The population size in most of the settlements is rapidly exceeding the carrying capacity of the land; available game and veld (bush) food within reasonable reach is diminishing, and grazing is deteriorating (Saugestad 2001a:134). There have been problems of loss of live-stock and wildlife due to disease and poor grazing.

Moving to the settlements has, in many cases, entailed a serious deterioration in women's previous economic status. The case of the San and Bakgalagadi women who were removed from the Central Kalahari Game Reserve is a case in point.

Firstly, it was the women among the San and Bakgalagadi that had greater numbers of goats in their possession, as many had used the money earned from the sale of handicrafts to buy small stock. When the Botswana government put the people and their livestock on the trucks to move them out of the Central Kalahari, some of the goats were left behind and lost to predators. Those goats that did get moved to the settlements were also exposed to predation and theft. Thus an important set of women's resources was decimated, thereby undercutting women's access to income and subsistence sources.

Another problem the women faced was that when the Botswana government gave livestock as compensation to people who had been removed from the reserve, the animals were given to male household heads and not to women, as government officials – most of whom were Tswana – judged that it was males who were supposed to be the ones who owned and controlled livestock.

Finally, the women also had to deal with the fact that the Land Boards were reluctant to give women certificates for residential and arable plots in the settlements. When asked why this was the case, land board members said that it was because males were supposed to be the household heads and it was they who should have the rights to homes and arable land. What ended up happening was that women who were removed from the Central Kalahari were left with fewer resources and less security of tenure over their homes and agricultural land than they had prior to their removal.

Over the years, there have been many attempts to improve the livelihood of San women through different income-generating activities based on their special skills. For instance, their skills in the collection and preparation of insects, like the mopane worm. Another profitable activity in the Kalahari Desert and adjacent areas in Botswana in which women are the primary participants is the exploitation of moth cocoons for silk production. From 1985-1988, Botswana Game Industries (BGI) purchased over 100 tons of cocoons from over 3,000 local collectors in northern and east-central Botswana.[9] Numerous women were involved in the cleaning and processing of the cocoons, and some of their products were sold directly to buyers from Zimbabwe, Italy and India. More recently, representatives of the Kuru Family of Organizations have worked with local people in Ghanzi District to raise cochineal, a small insect that feeds on the prickly pear cactus. Cochineal is a high value product used in the manufacture of carmine dye, a dye that is used in food coloring and cosmetics. The problem, however, was that the marketing of the product was not easy, and the program did not bring about the benefits that it had anticipated.

In many settlements, one of the few options for income generation is the production of crafts. A non-government organization, Gantsicraft, based in Ghanzi, Botswana, has assisted the San of the central and western Kalahari by purchasing crafts and other items, thus providing a source of income for local people. While both men and women produce and sell crafts, women earn the bulk of the funds. Kuru has also worked with local people to develop other crafts projects where the San traditional skills can be used – for instance painting and leatherwork. Several San women (as well as San men) artists have gained international fame for their paintings, which usually depict the animals and plants on which their life traditionally depended.

The manufacture and sale of ostrich eggshell items is an important source of income for many San households. The items are sold to the various craft organizations operating in rural Botswana. A problem facing women and other people who utilize ostrich eggshell products is that the government of Botswana established an *Ostrich Management Plan Policy* in 1994 (Botswana 1994b). This policy stipulates that people must have a license from the Department of Wildlife and National Parks (DWNP) before they can obtain and sell ostrich-related products. A fee must be paid in order to get the permit. Another stipulation is that ostrich eggshells are to be collected only from April to August, which limits the time that people can obtain them in the field. In addition, organizations involved in ostrich egg collection must establish a facility where the shells are kept, and the premises are inspected on a regular basis by the DWNP (1995).

There is some uncertainty over the timing of egg collection, general reporting procedures and the rights of people to collect eggs in the field. It has been argued by government officials that the manufacture of ostrich eggshell products by non-government organizations and community-based organizations is illegal because it contravenes another legal provision that states that only the holder of a Special Game License (SGL, a subsistence hunter's license) is allowed to manufacture articles from any trophy. A difficulty for SGL holders is that they are not allowed, under current law, to hold any other licenses besides their SGL. Thus, they cannot legally be given an ostrich egg-collecting license (Hitchcock and Masilo 1995). This has meant that women in the Kalahari have less access than in the past to craft products, and they are being out-competed by organizations and entrepreneurs who have been able to get licenses to obtain and sell ostrich egg products.

Similar concerns exist in tourism projects in Botswana, where it is men who get most of the cash-producing jobs (see Hitchcock, this volume). While women do get some work in the tourism industry, it is often as cleaners, maids and domestic workers for safari company managers. Women in the Kalahari and Okavango Delta regions of Botswana have pointed out repeatedly that the work that they do is not being rewarded at the same levels as that of men.

Changing Gender Relations

Draper (1975a, 1975b) notes that one of the effects of sedentarization on sex egalitarianism is to undermine it. This can take many forms. Once the Ju|'hoansi and other San shift their subsistence to animal husbandry and crop planting, sex roles become more rigidly defined and women's work is seen as "unworthy" of men. Women and girls appear to inhabit more restricted spaces. They gather wild plant foods but infrequently and seem more homebound, their time being taken up with domestic chores. Food preparation is more complicated. People have more possessions and better facilities and these things require more time and energy for maintenance. Housing is more substantial in settled communities than in the bush. The work of adult women is becoming more specialized, time consuming and homebound, and these women are quite willing to integrate their daughters into this work.

While women thus tend to stay in the village, the men are much more mobile: their work often takes them away from the village; they have more frequent interaction with members of other dominant cultural groups, and they thereby learn to speak Setswana and even English, which allows them to interact with tourists (see Hitchcock, this volume). Political affairs are the concern of men, not women. Men sometimes carry an aura of authority and sophistication that sets them apart from the women and children. Ranking of individuals in terms of prestige and differential wealth has begun in the settled villages.

A major aspect of these changes in gender roles is the decrease in women's autonomy and influence relative to that of the men. Women tend to become more isolated. One of the consequences of this isolation is that self-esteem is affected, as is the ability to influence decision-making at the community and family levels.

Another aspect is the increase in domestic violence and sexual abuses experienced by indigenous women. Alcohol contributes to spousal and child abuse, but alcohol-related violence is in general responsible for a substantial number of injuries to women, children and men and is a major cause of social conflict. This has notably been the case in the resettlement sites established by the Botswana government for those

177

people relocated out of the Central Kalahari Game Reserve (New !Xade, Kaudwane and Xeri) where alcohol-related and domestic assaults on women occur relatively frequently. San women in the settlements are also often the victims of sexual abuses committed by visiting non-San, and there are also cases of young San women in hostels at remote area schools being raped, abused and harassed, sometimes by teachers and school administrators. The drop-out rates of young girls from schools is high, in part because of teen pregnancy and fear on the part of girls about remaining in what they see as exploitative situations. As a result, there is a gender gap in school attendance among San in Botswana, especially in Grades 5, 6 and 7 (see Hays, this volume).[10]

The Health Situation

The San have traditionally exhibited some significant features in terms of population and health. In the 1960s, the Ju|'hoan San of Ngamiland had one of the world's slowest rates of population growth. The number of children born to women was between four and five. The average number of children who survived was slightly over two, meaning that the Ju|'hoan fertility was holding the population at the replacement rate. The reproductive health of women was relatively good, though there were cases of venereal disease and infertility.

Hunting-gathering Ju|'hoan San had very low serum cholesterol, low blood pressures that did not increase with age, and little in the way of heart disease. They were very active, going on forays for foraging and visiting purposes, carrying infants and engaging in extensive work activities both in their camps and in the bush. Their nutritional status was relatively good, high in vitamins and nutrients. The diet was also diverse, with as many as 150 species of plants and over 40 species of animals consumed. There were periods, however, when people went hungry, especially during the late dry season, and undernourishment was a problem with which the San had to contend.

Over the past few decades, the shift from nomadic foraging to sedentary crop and animal raising has impacted on people's health – positively and negatively. Population growth rates have risen to the point where some Ju|'hoan groups are increasing at a rate of 2.5% per annum (which would cause the population to double in 28 years). Some of the hypotheses proposed for the increased growth rates range from changes in patterns of breast-feeding and female activity levels to dietary and physiological shifts. Ju|'hoansi are taller and heavier now than they used to be. They also experience an increased life span. Because of the higher calorific diet, the reduced physical demands of settled life and the availability of Western-style health care, more Ju|'hoan

Handicraft manufacturing in the CKGR. Photo: Chris Erni

elders are living into their seventh and sometimes eighth decade of life.[11] This may prove to be particularly important for transitional populations. Older people remember the former nomadic life and have a better knowledge of the diversity of plants and animals and the different areas of the Kalahari in which they were found. As the San, Nama and other Kalahari populations become more aware of the fragility of the environment, the knowledge that only elders have of a lifestyle that was usually in harmony with nature will become more valuable as time passes.

On the other hand, diets today are higher in carbohydrates and refined sugars, and there are indications that adult-onset diabetes is on the increase among Ju|'hoansi, a process not dissimilar to that among other indigenous populations such as Native Americans (U.S. Indian Health Service 1991). In addition, cardiovascular disease is more common today than it was in the past. The San and Nama may be suffering more from the "diseases of development" - cancer and heart problems - but this situation is offset by the fact that they live longer and now have greater access to health services. Clinics and health posts have been established in the remote regions where the majority of San and Nama reside, and there are mobile health services that provide health care, immunizations and medicines to local people. Family planning services and information are more available than they were in the past.

Indigenous peoples in Botswana, as well as in other parts of southern Africa, however, face two major health problems, which also affect the population in general: malaria and HIV/AIDS. Malaria is endemic and, depending on the rains, sweeps the Kalahari in epidemics. In some instances, entire villages come down with malaria, so much so that the residents have difficulty collecting sufficient food or performing agricultural and domestic work. People will complain of hunger, and malaria often causes death, especially among children.

Southern Africa, and Botswana in particular, is said to be the global epicenter of HIV/AIDS in the new millennium. Although the HIV/AIDS rate among San seems to be much lower at present than is the case in the general population of Botswana and Namibia (estimated by some analysts to be as high as 15-30%, depending on the area), the infection rate is on the increase and it appears that San women in Botswana communities are becoming infected faster than men. Linked to the spread of AIDS has also been an increase in tuberculosis and other respiratory diseases. In general it can be said that indigenous women in southern Africa are collectively and individually highly vulnerable, in part because of their social and economic status, many of them being relatively poor.

Future Perspectives

It is only a decade ago that the first San organization – the First People of the Kalahari - was established. Its ultimate goal was to organize all the San in Botswana within a San Council but, otherwise, its objectives were to raise the awareness of San regarding their human and indigenous rights and more specifically to defend their land rights, notably in support of the residents of the CKGR. While these objectives were important to both men and women, the organization did not concern itself with the situation of women as such.

This is a common feature of many indigenous organizations: their leaders are men; their perspective is male-oriented; and their efforts are geared to face overall and vital needs that impact on their members in general. As noted in the introduction of this chapter, in the case of the San, the fact that gender relations had traditionally been relatively harmonious and egalitarian has meant that the need to secure the needs and interests of San women was not felt as urgent – not even by the women themselves.

However, the situation of San women has changed and they face new challenges. The changes are due primarily to external factors – land dispossession, resettlement and modernization. As people have become more sedentary, role differentiation has become more institutionalized, and changes have occurred in inheritance patterns, with a tendency toward greater patrilineality (passing property and other goods down through the male line), property rights and public policy decision-making (Draper 1975b, 1978). Changes in the economic systems due to globalization and an increase in the numbers of men affected by HIV/AIDS have meant that there are more female–headed households than there used to be. A disturbing trend is that there are more child-headed households in rural areas, too.

But the perceptions of San women have also changed; they are discovering alternative ways and are learning from other women's experiences. Today, indigenous women's groups are beginning to emerge, notably in connection with income-generating projects, and some of the bilateral aid agencies working in Botswana have developed policies that aim to promote gender and social equity. In recent years, a few San women have attended international meetings sponsored by various organizations including the United Nations, the World Bank and the International Work Group for Indigenous Affairs and, at the regional level, they have participated in conferences such as the San and Khoe Conference held in Gaborone in September 2003. This has given them the opportunity to meet other indigenous women, including San women from Namibia and South Africa, and share experiences, thereby increasing their own awareness of the problems they are facing as women and as indigenous peoples, and what kind of action they can take in order to improve their status.

Some San and Nama women in Botswana have argued that their socio-economic position is deteriorating in the face of globalization, trade liberalization and economic change. For this reason, they point out, they are in a "double bind". Clearly, greater attention has to be paid by Botswana and other southern African states to issues of gender, class and ethnicity. Human rights are peoples' rights, they say, but there are also rights that are inherent to individuals in societies that have varying traditions, values, customs and beliefs. Efforts must be made, therefore, to take cultural diversity and variability into consideration at the same time as promoting universal standards of human rights.

Acknowledgments

Funding for some of the research upon which this paper is based was provided by the Champe-Weakley Fund of the University of Nebraska-Lincoln to Christie Haney. Part of the data collection was supported by the U.S. Agency for International Development, the International Work Group for Indigenous Affairs and the Remote Area Development of the government of Botswana.

Notes

1 The UNDP *Human Development Report 2002*, pp. 237-240, Table 1, considers Botswana as a medium human development country.
2 Compare, however, this argument to that of Kenneth Good, 1992.
3 A landmark case was that of Unity Dow, a Motswana lawyer who, in 1990, challenged the Botswana government's *Citizenship Act of 1984* and the Botswana Constitution for discriminating against women. The High Court ruled in 1992 in Ms. Dow's favor and the discriminatory provisions in the *Citizenship Act* were overturned.
4 Some of the Nama came to Botswana during the German-Herero war in Namibia in the period 1904-1907. Eventually some of them settled permanently in Botswana after an agreement was reached between the British Protectorate administration and the German government of South West Africa. For a discussion of Nama (Khoikhoi), see Boonzaier et al., 1996.
5 Over half of the women Hitchcock interviewed in the east-central Kalahari in the late 1970s had collected tortoises and 30% had captured monitor lizards. Similar results were found in interviews by Melinda Kelly in the Nata River region in the mid-1970s (Melinda Kelly, personal communication, 1976).
6 These categories included (a) commercial land, (b) communal land, (c) reserved land, (d) Wildlife Management Areas, (e) specialized leasehold farms, (f) national parks and game reserves, and (g) land left either un-zoned or categorized as "investigation areas".
7 Republic of Botswana, *National Policy on Tribal Grazing Land,* 1975b:6.
8 Officers in the Rural Development Unit, Ministry of Finance and Development Planning, personal communications to Robert Hitchcock, 1985.
9 Alec Campbell, personal communication, 1988.
10 See also Kann, Mapolelo and Nleya, 1989; Felton and Becker, 2001: 36-46.
11 Patricia Draper, Nancy Howell, personal communications.

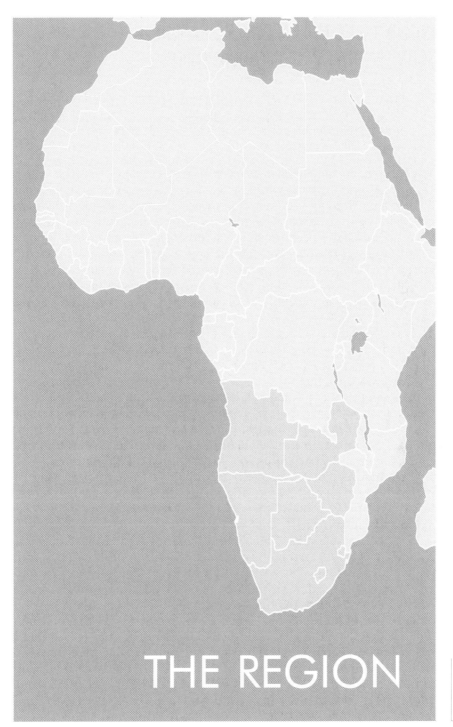

THE REGION

HUMAN RIGHTS AND PARTICIPATION AMONG SOUTHERN AFRICAN INDIGENOUS PEOPLES

Joseph Akpan, Ignatius Mberengwa,
Robert K. Hitchcock and Thomas Koperski

When addressing indigenous peoples' rights in southern Africa, one is confronted with a whole set of complex issues. First, what does the concept "indigenous peoples" mean? Second, do the individual governments of southern African countries recognize this concept and, if so, do they have protections for indigenous peoples built into their constitutions or national legislation? Third, are there policies and programs in place in the various southern African nation-states that deal directly or indirectly with indigenous peoples? Finally, to what degree are indigenous peoples able to participate in decision-making at the national, regional and local levels in southern African countries?

This paper deals with the question of indigenous peoples' recognition, human rights and participation in the context of three southern African nation-states: Angola, Zambia and Zimbabwe. Like other southern African states, these three countries were all colonies of European nations. Angola was a colony of Portugal while Zambia and Zimbabwe were colonies of Great Britain. Zambia and Zimbabwe were known as Northern and Southern Rhodesia and, at one stage, were part of a single administrative unit under British administration. Today, all three countries are independent nation-states (Angola, 1975, Zambia, 1964, and Zimbabwe, 1980). Angola and Zimbabwe went through lengthy periods of conflict both before and after independence, while Zambia was caught up in some of the struggles of its neighbors Angola, Namibia and Zimbabwe.

Angola, Zambia and Zimbabwe differ somewhat from Botswana, Namibia and South Africa, the other countries in southern Africa with populations that have been identified, either by themselves or by others, as indigenous (Suzman 2001a, b). Botswana, Namibia and South Africa all have programs that focus directly on the well-being of San and other minority populations. Namibia and South Africa have mother-tongue language programs that teach indigenous languages (see Hays, this volume). There are active non-government organizations that deal with indigenous peoples' issues. In the late 1990s, the Working Group of Indigenous Minorities in Southern Africa (WIMSA) began to focus attention on the situations facing indigenous peoples in Angola, Zambia and Zimbabwe (WIMSA 1998, 2003, 2004). While indigenous groups

Country	Population Size (July, 2003 estimate)	Size of Country (square kilometers)	Number of Existing Languages
Angola	10,766,471	1,246,700	41
Zambia	10,307,333	752,610	41
Zimbabwe	12,576,742	390,580	19
3 countries	33,650,546	2,389,890	101

Table 3. Data on Selected Southern African Countries with Indigenous Populations. Compiled by authors from official sources.

in all southern African countries are vulnerable, those residing in Angola, Zambia and Zimbabwe are especially so, in part because of conflict, resettlement and economic deprivation.

In the analysis presented here, we examine some of the on-the-ground situations of these indigenous or ethnic minorities. We look at the legislation and assess government policies, programs and development projects, with an eye toward determining whether they deal specifically with indigenous peoples or if they are more general in focus.

In this discussion, we address (1) civil and political rights, and (2) social, economic and cultural rights. We look more specifically at participation rights, land rights, water access and subsistence rights.

Indigenous Peoples in Southern Africa

Angola, Zambia and Zimbabwe have a combined population of 33,650,546 (see Table 3) and their size ranges from 390,580 sq km (Zimbabwe) to 752,610 sq km (Zambia) and 1,246,700 sq km (Angola). The three countries are diverse from a socio-linguistic perspective, with 101 different languages spoken (Grimes 2000). The groups defined as indigenous constitute very small minorities.

It should be stated at the outset that Angola, Zambia and Zimbabwe, like other southern African states, have constitutions that guarantee human rights and fundamental freedoms. While indigenous peoples are not recognized explicitly in the constitutions of any of the three countries, there are provisions for the protection of people from discrimination on the basis of race, tribe, political affiliation, disability, religion and social status. The question is: to what degree are constitutional provisions observed in practice?

Of southern Africa's contemporary peoples, those groups defined as indigenous tend to be over-represented in the categories of those lacking basic human rights, living below the poverty datum line and working for others under exploitative or unjust conditions (IWGIA 2003:398-413).[1] The indicators are painfully apparent: these groups usually have some of the lowest health and nutritional standards, the highest rates of unemployment, the lowest incomes, the highest infant mortality rates, the shortest life spans and the lowest degrees of political participation of the various categories of people in the countries in which they reside.

As noted in the annual reports of organizations such as Amnesty International, Human Rights Watch and the U.S. State Department's Country Reports on Human Rights Practices (2003),[2] human rights violations have occurred in all three countries, and the security rights of indigenous and minority peoples (that is, the right to life, liberty and freedom from torture or ill-treatment) have been a concern. There have been cases of human rights violations, including genocide and ethnocide (Souindola 1981; Hitchcock and Twedt 1997). As a result of conflict or deliberate government policy, members of indigenous groups have been displaced, have "disappeared" or have been tortured and otherwise mistreated. Many indigenous peoples have had to flee across borders and some have ended up in refugee camps in neighboring countries (for Angolans: the Congo, Namibia and Zambia; for Zambians: Namibia; and for Zimbabweans: Botswana).

Indigenous Peoples of Angola

Angola differs somewhat from other southern African states in which San are found today, in part because it experienced colonization by the Portuguese rather than the Dutch, Germans or British. Angola is located on the South Atlantic Ocean, with the Democratic Republic of the Congo to the north, Zambia to the east and Namibia to the south. It is a large country, 1,246,700 sq km in size, which achieved its independence in 1975 after a 14-year-long liberation struggle. Some parties, notably the National Union for the Total Independence of Angola (UNITA), refused to accept the results of the post-independence elections and began a civil war that lasted off and on for 27 years until a peace accord was signed in April 2002.

Angola is ethnically diverse, with 41 different groups speaking their own languages (Grimes 2000:8-11). Of these, some are considered by researchers to be Khoesan-speaking indigenous people, including the !Xu, Khwe and !Kung San (Barnard 1992; Robins, Madzudzo and Brenzinger 2001).

In 1960, Estermann (1976) estimated that there were 5,000 or more San in Angola. In 1987, Burger (1987:166) estimated the number to be

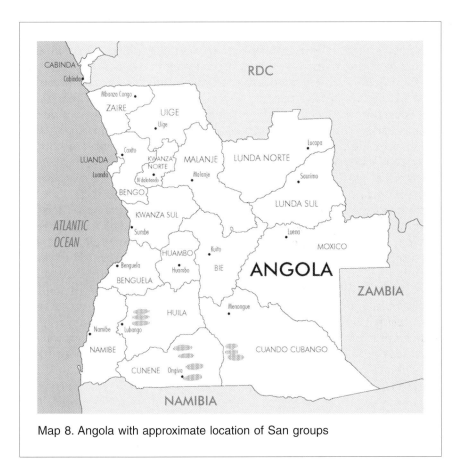

Map 8. Angola with approximate location of San groups

8,000. Fourteen years later, in 2001, it was estimated that there were fewer then 1,500 San in Angola (Suzman 2001a:5; Robins, Madzudzo and Brenzinger 2001:55).[3] The reduction over time in the numbers of San has been due primarily to conflict, which have resulted in many San moving across the border to neighboring Zambia or Namibia to seek refuge.

There are also San who were resettled out of Angola by the South African Defence Force (SADF). In the mid-1970s, as many as 6,000 !Kung and Khwe were resettled in Namibia when members of their groups joined the SADF, (Pakleppa and Kwokonoka 2003:7) and fought on the side of South Africa against the South West African Peoples Organization (SWAPO) in the 1970s and 1980s.[4] In July 2003, a detailed survey was undertaken of the San communities in southern Angola by WIM-SA, in partnership with two Angolan non-government organizations, Trócaire (the Irish Catholic Agency for World Development-Angola) and the Organização Crista de Apoio ao Desenvolvimento Comunitario (the Christian Organization Supporting Community Development, OCADEC) (ibid.). Contacts were made with over 2,000 San, primarily !Kung, in Huila, Cunene, Cuando Cubango and Moxico Provinces.

The WIMSA survey found that almost all of the San communities depended to a significant degree on food that they received in exchange for work that they did for their Bantu-speaking neighbors. Some of their subsistence was also derived from foraging. The majority were found to be highly vulnerable, impoverished and food-insecure. In addition, as Pakleppa and Kwononoka (2003:1) noted, "San communities throughout southern Angola experience social exclusion, discrimination, and economic exploitation".

Some of the !Kung of southern Angola had experienced difficulties in getting food relief from the government or non-government organizations, in part because other, more powerful, groups tended to divert it for their own needs. One of the authors was told in an interview in Namibia in 2001 that some well-to-do farmers hoarded the food aid in order to ensure that their San workers continued to be dependent on them. Many Angolan San felt insecure in the 27 conflict-years up to 2002, and it is only now that some San have begun to re-establish their communities and resume agricultural activities. Few of them receive much in the way of direct government assistance, in part because of the lack of extension work and development personnel in areas where warfare and conflicts prevailed. They are, however, getting help from some non-government organizations, some of them faith-based.

One of the principles of participatory development and human rights is that people should have the right to control their lands and resources (Davis and Soefestad 1995). On a theoretical level, San in Angola have the right to land that they have occupied for 20 or more years; in other words, they have customary rights under Angola's land law. Pakleppa and Kwononoka (2003:8) were told by the coordinator of the Human Rights Commission in Huila Province that the provincial government is willing to allocate land to San and will request that the Ministry of Agriculture issue title deeds to San "once their land needs have been established". In other words, assessments will have to be carried out by the Ministry of Agriculture before land allocation and land titling can occur. The danger here is that the assessors may decide that the land needs of San households are not significant, especially if they are seen as dependent on other groups who have land or they are engaged in foraging or small-scale craft production in order to generate income.

Another problem facing those Angolan San who have returned to their ancestral homes from other places now that the war is over will be the competition for land with local people. At the same time, there are well-to-do Angolans and outsiders, few if any of whom are San, who are attempting to establish claims to land and resources in areas that are inhabited by San. This situation is made even more complicated by the fact that the Angolan government has yet to define exactly the institutions that will be responsible for allocating land (Pakleppa and Kwononoka 2003:9). There is a Land Bill under consideration that does not recognize land rights acquired on the basis of customary occupancy. What this could mean for San and other poor Angolans is that their land rights will be overlooked in favor of private sector interests that have the cash to pay for land.

The Angolan San assessment revealed that virtually all of the San populations with whom they came in contact were considered to be highly vulnerable. For their purposes, vulnerability levels were determined on the basis of "the expected ability of people to maintain a minimum level of consumption until the next harvest" (Pakleppa and Kwonoidia 2003:19). These populations could presumably meet their minimum subsistence requirements during some seasons but they would be expected to experience privation and hunger during the lean season. They will also require food aid and medical intervention during at least some parts of the year. In order for this to be possible, the social and physical infrastructure of southern Angola will need to be repaired or constructed, and land mines will need to be cleared from roads, fields and border areas.

In some parts of southern Angola, access to water for San communities is problematic and people often have to walk long distances to obtain water. According to Pakleppa and Kwononoka (2003:23), some people who were growing gardens along water courses were forced to abandon them by other people, probably because of the perception that the gardens were in competition with domestic water needs. The provision of water facilities and water containers was seen by Angolan San as an important need.

From the standpoint of public participation and political rights, the San of Angola face some major constraints. There are few, if any, cases where San leaders have been recognized by the government or by local Bantu tribal authorities. San leaders do not have the same degree of authority as do non-San leaders, and they have little say in decision-making at the local level. Decision-making tends to be top-down, from non-San leaders and government officials to the San, who represent the bottom rung of the socio-political system. It is not surprising, therefore, that Pakleppa and Kwononoka (2003) describe Angola as a place "where the first are last". This is not to say, however, that Angolan San are unwilling to organize themselves in pursuit of human rights and development. There is a widespread awareness of the importance of human rights and social justice, and the Angolan San hope to capitalize on this awareness so that they can be, as one !Kung man put it, "equal to other Angolans".[5]

The Indigenous Peoples of Zambia

Zambia, 752,610 sq km in size, stretches from the Zambezi River in the south to Malawi and the Democratic Republic of Congo in the north, Tanzania to the northeast, and from Angola in the west to Mozambique in the east. The San of Zambia are the northernmost of contemporary San. Their living situations differ substantially from those of other San in southern Africa, with the exception of those living in Angola.

Zambia has the smallest San population of all the southern African countries, less than 300 people in total (Brenzinger 2001). They reside mainly in the western part of the country, on the border with Angola, in an area designated as a Game Management Area (GMA). The West Zambezi GMA, is 38,070 sq km in extent and contains two national parks: Sioma Ngweze in the southwestern part of the area and, with an extension of 5,726 sq km, the third largest in Zambia; and Liuma Plain National Park (3,660 sq km) further to the north. Some of the San living in the vicinity of the national parks attempt to sell crafts to the tourists who visit them. Like many people living on the peripheries of national parks, they feel that they should be able to benefit from at least some of the gate receipts from the people who visit the parks. The government of Zambia has not elected to move in this direction in the western national parks.

The San in Zambia should be seen as being transboundary in nature and, in the past, they moved back and forth across the Zambia-Angola border, depending on the security situation and the frequency of border patrols. They had relatives living on both sides of the Angola-Zambia border and they tried to maintain close social and economic links. Over time they experienced substantial changes, as many had to resettle, sometimes as a result of having to move out of conflict areas, sometimes due to efforts by the Zambian government to resettle them in new places.

The San status in Zambia is complex. A majority of them actually originate from Angola. This is the case of almost all the Khwe, who come from the Buma and Ngarange areas of Angola. The Ngweze Khwe came as early as in the 1920s and the Ngarange Khwe in the 1960s during the Angolan liberation war. The latter were registered officially as refugees by the United Nations High Commissioner for Refugees in 1971-72, and some of these Ngarange Kkhwe have been housed in the Meheba refugee camp located close to Solwezi in North-Western Province of Zambia for almost 30 years. They make up a small minority in the camp and, as a result, they feel highly vulnerable and with little ability to influence decision-making in the camp. Another group of Ngarange Khwe San are residing on the Sioma Plains in western Zambia and are subsistence farmers also engaging in foraging and small-scale business activities.

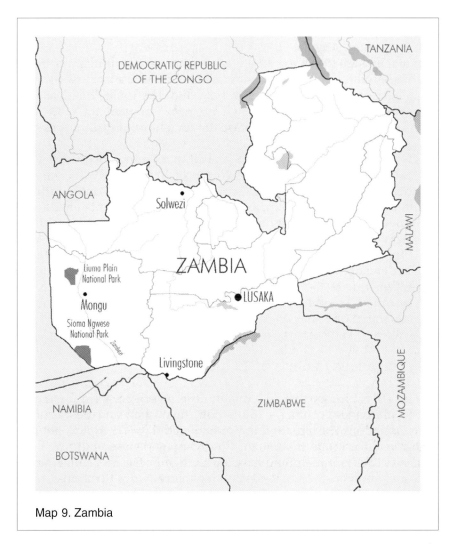

Map 9. Zambia

In November 1999, the San of Zambia were estimated to number less than 130 (Robins, Madzudzo and Brenzinger 2001) but the expansion of military operations into southeastern Angola in December of that year triggered a new migration wave. It was estimated that some 300 Khwe, many of them Ngarange Khwe, were among those who took refuge in Zambia.

It should be noted that the only San who receive regular assistance from government sources in Zambia are those residing in refugee camps. Those living outside refugee camps do not receive drought relief nor do they qualify for other Zambian government assistance. In other words, the Zambian government does not recognize San as being citizens, seeing them primarily as refugees or immigrants from a nearby country, Angola.

Some San admit having taken part in the various conflicts as fighters. Those who fought on the side of the Portuguese against the Angolan freedom fighters were viewed as traitors by some Zambians and Angolans. As a result, the San have attempted to maintain a low profile, not wishing to stand out in case they might be targeted for reprisals by various groups.

The Zambian Khwe who have spoken to representatives of San organizations such as the Working Group of Indigenous Minorities in Southern Africa (WIMSA) or to German anthropologist Matthias Brenzinger say that they wish to receive assistance from Zambia and from non-government organizations. At least one group of Zambian Khwe gets help from the Catholic Mission in Sioma.

There are some San who wish to see greater opportunities to take part in development and political decision-making in Zambia but they are fully aware of the constraints they face as a result of the perception that they are either refugees or supporters of institutions that challenged the nation-states of Zambia and Angola.

The Indigenous Peoples of Zimbabwe

The history of Zimbabwe, like that of other southern African nations, is one of change, conflict, exploitation, revolution and post-conflict transformation. The situation in Zimbabwe today is complex, not just with reference to the treatment of indigenous peoples, but in general. Zimbabwe is undergoing massive change in the new millennium, and land and constitutional rights lie at the center of this transformation (Naldi 2003).

Landlocked, Zimbabwe covers an area of 390,580 sq km, stretching from the Kalahari sands area in the vicinity of Hwange National Park in the west to the highlands on the Mozambique border, north to the Zambezi River, and south to the Limpopo River, which forms the border with South Africa. Zimbabwe is a rich country agriculturally, with some 2,200 sq km under irrigation. It is also rich in mineral resources, with substantial coal, gold, nickel, copper and chromium reserves. It supported a total population of 12,576,742 people in 2003, divided among 19 different ethnic groups each with its own language, culture and traditions.

In 2000, President Mugabe lost a referendum on a new constitution that his government had drafted, one that would have expanded the powers of the presidency. Particular emphasis had been placed by the Mugabe government on revising Section 16 of the Zimbabwe

Constitution of 1980, which guaranteed the right to property. The Mugabe government was blaming white farmers for encouraging opposition to the new constitution. In 2000, ex-fighters and some members of the ZANU-PF ruling party began to occupy farms and to intimidate people on the farms, including both farm owners and farm workers. Their goal was to force them off the land and to take over the farms for themselves. By 2003-2004, over half of Zimbabwe's 12 million people were threatened with starvation, and some were leaving the country for neighboring states. By the latter part of 2003, most of the whites and some 1.2 million black farm workers and their family members had been driven off the land. As a result, there were sizable numbers of internally displaced people in Zimbabwe, many of them unable to meet their food needs due to lack of supplies and the high prices that resulted from inflation.

Some people fled to Botswana where they found refuge in the UN-HCR camp at Dukwe. Botswana resorted to building what some describe as a "security fence" on the Botswana-Zimbabwe border, ostensibly to prevent movements of livestock across the border, which could bring diseases such as Foot-and-Mouth. But there were also rumors to the effect that the fence was set up in part to restrict movements of people across the border.

The two populations identified by themselves and by researchers, though not explicitly by the government of Zimbabwe, as indigenous are (1) the Tyua (Shua, Chwa) of western Zimbabwe, a San-speaking population, and (2) the Vadema (Doma) of Guruve District in the Zambezi Valley. These two populations are found in different parts of the country. The Tyua live in the west, in Matabeleland Province, on the border with Botswana, while the Vadema live in the northeast, to the east of Chewore Safari Area. In both cases, the indigenous populations have been affected by the establishment of national parks and safari hunting areas, and they have both experienced conflict-related trauma in the past several decades. The Vadema found themselves in the war zone during the liberation war (1968-1979) and some of them moved away to safer places, while some were relocated by the government to protected villages some 70 km away (Mberengwa 2000:55-6). Both indigenous groups claimed to have experienced difficulties in gaining access to land, resources, jobs and positions of authority.

The Tyua of Western Zimbabwe

The vast majority of the Tyua, who number some 2,000 – 2,500 people in western Zimbabwe, are former foragers who today have mixed economic production systems, combining pastoralism, agriculture and small-scale income-generating activities (Cashdan 1979; Hitch-cock 1988, 1999b; Madzudzo 2001).

The Tyua make up only a small portion (some 6%) of the population of Tsholotsho and Bulalima-Mangwe Districts (Madzudzo 2001:79). In the 1970s, they resided in small villages or dispersed and extended family compounds ranging in size from 10 to 120 people, where they depended upon crops (e.g. sorghum, millet, melons and beans), milk and meat from cattle and goats, food obtained through purchase or reciprocal arrangements with other groups, and a certain amount of foraging. Tyua women collected wild plant foods and made baskets and mats out of palm leaves, which they sold for cash or traded for non-local goods such as pots or ammunition. A fairly large number of Tyua work today for other people, including Ndebele and Kalanga, primarily as livestock herders, agricultural laborers or domestic servants. Hunting is practised by some of the Tyua, although arrests for violation of hunting laws do occur on occasion. A number of Tyua work for safari companies in Tsholotsho and Bulalima-Mangwe Districts, although unemployment has increased in the safari industry due to the instability in Zimbabwe in recent years.

From the perspective of the Tyua, the state has played a major role in limiting their access both to land and natural resources. The depletion of wildlife fueled concerns in the governments of Zimbabwe and Botswana that the resource potential of the region would be lost unless steps were taken to stop the killing. One way to deal with the problem, it was decided, was to utilize the "royal game" principle of Ndebele, Tswana and Shona chiefs and to declare wildlife species as state property. It was made illegal for individuals to kill game even if it invaded their fields or threatened their lives. As one Tyua expressed it, "The Europeans became the gamekeepers, and the Africans became the poachers".

In 1980 an incident occurred that resulted in increased concern on the part of both the Zimbabwe and Botswana governments about wildlife and human rights issues. Several Tyua and Kalanga who were hunting illegally inside Hwange National Park were detected by game scouts, who found the men near some animals they had killed. Reinforcements were called in, and a firefight erupted in which several Zimbabwe game scouts were killed along with some of the poachers. Subsequently, some of the people who were involved in the incident were hunted down and killed inside Botswana, according to testimony provided by some of the people involved.

In the 1980s and early 1990s, there were also reports of people from Zimbabwe who had gone to Botswana for the purposes of collecting firewood and other resources being shot by Botswana Defense Force personnel and police. Tyua who lost family members said that at least

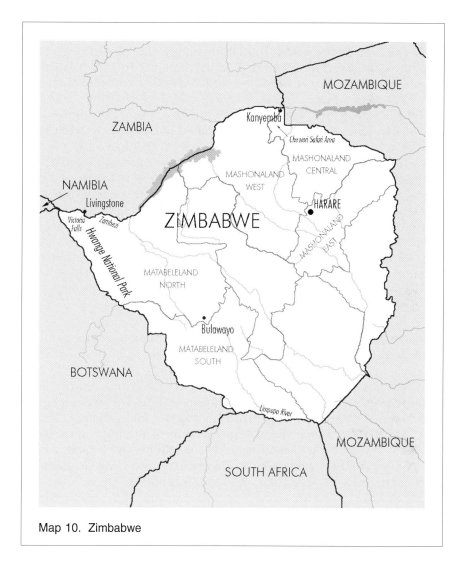

Map 10. Zimbabwe

some of the people who had crossed the border and been shot were women and children and that they were not involved in illegal wildlife procurement activities. The Tyua in both Botswana and Zimbabwe said that they were concerned with what they saw as "coercive conservation", in which people's human rights were being violated in the name of wildlife conservation.

In the 1980s Tyua and their neighbors in Tsholotsho and Bulalima-Mangwe Districts, the Kalanga, who represented 80% of the population, were caught up in a struggle between the government, dominated by the Shona, and the Ndebele. The Ndebele, who represented 14% of the population in the two districts, had been involved in the liberation struggle against the white minority regime but later expressed a desire for a certain degree of political autonomy in the Zimbabwean state. The Zimbabwean government under Robert Mugabe launched what they termed an anti-dissident campaign in Matabeleland that resulted in what may have been thousands of deaths, many of them civilians.

Tyua, Kalanga and Ndebele informants told one of the authors and a co-worker in 1992 that local people were the victims of what they termed a "genocidal policy" on the part of the Zimbabwean government. The old mines that dotted the area were filled with bones, the result of mass killings, one informant said.[6] Some of the Tyua said that they were targeted for execution by the government forces. Others said that they were moved out of the area to larger towns in southern Matabeleland so that the government could exert greater control over them.[7] By 1985, things were beginning to calm down, although a peace accord was not signed until 1988. Development activities in the area were severely curtailed during the 1980s as a result of the conflict and what some people felt was a deliberate government policy not to provide assistance to what was perceived as an opposition area.

In 1989 efforts began to be made to promote community-based resource management and rural social and economic development in the Tsholotsho and Bulalima-Mangwe Districts where the majority of Tyua reside. Under the *Parks and Wildlife Act* of 1975, the Tsholotsho and Bulalima-Mangwe District Councils began to devolve authority over benefits from wildlife to communities and wildlife committees under the Communal Areas Management Program for Indigenous Resources (CAMPFIRE). This program was aimed at increasing conservation while at the same time ensuring greater economic benefits to local people. The basic principle behind CAMPFIRE was the re-empowerment of local communities by providing them with access to, control over and responsibility for natural resources. A second principle was that local communities should have the right to make decisions regarding those natural resources and any activities that affect them. A third principle was that communities should receive the benefits from the exploitation of natural resources.

One of the problems with CAMPFIRE was that many of the decisions about resource management come from outside the producer community. This can be seen, for example, in the case of the Tsholotsho District Council, which refused to allocate decision-making power to lower-level institutions such as ward and village committees. Communities were informed by the district council that the money was going to be spent on a road and the construction of social infrastructure such as a clinic. Local people said that they would have preferred to get household level benefits in the form of cash pay-outs that could then be used to purchase food and other goods.

Another problem that arose in western Zimbabwe had to do with so-called problem animals – those animals that raided people's fields and villages and destroyed people's crops, livestock and homes. People were not allowed to take the law into their own hands; rather, they had to seek assistance from the Zimbabwe Department of National Parks and Wildlife Management game scouts to deal with problem animals. In the 1990s and into the new millennium, tensions were felt by local people in the Tsholotsho District who had to deal with elephants, lions and other animals that ranged out of Hwange National Park to the north, destroying their gardens and herds. Local people, including the Tyua, were upset that they could not go after the problem animals themselves.

Some of the Tyua who had been in the war, both the Zimbabwean war of liberation and the post-independence conflict between the peoples of Matabeleland and the government of Robert Mugabe, were able to establish themselves as local leaders, and some of them were elected to village and ward-level councils. At least one Tyua was a member of the Tsholotsho District Council. Some of these leaders have been approached by Tyua in the past several years in an effort to enlist their help in obtaining land. They have also been lobbied by Tyua who feel that Kalanga, Ndebele and other groups are being resettled in areas where Tyua have customary land rights.

There are Tyua that have expressed a desire for autonomy and decision-making power in western Tsholotsho, something that neither the government nor other groups seem willing to consider. Tyua have been able to participate in local and district-level political activities, and they have benefited from some of the community-based natural resource management projects in western Zimbabwe. At this stage, however, it is not possible to say that the Tyua have managed to reach a point where they have equal rights and can exercise their fundamental freedoms, particularly given the deteriorating socio-political and economic situation.

The Vadema of Northeastern Zimbabwe

It is possible to look at the effects of the CAMPFIRE Program on another population of former foragers in Zimbabwe, the Vadema (Vadoma, Wadoma, Tembomvura) of northeastern Zimbabwe. There are two groups of Vadema, one in the Chewore and Kanyembe area, and the other on the Angwa River, about 75 km to the south of Chewore. The Vadema today number approximately 800 and they reside in what is now the Guruve District, one of the first districts in Zimbabwe to have CAMPFIRE initiated (Hasler 1996; Mberengwa 2000).

The Chapoto Ward, where the majority of Vadema live, is in one of Zimbabwe's communal areas. It is a 300 sq km tract of land bounded on the north by the Zambezi River and the international Zimbabwe/Zambia border, on the east by the Zimbabwe/Mozambique border, on the south by the Dande Safari area and on the west by the Chewore Safari Area. Most of the flood plain areas of the region have been cleared for agricultural purposes, and people support themselves through a combination of agriculture, foraging and remittances from relatives, many of whom have left the Zambezi Valley to find work.

The Vadema pursue a mixed economic strategy that includes foraging, fishing, small-scale cultivation, honey collecting and a certain amount of hunting, some of which is done surreptitiously: the Vadema feel that they have to deal with what they see as "selective enforcement" by game scouts and police who tend to target Vadema in their anti-poaching patrols. The Vadema feel that they are being subjected to pressures because of their lifestyle, which was more heavily involved with wildlife and wild plant utilization than that of other groups.

The Vadema were resettled several times by the Rhodesian government, at least once because of the suspicion that they were supporting the freedom fighters who were seeking to overthrow the white minority regime that was in power. As the war increased in intensity in the 1970s, some Vadema were moved into a security village in Mashumbi Pools, some 150 km away from Chapoto Ward. By the late 1990s, a number of Vadema had shifted increasingly into agriculture, although they continued to collect wild plants, edible caterpillars and other bush resources. Some of the Vadema fall into the category of being "food insecure", living in households that find it difficult if not impossible to meet their basic needs. They said they felt they were being denied food because they were not supporters of the current government.

Guruve District is administered by a district council made up of councilors elected under the terms of the *District Councils Act of 1980*. The council is responsible for all of the development programs in the district. The people in the district feel that the district council is the main body deciding how to use the funds generated by CAMPFIRE programs, including the sale of animals and the income generated by safari operators working in the area. Some Vadema feel that the Chewore Safari Area, which was established on the western side of their area in the Katsuuku Mountains, cut into their traditional area and placed restrictions on some of their activities and limited their options.

The *Communal Land Forest Produce Act* (No. 20 of 1987) affected the ways in which the Vadema operated. This act governs the use of certain types of forest (timber) products in communal areas. Certain species of tree, which had in the past been important to people for economic, social and ideological reasons were, after 1987, off limits to local people. The act allows for district councils to engage in the exploitation and sale of forest products. The council is supposed to consult with the people of the district but, in practice, this was not always done.

One of the sentiments expressed by the Vadema was that they were ignored by the district council, which was taking the majority of the benefits for the council and paying little attention to the people of the district, especially those who were considered to be poor. The conclusion reached by many of them was that the CAMPFIRE program and other programs of the Zimbabwe government were not aimed at them but rather at other groups, including those associated with the safari industry. They noted that the beneficiaries of CAMPFIRE tended to be non-Vadema, such as the Chikunda, who dominate the wildlife committees in the district. As one Vadema put it, "We are the poorest of the poor; we have no say in what happens to us". Clearly, in the eyes of the Vadema, the CAMPFIRE program in the district had to become more participatory in its approach and the ways in which benefits were distributed. The conclusion drawn by the Vadema was that they were subjected to top-down development planning and a government system that did not take into consideration their cultural backgrounds, values and traditions.

Conclusions

An examination of the constitutions, legislation, programs and policies of three southern African states: Angola, Zambia, and Zimbabwe, reveals that all of them are committed, at least on paper, to promoting basic human rights and social justice. While none of the states has signed the only convention to deal specifically with indigenous peoples' rights, ILO Convention No.169, they have signed some of the major human rights instruments: the United Nations Charter, the International Covenant on Civil and Political Rights, the International Covenant on Economic, Social and Cultural Rights, and the Convention on the Elimination of All Forms of Racial Discrimination. They have all signed the African Charter on Human and Peoples' Rights and the Convention Governing the Specific Aspects of Refugee Problems in Africa (Hamalengwa, Flinterman, and Dankwa 1988; UNHCR 2004). It must be emphasized, however, that being a signatory to an international human rights convention or having a constitution that proclaims that humans rights and fundamental freedoms are protected does not mean that people in Angola, Zambia, Zimbabwe, nor any other country for that matter, can expect to be exempt from violations of human rights.

As this chapter has shown, violations of constitutional guarantees and human rights conventions and covenants are commonplace in Angola, Zambia and Zimbabwe. In some cases, there are human rights violations that indigenous peoples experience to a significant degree compared to some other populations in these countries. To take one example, it is not unlikely that members of indigenous groups that have committed crimes will get stiffer jail sentences than members of dominant groups that have political power.

Members of indigenous communities experience greater difficulties than other groups in accessing positions of leadership and authority, especially at the regional and national levels. Governance structures of indigenous communities are sometimes organized in such a way that public consensus is sought before decisions are taken (Davis and Soefestad 1995; Horn 1996; Nettleheim, Meyers, and Craig 2002; Hodgson 2003). Unlike Botswana, Namibia and South Africa, the governments of Angola, Zambia and Zimbabwe do not have programs targeted specifically at groups that can be characterized as indigenous minorities.

The three countries do not have education programs that include mother-tongue language education or culturally-oriented assistance for pre-school and primary school-age children. In general, the educational and literacy levels of indigenous peoples in Angola, Zambia and Zimbabwe are extremely low. Their health status is also lower than is the case for more urbanized, majority populations. The Southern African Development Community and the African Union have both held meetings where the needs and rights of indigenous peoples have been discussed, but they have yet to devise any specific programs to promote indigenous peoples' rights.

In spite of the constraints to public participation and equality before the law, indigenous peoples in Angola, Zambia and Zimbabwe are seeking actively to assert their rights. They are interested not only in civil and political rights (first generation rights) and economic, social and cultural rights (second generation rights) but they also wish to affirm the new generation of rights, including the right to development and the right to a healthy environment. They see the value in both individual rights and collective rights. They want to ensure that they have the rights to freedom of expression, assembly and political opinion and the ability to participate, as full partners, in the democratic process. Virtually all of the members of indigenous groups to whom the authors have spoken expressed a strong desire for democratic rights, cultural rights and intellectual property rights.

Clearly, indigenous peoples are faced with many challenges in their efforts to promote human rights, participation and social justice in southern Africa. These challenges include government hostility or lack of concern for the needs of indigenous peoples, the lack of resources to promote wide-ranging development in areas where indigenous peoples are found and, in some cases, a lack of management and institutional capacity at the local level. Fortunately, indigenous peoples in Angola, Zambia and Zimbabwe have some new partners with whom to work, including civil society groups that have emerged over time, some of them oriented directly toward addressing the needs of marginalized populations. As one Tyua community leader said, 'Without the help of civil society and the international human rights movement, we would not be making progress toward the realization of our goals of having fully recognized human rights and equal justice".   ❏

Notes

1   See also Hitchcock, 1994:1-24; Young, 1995; Suzman, 2001a, 2001b; Barnard and Kenrick, 2001; Robins, Madzudzo, and Brenzinger, 2001.
2   See also Africa Watch, 1989; Minority Rights Group, 1997: 472-474, 527-531; Alexander, McGregor, and Ranger, 2000; Robins, Madzudzo, and Brenzinger, 2000; Pakleppa and Kwononoka, 2003.
3   It should be noted that the estimate of the numbers of San in southern Angola by Pakleppa and Kwokonoka (2000:5, Table 1) was 3,400.
4   It was members of these groups who, in 1990, opted to be moved to South Africa where they were put up in tents on a military camp at Schmidtsdrift near Kimberley (see Chennells and du Toit, this volume).
5   Angolan !Kung informant speaking to Robert Hitchcock, Kapatura, northern Namibia, August 1999.
6   Statement by an individual who asked that his identity be kept confidential, speaking to Robert Hitchcock and Fanuel Nangati, Tsholotsho District, Zimbabwe, June 1992.
7   Statements by Tyua informants to Robert Hitchcock and Fanuel Nangati, Tsholotsho and Bulalima-Mangwe Districts, June-July 1992.

NATURAL RESOURCE MANAGEMENT AMONG KALAHARI SAN: CONFLICT AND COOPERATION

Robert K. Hitchcock

M any of the issues facing indigenous peoples today - including the San and Khoe of southern Africa - are the result of global processes, such as economic development, the transboundary movement of goods and services, environmental change, and competition for resources. Today, another global process, the world wide effort of indigenous peoples and their supporters to develop and enforce international standards relating to indigenous rights, has the potential to redress some past injustices and ameliorating present circumstances.

For the 350-400,000,000 indigenous people on the planet today, it is crucial to identify and implement the best combination of legislation, policies and governance systems in an effort to promote human rights and to enhance living standards. This must be done in such a way that societies, economies, habitats and ecosystem processes are protected so that future generations can sustain themselves. Indigenous peoples have experienced a drastic reduction in their land and resource access over time. In the United States, for example, Native Americans had surrendered 2 billion acres through treaties by 1887, leaving a residual 140 million acres. Another 90 million acres was lost through the allotment policy that operated to privatize Native American lands until 1934. As a result, today Native Americans retain less than 1 percent of the land in the United States (Sutton 1985). In Australia, aboriginal title to land was not recognized by colonial authorities. Instead, the land was defined as terra nullius (empty land) and was assumed to be without the impediment of indigenous rights (Young 1995). The Crown assumed title over the land, which it disposed of as it saw fit. When their lands were lost, Aboriginal peoples and Torres Strait Islanders also lost livelihoods, graves and other sacred sites, and belief systems. European colonizers offered in return their form of civilization, based on Christianity, individualism and private property ownership.

In recent years indigenous peoples have re-asserted their rights to traditional homelands and have challenged the assumptions and mechanisms that resulted in their dispossession. In doing so, they have extracted some concessions from the still-colonizing powers that govern them. In Canada, for example, the 1982 Constitution Act formally recognized for the first time the inherent aboriginal rights of First Nations, paving the way for Supreme Court decisions that confirmed their original title to the land. And in Australia, since the June 3, 1992 High Court decision in *Eddie Mabo and Others v The State of Queensland*, which affirmed aboriginal title, Aboriginals and Torres Strait Islanders have had the opportunity to prove their rights to ancestral lands and to be compensated for their losses (Young 1995).

In Africa too, sizable numbers of indigenous people have been dispossessed of their ancestral homelands but have generally not had the same opportunities to assert their rights, especially in those areas that have been declared "state lands". In such countries as Angola, Botswana, Namibia, Zambia, Zimbabwe and, until recently, South Africa, indigenous peoples have largely been unable to get legal rights to land recognized. This is due in part to the fact that the governments of southern Africa nation-states do not recognize aboriginal title and to the fact that such states as Botswana do not recognize their San and Khoe citizens as indigenous. The purpose of this chapter is to assess some of the evidence of conflicts and cooperation among indigenous peoples in southern Africa, particularly those who historically have foraged for a living, as they relate to land and wildlife conservation, preservation and sustainable use. Particular emphasis is placed on the Ju|'hoan San of the northern Kalahari Desert who today are engaging in efforts to reclaim lands that they have lost, to obtain greater rights to natural resources, to take part in ecotourism activities and to promote community-based conservation and development. I examine the community-based natural resource management programs that are on-going in northwestern Botswana and northeastern Namibia. I then draw some general conclusions about integrated conservation and development programs as strategies for enhancing local livelihoods and security of tenure over land and resources.

Indigenous Peoples and Land and Resource Rights

In some parts of the world, "indigenous" identity has taken on added political and economic significance because it is used to claim title over blocks of land, certain types of resources, development assistance, or recognition from states and intergovernmental organizations (Hitchcock 1994; Young 1995). Indigenous organizations, local leaders and advocacy groups all maintain that it is necessary to gain not just de facto control over land and resources but also de jure control. One way to do this is to negotiate binding agreements with states, while another is to seek recognition of land and resource rights through the courts. A problem facing the San and other indigenous peoples in southern Africa is that the process of turning common property rights into nationally recognized legal rights is extremely complex.

Indigenous peoples in southern Africa have sought to have their civil, political, social, economic and cultural rights recognized for several decades. They have done so through a number of means, using passive resistance methods like labor strikes, boycotts, blockades, teach-ins and sit-ins, demonstrations and civil disobedience. Indigenous and other peoples have engaged in strikes for better pay and working conditions, as occurred, for example, when a group of Hai‖om San blockaded a road into Etosha National Park in Namibia in October 1997. Other indigenous groups have taken legal cases to court, as was seen in the case of the Nama of the Richtersveld of South Africa, who won a legal case in the Constitutional Court of South Africa in October 2003 (see Chan, this volume). The land claim of the ‡Khomani San of South Africa too, on the other hand, was settled out of court and meant that they received some land and cash compensation and will have the right to resource access in the Kalahari Gemsbok Park (see Chennells and du Toit, this volume).

Another problem faced by many indigenous peoples in southern Africa when claiming their land and resource rights is the standing controversy between wildlife conservation and development, which creates numerous conflicts as indigenous peoples' ancestral homelands are taken over by the nation-states to establish national parks, game reserves, monuments and sanctuaries.

On the one hand, policy makers often favor strict preservation of habitats and wildlife and other natural resources; on the other people at the grassroots level favor a community-based conservation approach that allows local people to benefit from natural resources (Hulme and Murphree 2001). Such conflicts can be seen in the debates over community-based natural resource management in Botswana and Zimbabwe, for example, with various government officials arguing that resources should be in the hands of the state and people and non-governmental organizations at the local level, saying that communities should have the right to benefit from natural resources.

Conservation-development conflicts are illustrated well in the arguments over the Central Kalahari Game Reserve (CKGR), the largest game reserve in southern Africa at 52,730 square kilometers. The CKGR was established in 1961 to protect unique habitats and the people who depended upon them. In 1986, Government of Botswana decided to resettle the resident populations outside of the reserve in order to "promote development" and to "protect the environment" (see Taylor, this volume). The people of the reserve, the G|ui and G‖ana San and Booloongwe Bakgalagadi, argued that they should be allowed to maintain their land and resources rights in the Central Kalahari.

In February 2002, the Botswana government relocated several hundred people out of the Central Kalahari Game Reserve, settling them in three government-sponsored settlements on the peripheries of the reserve. Developments in the settlements have taken the form mainly of the provision of social and physical infrastructure (the establishment of schools, health facilities, water points, and offices). In these settlements, there is intense competition for jobs, income, and resources and relatively high levels of interpersonal conflict. Unemployment levels are high, and many of the residents felt themselves to be worse off compared to life in the Central Kalahari. Some of the residents even called the largest of the three settlements, New !Xade, "the place of death" because of the number of people who died mysteriously or who suffered from alcohol-related problems.

As a result of the problems they were facing, some of the people in New !Xade, Kaudwane, and Xeri chose to move back into the Central Kalahari Game Reserve in 2003-2004. As one former Central Kalahari resident put it, "It is better to be in a place where we have freedom and wild foods than a place where there is no freedom and dependency on the government for a living".[1]

Wildlife Conservation Strategies

Wildlife conservation strategies in Africa generally fall into four major categories: (1) species protection, (2) habitat protection, (3) control of trade in wildlife products, and (4) community-based conservation (CBC). Species protection is done through the enactment of wildlife legislation that stipulates that certain animals are off-limits either all of the time or at certain periods of the year. Wildlife and conservation laws have resulted in substantial numbers of Africans losing their rights to hunt and gather wild natural resources, or having to obtain a license from the government. In some parts of Africa, local people are not allowed to hunt, but safari hunting companies are allowed to do so. This is the case, for example, in Zambia and Zimbabwe. In order to enforce the legislation on wildlife exploitation and trade, African governments have established units within departments of wildlife and national parks to monitor wildlife areas. One result of this enforcement is the detention of local people for contravening wildlife conservation legislation and there have been numerous instances in southern Africa where local people have been arrested and jailed for engaging in what they believed to be culturally appropriate behavior.

The second category of species conservation is habitat protection. In Africa, this is done primarily through the establishment of conservation areas, such as national parks and game reserves. South Africa, which is ranked as the third most biologically diverse country on the planet, has some 6% of its territory of 1,219,912 sq km devoted to conservation areas and at least 77 protected areas. Botswana has 17% of its land devoted to national parks and game reserves, and another 34% is classified as Wildlife Management Areas.[2] In Namibia, some 60,000 sq km of communal land in the country is devoted to community-based conservation and development in the form of conservancies, areas of land over which communities are able to gain rights to the benefits from wildlife resources.[3]

A problem with the habitat protection or preservation approach is that all too often, local people are forced to leave areas that in many cases they have occupied for generations, sometimes for centuries. In numerous instances, when protected land was declared, people had to move to other areas that were more marginal ecologically and where population densities were higher (Hitchcock 1997, 2000, 2001). One outgrowth of these processes was that competition for resources increased in the buffer zones around protected areas. Many people in these areas became impoverished, and some of them left their homes in order to seek work and alternative sources of income and subsistence, a process that had impacts on the stability of families and communities.

In southern Africa, the people who were required to leave their homes because of the declaration of blocks of land as conservation areas were often hunter-gatherers and part-time foragers. Table 4 presents data on conservation areas in southern Africa that resulted in the involuntary resettlement of local populations. Data collected among some of the people who were resettled reveals that many of them consider themselves worse off than they were before they were moved out of their areas. This was the case, for example, among the Hai‖om San of northern Namibia, who lost access to Etosha National Park in 1954. Many of the Hai‖om became landless laborers on commercial farms or moved into communal areas where there were already sizable numbers of people (Widlok 1999:34-35). Similar conditions faced the Tyua of western Zimbabwe who were moved out of Hwange National Park in the 1920s (Hitchcock 1995; Akpan et al., this volume).

The third strategy of wildlife conservation is that related to the control of trade in wildlife products. There are several levels at which this conservation strategy is implemented. At the international level, control of trade is done through legislation relating to endangered and threatened species, notably the Convention on International Trade in Endangered Species of Flora and Fauna (CITES). CITES is one of the more visible examples of international environmental law currently in force.

The control of trade is based on the assumption that wildlife products have an economic value that can be determined in monetary (e.g. dollar, Euro, yen, mark or pound) terms. An elephant, for example, has certain High Value Body Parts (notably tusks, which are made of ivo-

Park or Reserve Area, Establishment Date, Size	Country	Comments
Central Kalahari Game Reserve (1961), 52,730 sq km	Botswana	Over 1,100 G|ui, G||ana, and Boolongwe Bakgalagadi were resettled outside the reserve in 1997 and 2002
Chobe National Park (1961), 9,980 sq km	Botswana	Hundreds of Subiya and some San were resettled in the Chobe Enclave, where 5 villages are in 3,060 sq km area
Moremi Game Reserve (1964), 3,880 sq km	Botswana	Bugakwe and ||Anikhwe San were relocated out of Moremi, one of the first tribal game reserves in the 1960s
Tsodilo Hills National Monument, (1992), declared a World Heritage Site in 2001, 225 sq km	Botswana	Ju/'hoansi San were resettled away from the hills in 1995 but continue to use resources there
Kalahari Gemsbok Park (1931), made a transfrontier park in April 1999, 37,991 sq km	South Africa, Botswana	‡Khomani San were resettled out of the park in the 1930s, some of whom remained on the peripheries
Etosha National Park (1907), 22,175 sq km	Namibia	Hai||om San were resettled outside of the park and sent to freehold farms in 1954
West Caprivi Game Park (1963), 5,715 sq km	Namibia	Khwe San and Mbukushu were resettled in the early 1960s and some San in the 1980s
Hwange (Wankie) National Park (1927), declared a national park on January 29, 1950, 14,620 sq km	Zimbabwe	Tyua were rounded up and resettled south of Hwange Game Reserve in the late 1920s

Table 4. National parks, game reserves and conservation areas in southern Africa that resulted in the involuntary resettlement of local populations. Data compiled by author from interviews and archival information.

ry). Elephants have since 1989 been on Appendix I of CITES, which means that no trade of elephant products can be undertaken. According to local people in western Zimbabwe, including Tyua and Ndebele, the "elephant ban" has had negative effects on their livelihoods, which included the production and sale of crafts made of ivory and other elephant parts (e.g. bracelets made of elephant hair) (Hitchcock 1995). The increased number of elephants in these areas has also had direct impacts on the agriculture of local people as elephants have invaded fields and gardens and destroyed crops. Similar processes are at work in the Nyae Nyae region of Namibia, where the Ju|'hoan San have been having to cope for years with large numbers of elephants, that have destroyed their boreholes.

While wildlife ownership resides with the state in Africa, this is not the case for wild plants on communal land. The laws of most African countries do not specify ownership or use rights of wild plant products, including those that local people use for medicinal purposes. Plant products, with few exceptions, are essentially open access resources. It is for this reason that multinational corporations, including large-scale pharmaceutical companies, have been able to obtain wild plants, which they analyze, get patents for and then use the genetic materials to develop medicines and other economically significant products.

Currently, there is considerable controversy between indigenous peoples and multinational corporations regarding intellectual property rights and efforts are being made by San and other groups to obtain benefit-sharing agreements with multinational corporations and scientific research institutions (for a recent example see Chennells and du Toit, this volume). There are indigenous groups who want to see greater controls exercised over the exploitation and movement across borders of plants and other economically valuable products, and they have argued for strengthening sections of CITES and the Convention on Biological Diversity (CBD) in order to ensure that valuable resources receive greater protection. As one San representative put it, "We would like to see CITES and the Convention on Biological Diversity used to control the exploitation and trade of important species that we depend on for our survival".[4]

A fourth major conservation strategy in Africa is community-based conservation (CBC) or community-based natural resource management (CBNRM), an approach that combines conservation with economic development. The main idea behind community-based conservation is that communities get the rights to the benefits from natural resources. This is done through the passage of legislation to allow local or regional bodies to profit from conservation areas and from activities that take place in conservation zones such as tourism.

In recent years, San in Botswana, Namibia, South Africa and Zimbabwe have been able to benefit from community-based natural re-

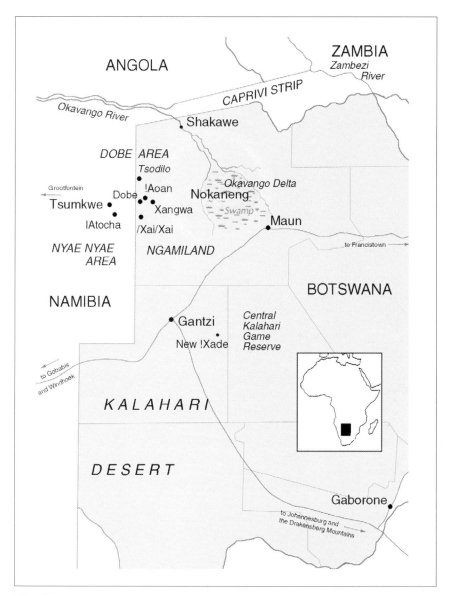

Map 11.
Conservation areas in Northeastern Namibia and Northwestern Botswana

source management projects that have tourism as a component (Hitch-cock 1995, 2000, Wyckoff-Baird 2000). Some of these projects are imple-mented in the buffer zones around national parks and game reserves in South Africa, notably around the Kalahari Transfrontier Park (for-merly the Kalahari-Gemsbok National Park), and in Namibia, partic-

209

Name of trusts and founding date	Controlled hunting areas, size in km^2	Composition and size of population	Project activities
Sankuyo Tshwara-gano Management Trust (STMT), 1995	NG 34, 870 km^2	Bayei and Basubiya 345 people, 1 village	Ecotourism, safari hunting concession, craft sales, campsite
Xai/Xai Tlhabololo Trust, 1997	NG 4, 9,293 km^2 NG 5, 7,623 km^2 (16,966 km^{2}total)	Ju|'hoansi San, Mbanderu, 400 people, 1 village	Leasing out portion of quota, crafts, community tourism
Mababe Zukutsama Community Trust, 1998	NG 41, 2,045 km^2	Tsegakhwe San, 400 people, 1 village	Ecotourism, some of the hunting quota leased out to a safari company
Jakotsha Community Trust, 1999	NG 24, 530 km^{2}Tsumkwe District West, 8,457 km^2	Mbukushu, Herero and ||Anikhwe San, 10,000 people, multiple villages	Community tourism, makoro (canoe) poling, basketry and other craft sales
Teemashane Community Trust, 1999	NG 10 and NG 11, ca. 800 km^2	Mbukushu, Bayei, Bugakwe San, ||Anikhwe San, 5,000 people	Community tourism, campsite, cultural trail, craft sales
Okavango Community Trust, 1999	NG 22, 580, km^2, NG 23, 540 km^2	Bugakwe San, Bayei, Mbukushu, ||Anikhwe San , Dxeriku, BaTawana, 2,200 people, 5 villages	Safari hunting and photo-based tourism
Khwaai Community Trust, 2000	NG 18, 1,815 km^2 and NG 19, 180 km^2	Bugakwe San, Tawana, and Subiya, 360 people, 1 village	Ecotourism, craft sales, work at safari lodges, auctioning off hunting quota portion
Nyae Nyae Conservancy, Namibia, 1998	Nyae Nyae area, Tsumkwe District East, 9,003 km^2	Ju|'hoansi San, 2,200 people, 37 villages	Community-based tourism and safari hunting
Nǂa Jaqna Conservancy, July 2003	Tsumkwe District West, 8,457 km^2	!Xun (Mpungu, and Vasekela San), 4,500 people, 24 villages	

Table 5. Community trusts in Botswana's Northwest District and conservancies in Namibia involved in integrated conservation and development activities including ecotourism. Data compiled by author.

ularly in the Caprivi Strip area where there are a number of national parks and reserves and in the Nyae Nyae region of northeastern Namibia (for a list of some of the places where tourism is taking place in Botswana and Namibia, see Table 5). In other parts of southern Africa the CBNRM related tourism projects are conducted in areas that are ecologically or culturally significant but that are not associated with protected areas. Some of the tourism operations have generated fairly sizable returns, a portion of which has gone to the community trusts overseeing the tourism operations. This was the case, for example, at /Xai/Xai in northwestern Botswana, where the /Xai/Xai Tlhabololo Trust earned thousands of Pula during the latter part of the 1990s and early part of the new millennium. It was also the case for some of the community trusts in and around the Okavango Delta or northern Botswana and the conservancies in the Caprivi Strip region of Namibia.

Much of this tourism is ecotourism, defined by the World Conservation Union (the IUCN) as "environmentally responsible travel and visitation to relatively undisturbed natural areas in order to enjoy and appreciate nature (and any accompanying cultural features, both past and present) that promotes conservation, has low visitor impacts, and provides for beneficially active involvement of local populations". The problem for the San is that in spite of the rhetoric about public participation and the benefits of tourism that are supposed to accrue to local populations, more often than not ecotourism serves to dispossess poor local people and has only limited social and economic benefits – and many risks – for them.

Community-Based Conservation, Ecotourism, and Development: the Case of Tsodilo Hills

Such a situation can be seen in the case of the Tsodilo Hills of northwestern Botswana, now a national monument where Ju|'hoan San and Mbukushu, a Bantu-speaking group, have resided for generations.

The Tsodilo Hills contain the largest concentration of rock art in Botswana and a number of important archaeological and historic sites. The paintings and engravings in the Hills demonstrate a variety of different kinds of images, some of which include animals, both wild and domestic, herding or stealing of livestock, and possibly the performance of trance healing rituals. Tourists have been visiting the Tsodilo Hills for many years, and the Ju|'hoansi and the Mbukushu who originally were living at the base of the hills in two small villages have been able to make small sums of money by taking tourists on visits to the rock art sites and selling crafts to them.

In the latter part of the 1970s, archaeologists working in cooperation with the National Museum and Art Gallery of Botswana began an extensive rock art and archaeological site recording effort in the Tsodilo Hills with an eye toward coming up with an integrated land use plan and gaining World Heritage site status. One of the recommendations that came out of this work was to increase the protection of the area and, at the same time, a second recommendation was to make the Hills more accessible to tourists.

The Tsodilo Hills were gazetted under the Ngamiland District Land Use Plan in 1991 as NG 6, which has an area of 225 square kilometers. It was zoned by the North West District Council as a photographic safari area, where ecotourism can take place. The Tsodilo Hills were declared a World Heritage Site in 2001, and today, they represent an important tourism destination in Botswana with as many as 5,000 – 10,000 visitors per year.

There is a small museum that is part of the National Museum and there are camping places and facilities for tourists such as showers and toilets. These developments, however, have had a price. In 1995, at the request of the government of Botswana, the Ju|'hoan San community was moved from their village at the base of the Male Hill in Tsodilo to a place about 5 km south of the Hills. This was done, as the government of Botswana put it, "in order to enhance the tourism potential of the Hills and protect the natural resources and cultural heritage of Tsodilo". In 1999 this settlement had about 40 people residing there, while the Mbukushu village, which had not been relocated, had approximately 110 people.

The Ju|'hoansi speak frequently about the fact that the government of Botswana has, to their way of thinking, treated their non-San neighbors, the Mbukushu, preferentially in the development of the Tsodilo Hills. They note that the government moved them, the Ju|'hoansi away from the hills but left the Mbukushu where they were. This situation meant that the Mbukushu were usually the first group of people that tourists visiting the Tsodilo Hills saw on their way in, and it meant that members of the Mbukushu community were often tapped to serve as guides to the rock paintings in the Hills. Another effect of the move of the Ju|'hoansi was that they now had to walk some 5 km each way in order to get water from the borehole built near the new museum facility.

As the Ju|'hoansi asked a team of reviewers of the Trust for Okavango Cultural and Development Initiatives in August 1999, "Why is it that the Mbukushu get to remain close to the Hills where they can greet tourists, while we Ju|'hoansi have to live in a waterless place and have to walk a long way in order to get water and to sell goods to tourists?"[5] It should be noted that even though there are some disagreements between the Ju|'hoansi and the Mbukushu over the tourism issue, both groups benefit from the presence of tourists, who use them as guides and camp workers, purchase crafts and other goods from them and leave clothing and other items for local people.

On the other hand, interviews of the people in the Tsodilo Hills indicate that there are mixed feelings about the presence of tourists.[6] Some of the Ju|'hoansi and Mbukushu residents of the Hills expressed a desire for the visitors to be more careful about the ways in which they treat the environment and the residents of the area. Tourists, they said, often drive off the roads in four-wheel drive vehicles, destroying sensitive habitats. The tourists also have a tendency to build large fires that draw heavily on local firewood resources. In addition, they noted, tourists have been known to spray water and Coca Cola on the rock paintings in order to make them stand out so that they can photograph them, eroding the paints and making the features less visible. The local people understand the value of having tourists. At the same time, they realize the importance of conserving the habitats and the rock art and culturally significant sites in the Hills.

The San and Mbukushu have asked for guidance in creating tourism brochures that address appropriate ways for tourists to behave with respect to the rock art, people and environments of the Tsodilo Hills. Local residents, when interviewed about the effects of tourism, said that they saw tourists as a "necessary evil". Tourists bring money, they noted, but the tourists also exploit the human and natural resources of the area to their own advantage. A few Ju|'hoansi and Mbukushu adults said that they were worried about their children being exposed to alcohol, physical abuse, and sexually transmitted diseases, including HIV/AIDS, from tourists.

The Ju|'hoansi have sought the assistance of San organizations and human rights groups[7] to advocate for their land, resource and development rights. Local people have also worked with government institutions, such as the Remote Area Development Program of the North West District Council. One of the aims of the Ju|'hoansi and Mbukushu is to form a community trust so that they can benefit more directly from the natural resources in the Hills and have a greater say over the ways in which those resources are used.[8]

As the Ju|'hoansi stress, the objective of the Botswana government, to ensure that development in the country is sustainable, is a good one. Ju|'hoansi and NGO spokespersons argue for emphasis to be placed on sustainable tourism, which is defined by the World Tourism Organization as "Development which meets the needs of present tourists and host regions while protecting and enhancing opportunities for the future...[and] while maintaining cultural integrity, essential ecological processes, biological diversity, and support systems".

Whether or not the integrity of the ecological and social systems in Tsodilo is being protected is open to question. Ju|'hoansi and Mbukushu point out that their cultural systems have been transformed substantially as a result of development initiatives and the presence of tourists. According to local parents, children no longer wish to go through rituals that were performed in the past unless there is a way that they can be paid for doing so. They also point out that while the Botswana government attempted to help them by providing some training and occasional jobs, it was also the government that moved the Ju|'hoansi away from the Tsodilo Hills against their will. In addition, the Botswana government has erected fences around the hills, which have disrupted the movements of wildlife. While water is available to tourists, who have only to turn on a tap, the Ju|'hoansi have to spend several hours a day walking to the same taps and then they have to carry the water in buckets back to their homes 5 km away.

Today, areas around the tourist camps in Tsodilo have been denuded of firewood. Women and children, who are the members of San communities who usually collect firewood and water, have to walk long distances to get resources. The people in the Tsodilo Hills admit their own culpability in the overexploitation of some of the resources. They point out, for example, that they have collected thatching grass for construction of their homes, and they have on occasion sold some of the grass to outsiders who pay cash for the resource. This is done, they admit, in spite of the fact that the area and its resources are protected under Botswana government legislation. Nevertheless, as local people hasten to point out, they have less impact on the environment than do the tourists and government officials who work in the area. Tourists and development workers, in their opinions, should be just as concerned with sustainable natural resource management and development as they are. Integrated conservation and development programs, they note, are - by their very nature - multi-stakeholder efforts that require the collaboration of many people.

One of the problems that both of the communities in Tsodilo have noted is that they have to compete with one another for jobs, opportunities to guide tourists and craft sales. They feel that it would be better if the community trust that they hope to establish could be structured in such a way as to have sub-units that work directly with groups of producers such as craft manufacturers and tourism guides. They also feel that the trust will have to pay better attention to ensure that all members of the two communities gain access to income and employment, not just the members of the trust board. Cooperation among the two different ethnic groups is possible, they say, as long as they both feel that they have decision-making power and are able to benefit equally from tourism, development-related jobs through the National Museum and District Council and private safari operators who visit the Hills with their clients.

Gender-related Impacts

A major problem with ecotourism projects is that they tend to have differential and sometimes negative gender-related impacts. As seen in southern Africa, hunting-related projects tend to favor males, as do those projects that have employees that serve as guides (Hunter, Hitchcock, and Wyckoff Baird 1990). Often, men are more familiar with English, Afrikaans or German and thus it is they who get to interact with the safari clients. In some cases, women do get jobs, notably where they work as domestics in tourism lodges, and women do make crafts that are sold to tourists. But, in general, males tend to benefit more from tourism development than females in southern Africa.

These gender-related differences can be seen in other areas of southern Africa besides Tsodilo, one example being the case of /Xai/Xai, an Ngamiland community that lies to the south of the Tsodilo Hills on the Botswana-Namibia border. The /Xai/Xai Tlhabololo Trust is the oldest community trust in Botswana, having been founded in 1997. /Xai/Xai is located in a community-controlled hunting area (CCHA) known as NG 4, which is 9,293 sq km in size. People at /Xai/Xai also have rights to wildlife in NG 5 (7,623 sq km). Just to the north of /Xai/Xai are the Aha Hills and beyond that, the communities of Dobe, !Xangwa, !Kubi, and Mahopa, all of which lie in NG 3, another community-controlled hunting area.

The /Xai/Xai population in the late 1990s was between 350-400, the majority of whom were Ju|'hoan San and about a quarter of whom were Herero. The community trust council was made up of both Ju|'hoan and Herero members, but interview data suggests that the Herero tended to dominate the discussions and had a more substantial say in decision-making about trust-related matters. The activities of the /Xai/Xai trust area included leasing out a portion of the wildlife quota to a safari company, keeping a portion of the wildlife quota for subsistence hunting purposes, commercial craft production and sale, and cultural tourism.[9] At /Xai/Xai the amount of money earned from natural resource management activities in 1995-96, before the trust was formed, was P22,100 (the Pula at the time was worth about US $0.46). Of that total, craft sales generated P13,500, tourism generated P8,000 (benefiting 20 people) and consumer goods sales generated P600. In 1998-99, in the first and second years of the trust, the returns for /Xai/Xai totaled P80,000. Of this total, hunting generated P40,000, 80% of which went to men and 20% to women, photo tourism generated P20,000, 60% of which went to women and 40% to men, and craft production generated P20,000, all of which went to Ju|'hoan women.[10]

The majority of people who were employed by the safari operators who had the lease concession in /Xai/Xai in the late 1990s and 2000 were males. In 1997, 28 people had jobs, in 1998, 31, 1999, 45, and in 2000 24 people were employed.[11] When tourists visited the /Xai/Xai area and dances were held, the majority of the participants were Ju|'hoan women, but these occasions were few and far between. The women of /Xai/Xai also formed their own craft production and marketing operation, !Kokoro Crafts, which generated some income for its members. The primary source of jobs and income for the members of the trust, however, came from the safari hunting and tourism operations. Some of the people in the community invested this income in the purchase of livestock, while the majority bought food and other household necessities. Most of the funds generated by the /Xai/Xai trust that came from the joint venture agreement with the safari operator were invested in community level projects, including the construction of a trust office, a community hall, two campsites and an air strip. Fees are supposed to be paid by visitors to the NG 4 area, with the revenues going to the trust.

According to interviews by Masilo-Rakgoasi (2002), most people in the /Xai/Xai community felt that they did not benefit directly from the investments of the /Xai/Xai Trust. They did admit to getting some money through craft sales, participation in dances, and taking people out on hunting and animal tracking trips. One man to whom the author spoke in 2001 said that some tourists to the /Xai/Xai area were very interested in the tracking abilities of Ju|'hoansi. Ecologists who visited the Ju|'hoansi were also interested in these abilities, which have been demonstrated to have ecological significance.[12] One benefit that the people of /Xai/Xai said that they saw from the community trust's operations was the provision of game meat by safari hunting clients, which added to the protein levels of households. At the same time, it should be noted that there was a sense in the /Xai/Xai community that the distribution of the meat was inequitable, with adult male hunters getting the majority of the meat and women, children and the elderly receiving smaller portions.

For comparative purposes, it is useful to look at another case where Ju|'hoan San have been able to establish a community-based natural resource management program that generates income from safari hunting, photo tourism, and craft production: the Nyae Nyae Conservancy in Namibia. The Nyae Nyae Conservancy is the oldest in Namibia, having been founded in 1998.[13] In Namibia, conservancies are locally planned and managed multipurpose areas that have been granted wildlife resource rights under an amendment to *The Nature Conservation Ordinance of 1996*. By 2002, there were over a dozen conservancies in Namibia, some of which had majority San populations (see Table 6). More than 20% of the communal land in Namibia is now under conservancy status. Some of the conservancies have done reasonably well in terms of generating income for their members. In the mid-1990s, Nyae Nyae generated N$17,400 (the Namibian dollar at the time was worth about

Young San women performing for tourists. Photo: Arthur Krasilnikoff

US $0.25) through photographic safari operations and N$5,000 was generated through game ranching, which had a tourism component.[14] One safari company based in the northern part of the Nyae Nyae region, Namibia Adventure Safaris and Tours, charged N$350 for a full day's traditional hunting. Only a small portion of those funds went to the 2 or 3 adult male hunters who took part (N$40 each). Traditional dancing paid N$25 per person, with most of the funds going to women but, as was the case at Tsodilo and /Xai/Xai, these dances were held infrequently.

In 2002, the Nyae Nyae Conservancy generated N$956,500.[15] Of this amount N$477,672 was distributed as benefits to the 770 adult members of the conservancy, N$620 per person or less than US $100 (US $1 = N$7.5). The safari operator that had the concession in the Nyae Nyae Conservancy, African Hunting, employed 26 men and 2 women (Weaver and Skyer 2003). Approximately 16% of the income earned by residents of the Nyae Nyae area in 2002-2003 came from craft sales.[16] As in /Xai/Xai, an important side benefit of the safari hunting was the meat that came from the animals killed by the safari operators' clients. Overall, tourism returns represented less than a quarter of the income of the households in the Nyae Nyae area.

As was the case with the Nyae Nyae Conservancy, the /Xai/Xai Trust had a joint venture agreement with a partner, a safari company.

The relationships between community-based organizations and safari companies operating in a conservancy or a community-controlled hunting area in the case of Botswana have been largely positive, but disagreements have occurred, for example, over the numbers of jobs for local people to be provided by the joint venture partner. Sometimes there have been outright conflicts between communities and safari operators, as occurred, for example, in /Xai/Xai when one safari operator who had a concession to work there was dismissed for allegedly having engaged in what a number of community members saw as unethical behavior.

In spite of some of the difficulties, most community members have wanted to have joint venture agreements because the economic returns are substantial, and at least some people are able to obtain jobs or access to markets for their products. In general, those community-based natural resource management programs where there have been joint venture partnerships have tended to fare better economically than has been the case with community organizations that undertook activities on their own.

Community Organization Leadership Issues

One of the problems facing the community-based organizations (CBOs) in Botswana that have sizable numbers of San is that the government is often unwilling to recognize San leaders and, by extension, does not recognize CBOs whose elected leaders are San. A prevailing assumption in Botswana government circles has been that San communities lacked formal leaders and that they did not have organized political institutions. Discussions with San have revealed that virtually all communities traditionally had people who they respected and whose suggestions they frequently chose to abide by. These leaders made decisions, adjudicated disputes and represented the community in discussions with outsiders. In some cases there were groups of elders who formed what might be described as community councils. These people had a significant say in civil matters, such as how to handle disruptive individuals. They were also important in decision-making when other people requested that they be allowed to enter their areas in order to use local resources.

Some of the San leaders were essentially resource managers, people who had a long history of occupancy in an area, who were knowledgeable about local resources, and who frequently were approached by other people when they wished to seek rights of access to local resources. Among the Ju|'hoansi, these individuals are known as *n!ore kxausi*, a
term that refers to territory headmen or, as some people put it, "own-

ers". The territories, *n!oresi*, were overseen by individual Ju|'hoansi who had long-standing customary rights to the areas in question. It was often these individuals who were elected to important positions in community trusts involved with conservation activities.

Public policy was traditionally a product of extensive consultation and discussion among the members of San groups, with all adults and sometimes children having the opportunity to participate. Decision-making was generally done on the basis of consensus. The politics of San communities were such that individualism was tolerated and in fact was admired. Those people who engaged in socially inappropriate behavior (stealing, fighting, adultery or overuse of resources) were usually dealt with by peers, who intervened to stop fights and who remonstrated with them, urging them to stop acting in negative ways. People who continued to act in ways that were disapproved of by other members of their communities were subjected to social pressure, which usually took the form of comments and criticisms made by other members of his or her group.

As Marshall (1976:350) notes, the Ju|'hoansi and other San had customs that helped them to avoid situations that were likely to arouse ill will and hostility among individuals within groups and between groups. These customs included (1) meat-sharing, (2) gift-giving and (3) extensive public discussion of events and ways to deal with issues of concern to the group. Among the Ju|'hoansi the meat of wild animals was shared among members of a group, usually along lines of kinship and friendship. There were some gender and age differences in terms of who was allowed to get which parts of an animal, and the degree to which there was true equality in sharing and goods distribution has been questioned by some analysts. Nevertheless, sharing was, and in many cases still is, something that is seen by most if not all San as an activity that is important to maintaining good social relations among people (Lee 1979).

According to the Commissioner of Customary Courts in the Ministry of Local Government, San communities have been involved in electing headmen for a number of years. Some of these headmen have been recognized officially by the Tribal Administrations in their respective districts, and their status has been confirmed by the Minister of Local Government under the *Customary Courts Act* (1975) and the *Chieftainship Act* (1987). Some of the leaders elected by San communities have been very effective at representing their constituents. There have been a number of cases, however, where headmen were elected in communities but were not recognized or have yet to be recognized officially. There have also been cases in which non-local people have become headmen, sometimes to the chagrin of resident members of the community. It is important to note, however, that there have been relatively

Name	Region	Size in sq km	Number of Members	Date of Registration
Doro !Nawas	Kunene	4,073	430	Dec 1999
Ehi-Rovipuka	Kunene	1,975	500	Jan 2001
#Khoadi //Hoas	Kunene	3,366	1,600	June 1998
Kwandu	Caprivi	190	1,800	Dec 1999
Marienfluss	Kunene	3,034	121	Jan 2001
Mayuni	Caprivi	151	1,500	Dec 1999
N‡a Jaqna	Otjozondjupa	8,547	1,344	July, 2003
Nyae Nyae	Otjozondjupa	9,003	752	Feb 1998
Oskop	Hardap	95	95	Feb 2001
Purros	Kunene	3,568	85	May 2000
Salambala	Caprivi	930	4,000	June 1998
Torra	Kunene	3,522	450	June 1998
Tsiseb	Erongo	8,083	950	Jan 2001
Twfilfontein-Uibasen	Kunene	400	61	Dec 1999
TOTAL 14	5 regions	46, 937 sq km	13,688	

Table 6. Conservancies in Namibia's communal areas Note: Data obtained from the Directorate of Environmental Affairs, Ministry of Environment and Tourism (MET), Namibia.

few instances in which the elections of headmen have been challenged. This is the case in spite of the fact that sometimes the government of Botswana has appointed outsiders, most of whom are non-San, as headmen in communities where the majority of residents are San.

One of the criteria for becoming a headman in Botswana is that the individual must have the ability to read and write. This requirement has been problematic for many San since a significant proportion of the adults are non-literate. It is interesting to note that some San groups have figured out innovative ways to get around this problem. In the case of Ka/Gae in the Ghanzi District, for example, a young school-educated man was appointed as headman, but he had a close adviser who was an elderly individual that was illiterate but well respected. There have also been cases where the government relaxed its requirements, allowing non-literate people to become headmen.

There is both conflict and cooperation among community members when it comes to the management of local institutions, including village development committees and community trust councils. Some of the conflicts are between individuals vying for positions in the institutional leadership. In the case of the community trust councils, some of the conflicts have been between different ethnic groups in the community, with the Ju|'hoansi feeling, apparently with some justification, that other groups were more influential than they were in decision-making at the community level. In the Nyae Nyae area of Namibia, on the other hand, since nearly all of the members of the Nyae Nyae Conservancy were Ju|'hoansi, the conflicts over access to positions in the Conservancy Council were based more on where people were from in the region. In all three case areas, women, children and the elderly felt that they had less opportunity to take part in community trust activities than did adult males.

Problems and Lessons Learned

While governments and international organizations such as the World Conservation Union (IUCN), the World Bank, the World Trade Organization (WTO), the World Tourism Organization, and the U.S.-based International Ecotourism Society and many environmentally oriented non-government organizations argue for the utility of ecotourism and sustainable tourism, it is clear that a great deal of work needs to be done to ensure that tourism has positive social, economic, and environmental effects at the local level.

As can been seen from the three cases presented in this chapter, a major problem in a number of the community trusts is that of social exclusion, or what community members might define as discrimination. Some groups, especially the San, have had less chance to participate than other groups in decisions regarding the trust management and operations. In the opinion of Masilo-Rakgoasi (2002), one of the reasons that there were difficulties in the community-based organization in /Xai/Xai was due to the lack of sufficient grassroots mobilization of the full range of community members. Part of the problem also relates to language difficulties since the majority of CBNRM-related business and community-level discussions are held in Setswana, the national language of Botswana (along with English), which some members of the communities do not speak. What this means, in effect, is that the elderly and those who have had less opportunity to learn other languages besides their mother tongue are not able to participate as extensively as other people in the deliberations of the community-based organization; they also have greater difficulty in obtaining information on government and NGO policies and plans.

There are also community members who feel excluded because they receive less than others in terms of economic and social benefits from the CBNRM activities. Even within the trust membership, people feel that there can be inequities in the distribution of benefits, especially jobs, income, and meat. As a result, the legitimacy of the leadership of the community councils has been questioned and a number of people have said to NGO workers that they would like to withdraw their membership of the community trusts, while others want to establish their own independent community-based organizations. Alternatively, some community members have expressed a desire to return to the former system, when individuals had access to Special Game Licenses and other forms of livelihood supports from the Botswana government.

Another important problem is that the important goal of poverty alleviation in a number of cases has not been achieved. While a number of the CBNRM projects in Botswana and Namibia have been able to generate at least some income, there have been problems particularly pertaining to inequities in the distribution of benefits, which has led to local conflicts.

The income-generating projects have not been as effective as people hoped in generating funds for use by individuals, and thus many people continue to live below the poverty line. A major issue relates to the control of the benefits from the CBNRM activities, which largely lies in the hands of the management of the community trust boards. The flow of benefits to the household and individual level is minimal, resulting in dissatisfaction and concern on the part of a number of the community member. Elites in the communities, who are largely in control of the community trust councils, are not always equitable in the ways in which they share benefits that derive from the CBNRM activities, and they do not always take into consideration the views of the more marginalized members.

It is interesting to compare the economic returns to people in the three areas. The two areas where there is a combination of safari hunting and photographic tourism, /Xai/Xai and Nyae Nyae, generate relatively sizable returns for the community trusts. In the Tsodilo Hills, where people have not yet been able to form a trust, economic returns to individual households tend to be lower. This is not to say that community-based natural resource management projects based solely on photographic tourism are less viable economically than those that combine safari hunting with wildlife-related and cultural tourism. If photographic safari tourism operations are well-run, they can generate substantial returns for the communities that take part in them.

CBNRM programs have not resolved the significant conflicts between conservation and development, which exist in northern Botswana and northeastern Namibia like in other parts of southern Africa. It is also an open question as to whether CBNRM projects have enhanced the balance between conservation and development.

While people from the North want to see "pristine habitats and culturally diverse populations", people from the South generally want eq-

Mothomelo (GKGR) resident showing his Special Game License. Photo: Chris Erni

uitable development, access to resources and the chance to have secure livelihoods. The question that the San, Mbukushu, Herero and others ask is why conservation and development appear to be geared more toward helping the rich instead of the poor.

Tourism development and conservation were used as justifications for the removal of people from some of the best-known protected areas in southern Africa (see Table 4) But, as the people that were resettled point out, the people who subsequently have used the parks and reserves have, in many cases, tended to be tourists who were relatively well-off and who often came from other countries.

In all three cases addressed in this chapter, the Tsodilo Hills, /Xai/Xai, and Nyae Nyae, the Ju|'hoan San and their neighbors have been able to derive some benefits from ecotourism. At the same time, as local people in all of these places pointed out, the majority of the benefits from tourism went to the safari operators and companies rather than to the residents of the areas. A number of San have pointed to some of the successes of cultural tourism in South Africa, Zimbabwe and other parts of Botswana (e.g. Ghanzi District, see Bollig et al. 2000). They have said that more investment should be made in promoting culturally oriented community-based tourism since, in their opinion, it tends to provide more benefits to certain segments of the population, including women, children and the elderly.

The Ju|'hoansi and other San in the new millennium are arguing for sustainable tourism development that benefits not only the tourists but also the hosts. They have sought to get non-government organizations, human rights groups and social scientists to advocate on their behalf (Hitchcock 2004). Unfortunately for the San and their neighbors, the Botswana government has not always responded positively to the requests of local people to have more defined rights to resources in protected areas such as the Tsodilo Hills and the Central Kalahari Game Reserve.

It is apparent that community-based integrated conservation and development programs are not easy to implement. In spite of their complex nature, San communities have chosen to embark on them and to attempt to use these programs to their advantage. Judging from the experiences of Namibia and Botswana, steps are being taken toward more localized control of resources through legislation that allows for the establishment of conservancies and community trusts. The question remains as to whether these kinds of institutions provide sufficient control over land and resources for local people to facilitate social and economic development and at the same time conserve resources for the future.

In order to get around these kinds of problems, non-government organizations should seek to strengthen the institutional capacity of community-based organizations, especially in the areas of project administration, financial management and reporting. It is also evident that there need to be greater efforts to promote more participatory approaches to decision-making regarding community-based natural resource management.

CBNRM programs should be monitored very carefully in order to ensure that they do not overtax the environment or the institutional capacities of the community-based organizations involved. It must be emphasized that the constitutional, management, organization and administration systems of CBOs should not be overly complex. The devolution of authority must be done through negotiation and interaction rather than through statutory mandate and the imposition of strict rules and conditions. Crucial to the success of a community-based organization are transparency, openness and flexibility. Community-based organizations and non-government organizations must be allowed to set their own priorities and mobilize themselves to achieve the goals that they set for themselves. At the same time, NGOs and CBOs should understand their obligations to their funding agencies and the organizations that support them. Mechanisms must be in place that foster accountability and responsibility and not just participation.

Natural resource management and governance regimes must also take account of diverse interests. Careful attention must be paid to constraints within governments and the private and non-government sectors and in CBOs in terms of the ways in which they treat specific groups such as ethnic minorities, women, children or people who are perceived as being non-members or those who are "outside the universe of obligation". If it is determined that there are biases in the ways that groups are treated, efforts must be made to ensure that all actions are equitable and that they do not either favour or harm a specific group. At community level it is very important to implement methodologies that are sensitive to community and individual variation and to ensure that gender, age, power, occupational and class characteristics are taken into consideration. All members of the community, not just the elites or members of specific ethnic groups, should have a significant say in the operations of community-based organizations; in other words, careful attention should be paid to issues involving equity since equity and fair treatment are key to successful sustainable development and natural resource management.

The implementation of community-based natural resource management activities is both time-consuming and labour-intensive. Working at the rhythm of communities is critical in local-level development. Democracy, equity, participation, open-ended consultation, information, sharing and group and individual responsibility are all keys to success in CBNRM and development project implementation. Government, non-government organizations and communities should be more willing to allow bottom-up decision-making and be more open to allowing local people, regardless of their ethnic, class, religious or social backgrounds, to make their own choices regarding conservation, development and governance and to benefit from the CBNRM and other activities being implemented.

It is in the best interests of community-based natural resource management and local communities if the state and other agencies recognize those communities officially as proprietary units with de jure rights for land, wildlife, veld (bush) products, minerals, and other natural resources over which they maintain legal control in perpetuity. One of the problems that has arisen in southern Africa is that the degree to which communities actually have control over their own land is limited by the nature of the government's conservation and land legislation. The land authorities or ministries involved with wildlife and natural resources ultimately retain control over the land and resources. There have been cases in Botswana, for example, where the Department of Wildlife and National Parks decided not to allocate the wildlife quota to a community. There have also been cases where there were conflicts between communities and the government over the numbers and types of animals to be allocated as part of the quota. In addition, there has been uncertainty over whether community trusts in Botswana were going to be able to continue to retain control over the revenues that they generated from CBNRM activities.

In the face of increasing human pressures on the environments and economies of southern Africa, it may well be time to employ a more participatory approach to conservation and development, one that allows for greater community control over resources. This way, conflict will give way to greater cooperation, and the community-based natural resource management projects in the region will have greater chances of success.

Acknowledgments

Earlier versions of this paper were prepared for presentation at the Ninth International Conference on Hunting and Gathering Societies (CHAGS-9), University of Edinburgh, Edinburgh, Scotland, September 9-13, 2002 and the 64th annual meetings of the Society for Applied Anthropology, Dallas, Texas, March 31st – April 4th 2004. ❑

Notes

1   Statement by resident of New !Xade to R. Hitchcock, March, 2004.
2   Data from the Department of Wildlife and National Parks, Ministry of Environment, Wildlife, and Tourism, Republic of Botswana. Wildlife Management Areas are blocks of land in rural Botswana which were designated as areas within which wildlife utilization and development programs can be carried out. In 1986, these WMAs, along with national parks and game reserves, constituted some 37% of the land of Botswana, or over 200,000 sq km (Botswana 1986).
3   Ministry of Environment and Tourism, Namibia; (see also Harring, this volume).
4   Joram /Useb, personal communication, 2003.
5   TOCaDI members, personal communication to Kuru Development Trust Review team, August, 1999.
6   These interviews have taken place over time in Tsodilo, with data collection in 1976, 1978, 1981, and 1999 by Robert Hitchcock.
7   These organizations included the Trust for Okavango Cultural and Development Initiatives (TOCaDI), the Working Group of Indigenous Minorities in Southern Africa (WIMSA) and DITSHWANELO, the Botswana Center for Human Rights.
8   The formation of a trust has been delayed in part because the Hills are zoned as a National Monument under the Botswana National Monuments and Relics Act, but the trust is currently in the process of being registered.
9   For a discussion of the /Xai/Xai trust and its activities, see Hitchcock, 2000; Rozemeijer, 2001; Masilo-Rakgoasi, 2002.
10 Charlie Motshubi (former employee of SNV Botswana), personal communication, 1999.
11 Nico Rozemeijer, Charles Motshubi and Bernard Horton, personal communications, 2000.
12 See Stander et al., 1997:329-341.
13 For discussions of the Nyae Nyae Conservancy and the Ju|'hoansi, see Biesele and Hitchcock, 2000: 305-326; Wyckoff-Baird, 2000:113-135; 2003; Weaver and Skyer, 2003.
14 Megan Biesele, Barbara Wyckoff-Baird, Chris Weaver, personal communications, 1995, 2001.
15 see Berger et al., 2003.
16 Polly Wiessner, personal communication, 2003.
17 John Ledger, Mike Mentis, personal communications, 2004.

INDIGENOUS RIGHTS IN EDUCATION:
THE SAN OF SOUTHERN AFRICA IN LOCAL AND GLOBAL CONTEXTS

Jennifer Hays

S ince the World Conference on Education for All, held in Jomtien, Thai–land, in 1990, the global initiative to provide primary education for *all* of the world's children has gained momentum. The assumed correlation between education and empowerment is so completely interwoven into development and educational discourse today that it has become virtually unquestioned; indeed, education is guaranteed in numerous international documents as a fundamental human right. In keeping with the global emphasis on *Education for All* and *Educational Rights,* southern African government bodies responsible for education, and concerned non-government organizations, are working to provide access to the formal education system for San communities, whose participation level in government schools is historically the lowest in the region. However, the experience of San children in formal education systems across southern Africa continues to be characterized by high drop-out rates and low success rates. San communities everywhere express disappointment and frustration with their lack of educational options.

This chapter argues that *education* is usually understood too narrowly, as meaning only *formal education*. Indigenous peoples in many parts of the world have long recognized that formal education serves primarily to undermine their own skill base and value systems without replacing them with viable alternatives, and many are now beginning to claim their right *not* to be assimilated through mainstream, formal education systems. Drawing upon these global trends, and using the Nyae Nyae Ju|'hoansi of north-eastern Namibia as a case study, this chapter argues that our concept of "education"- what it *is*, and what it *is for*- must be broadened and diversified if the goal of *Education for All* is to be either realistic or beneficial for San communities.

Southern African Background

Across southern Africa, San communities have specific problems with education that transcend linguistic groups and national borders; these have been well documented.[1] The high drop-out rate (and thus low success rate) of San students has been attributed to a great number of factors, including the lack of mother-tongue education for most San communities, cultural differences between the home and school, cultural practices (such as hunting trips or initiation ceremonies) that keep students away from school, frequent abuse at the hands of school authorities and other students, and the alienating experience of boarding schools (often necessitated by the great distances between their home villages and the schools). Although some of these problems are shared with other minority groups in southern Africa, in San communities they are compounded by their extremely marginal social status and their general lack of access to land and other resources.

Southern Africa's recent history of apartheid, with its forced separation of people based on language and ethnicity, has had far-reaching effects on attitudes towards minorities, on language and education policy, and on educational options in the region. The use of mother-tongue education as a tool for separation and oppression during the apartheid era has made southern African governments and citizens understandably wary of educational initiatives that seem to promote "separate education", or education in one's mother tongue, at the expense of the dominant language. The pedagogical soundness of mother-tongue education during the early years is recognized, however, and educational bodies in southern Africa are, in theory, committed to providing this option for all of their citizens. What this means *in practice*, however, varies greatly among southern African countries.

The following sections will briefly outline the educational situation in South Africa, Botswana and Namibia.[2] The approach of southern African governments to the problems that San students face in the state education systems reflects their attitude towards indigenous minorities in general. While the degree of tolerance for cultural and educational differences varies, ultimately all three countries emphasize formal education. Although efforts have been made below to provide a statistical illustration of the level of participation of San children in government schools, these figures must be understood as very rough. Gathering accurate statistical data on this topic is difficult for a number of reasons. Identity can be confusing; sometimes San children do not identify themselves as such, leading to an under-representation in official statistics. Or, as is the case in Botswana, official data may not be disaggregated by ethnic or linguistic group. San children also often attend school irregularly; they might thus be over-counted if numbers are gathered at the beginning of the year, when attendance is usually at its highest. On the other hand, many San children see themselves as "school-goers" even if they do not attend consistently; further complicating the goal of an accurate statistical portrayal of San school attendance.

Despite the problems with collecting and interpreting data, the figures that are available paint a bleak picture. Compared to other ethnic groups, the San attend government schools at far lower rates, and have higher numbers of drop-outs, than other ethnic groups. Furthermore, the quality of education available in areas with high San concentrations is generally much lower than in other places.

South Africa

In South Africa, a progressive constitution that promotes "unity in diversity", a current educational policy that emphasizes the need for flexibility and creativity at the local level, and a current cultural fascination with the San all contribute to an attitude of willingness to accommodate indigenous minorities' educational needs. In this spirit, the Northern Cape Education Department has taken on the task of working to integrate San and Nama languages and cultures into the province's education system.[3] Although the initiative is there, South Africa has a high number of marginalized rural minorities and the educational needs of these populations often exceed the resources available to address them (see also Chennells and du Toit, this volume, for additional information on education rights and initiatives in South Africa).

Current South African education policy encourages mother-tongue education for the first three years. The history of this approach (albeit enforced) during the apartheid era has facilitated the creation of curriculum materials in the eleven official languages, and government funding is earmarked for this purpose. The Khoe and San languages, however, were actively suppressed during the apartheid era as these populations were forcibly assimilated into the "coloured" ethnicity, for which Afrikaans was a primary linguistic marker. There was thus virtually no development of any of the Khoe or San languages for educational purposes. Today, although the Khoe and San languages are recognized, as they are not official languages there is no government funding available for their development.[4]

As a result of decades of linguistic persecution, today most San and Nama populations indigenous to South Africa speak Afrikaans as a first language with only a few elders still speaking their original mother tongue. For such groups, "mother-tongue" education is more an issue of language restoration than of effective pedagogy, though still a crucial aspect of community development. Efforts are being made in this direction with the cooperation of linguists, and for the Nama, drawing upon the extensive educational materials available in Namibia.[5]

The largest San community in South Africa, however, is the community of re-settled !Xun and Khwe soldiers (originally from Angola and Namibia) and their families, whose children *do* speak San languages as their first language. The school at Schmidstdrift,[6] !Xunkhwesa Combined School, is the largest San-only school in all of southern Africa, with 1190 learners in pre-school through Grade 12.[7] The language of education there is currently Afrikaans but, in cooperation with language development initiatives in Botswana and Namibia, efforts are being made to develop curriculum materials in !Xun and Khwedam; the Grade 1 materials are expected to be implemented in early 2004.

Botswana

Botswana's educational approach to San communities is in many ways the inverse of South Africa. An important part of Botswana's state-building strategy since independence has rested upon the identification of all of its citizens with the *Batswana* ethnic identity. Largely a reaction to its uncomfortable proximity to the formerly apartheid South Africa and Namibia, Botswana's ideal of homogeneity resulted in a general policy of non-recognition of ethnic minorities. This stance is reflected in their approach to education and is particularly evident in language policy. The building of a national Batswana identity has relied heavily upon the promotion of *Setswana* as the primary language of its citizens. Setswana is the national language of Botswana, and English the official language; the use of any other languages for public functions, including education, has been strongly discouraged. While Botswana does recognize the right to mother-tongue education, the "mother tongue" is assumed to be Setswana, despite the fact that at least 18% of the country's citizens have other home languages (Botswana 2003b). Accordingly, the first years of school are taught in Setswana before switching to English as the medium of instruction by Standard (Grade) 4 (Botswana 1994a).[8] There is no provision for mother-tongue primary education for minority-language children. This is undoubtedly a serious educational obstacle for San students (and other linguistic minorities), who must begin primary school in a foreign language (Setswana), then switch to another (English) before they have even mastered the first.

Although Botswana has one of the most successful formal education systems in Africa, claiming universal basic education of up to ten years, San children do not reap the same benefits as children of more dominant groups in the country. Accurate statistics for the participation of San students in Botswana's schools are difficult to obtain as the government does not disaggregate data by ethnic group, but all indications are that San students attend at much lower rates and drop out much more than students from other ethnic groups. Botswana's Remote Area Development Programme (RADP), which provides support services and material goods to remote communities, has a special focus on educational needs. Children from settlements without schools are transported to boarding schools where they are provided with school clothing, food and hostel accommodation while attending school.[9] (See also Mazonde this volume). Official figures are not available and there is significant local variation, but a common estimate is that more than 80% of the RADs nationwide are San, and that this number approaches 100% in some areas. The Ngamiland district has the highest concentration of San, but there they only make up about 10% of the population. In the Ghanzi district, which also has a high number of San residents, they make up only about 5% of the population (Le Roux 1999:17). When we compare these figures to the percentage of San defined as "RADs" it is clear that the San are vastly overrepresented in this category.

The government of Botswana invests a great deal of resources in providing RAD children with the opportunity to attend government schools, at least up until Standard 4. Unfortunately, however, these schools, and the hostels, tend to be very unsympathetic places for San students. The idea of separating parents and children is foreign to San culture; the pain and alienation that San students feel at boarding schools can be acute and many of those who drop out cite missing home and family as their reason for leaving. Abuse by hostel staff and other students, poor hostel conditions, stigma experienced by the San as "RADs" and a general lack of cultural sensitivity exacerbate the situation. The subjects are taught in a foreign language, cultural representations in curriculum materials represent the perspective of the dominant group, and teaching styles are derived from the dominant culture (Nyati-Ramahobo 2003). These factors further reinforce the marginality of San language and culture within the schools and make it more difficult for them to succeed in that environment. A review of the latest educational statistics reveals that the four districts with the highest percentage of RAD learners have significant differences from the rest of the country.[10] These include higher numbers of drop-outs; a disproportionate number of untrained and deserting teachers; and a shortage of classrooms and teachers and library resources (Botswana, 2003a).

Botswana's educational approach to marginalized students is thus characterized by the investment of substantial resources in attempts to incorporate San students into the formal education system. From the perspective of the government, they are working hard to provide San children with the same opportunities as the rest of the population. There is some evidence that this approach is resulting in a higher number of San students moving forward through the education system.[11] Critics, however, call the approach assimilationist, and point to the lack of respect for San languages, culture, community and knowledge within the current educational options.

Namibia

Of the three countries, Namibia has made the most progress towards ensuring mother-tongue and culturally appropriate education for the first three years of school for San minorities. Namibian educational policy recognizes the pedagogical soundness of mother-tongue education during the early years of schooling and is also sensitive to the function of language as a medium of cultural transmission (Namibia 1997). As in South Africa, mother-tongue education until Grade 3 is encouraged, but the lack of curriculum materials in San languages has been a primary obstacle to implementing this option for San learners. Recently, however, the National Institute for Educational Development (NIED), a directorate of the Ministry of Basic Education, Sport and Culture (MBESC), has spearheaded the effort to create mother-tongue educational materials in San languages, the first being Ju|'hoansi; similar plans are also underway for !Xun and Khwedam.[12] These efforts still have some way to go, however, and at present only a very small minority of San children have the option of attending a school where they are taught in their mother tongue, or which recognizes and respects their unique culture.

In addition to an overall lack of schooling that recognizes and validates their language, culture and background, San learners experience barriers to formal education stemming from poverty, low socio-economic status, stigma surrounding their culture, and "remoteness" - most San students live very far from government schools. In an attempt to address these challenges, Namibian educational policy also makes explicit provisions for remote and otherwise marginalized students. The Intersectoral Task Force on Educationally Marginalised Children, under MBESC, has identified San children as one of the three major "educationally marginalized" groups in the country.[13] The document "National Policy Options for Educationally Marginalised Children" emphasizes the need for flexibility in several places. In Part V, section 13, "Policy Implementation" it says:

> The main theme of this policy is **flexibility**. It is necessary to use a number of unconventional approaches in order to achieve education for all educationally marginalised children. (Namibia 2000:31; emphasis in original)

Such policies create an environment in which innovative education projects may be implemented for San communities. One of the most progressive, and perhaps the best known of these is the Nyae Nyae

Village Schools Project (VSP) located in the Nyae Nyae Conservancy of north-eastern Namibia, a community-based mother-tongue education project that attempts to address many of the numerous problems that Ju|'hoan children of Nyae Nyae face in education. (This project is described in greater detail below). However, despite the environment of respect for cultural and linguistic diversity, San children, including the Ju|'hoan beneficiaries of the progressive Nyae Nyae VSP, continue to drop out of government schools in disproportionate numbers.

Obtaining accurate estimates of San participation is also difficult in Namibia, even though breakdowns by ethnicity are a part of the figures. Students may not identify themselves as San, leading to a lower count; on the other hand, counts taken near the beginning of the school year may not reflect drop-out rates and irregular attendance.[14] Figures from the UNDP from 1998 estimate that less than 20% of San children were enrolled in school that year; government figures from the same year calculate about 25-30% (UNDP 1998; EMIS 1998, from Suzman 2001b). These figures are very low, but indicate a dramatic rise in attendance from the early 1990s when the enrolment of San children was closer to 10-12%. However, there is also a dramatic drop-off in attendance in higher grades; for 1998 there were 2,723 San learners in lower primary, the figure drops to 803 by upper primary and by senior secondary there were only 19 learners identified as San. Despite Namibia's progressive policies and concern for educationally marginalized children, San children's participation in the mainstream education system continues to be extremely low, especially from upper primary school onwards.

Although these three countries differ significantly in their approaches to education for San minorities, all three emphasize formal education, based upon Western models. Guided by the global discourse of *Education for All*, the primary focus of attention is upon removing the entry barriers for San students to government schools. The right of San communities and their children to have access to formal education is crucial, and is something that San people say that they want and need. However, providing such access is not the whole answer to the question of educational rights for the San. The section below interrogates this limited definition of education, and the discourses based upon it.

What is "Education?"

Since 1948, access to education has been recognized as a fundamental human right. Article 26 of the Universal Declaration of Human Rights states that everyone has the right to education, that elementary education shall be free and compulsory, that education shall be directed

Children in Nyae Nyae, Tsunkwe District East, Namibia. Photo: Diana Vinding

to the "full development of the human personality and to strengthening of respect for human rights and fundamental freedoms". Numerous subsequent documents have re-emphasized this right, including the International Covenant on Economic, Social and Cultural Rights, the Convention on the Rights of the Child, the Convention against Discrimination in Education, and the World Declaration on Education for all. However, as Spring (2000) points out, none of the international documents addressing education provide a justification for, or a definition of, education. What *is* education?

When we speak of "education", most of us normally think of a particular kind of education, referred to in this paper as *formal education*. We think of a teacher in front of a class, in a room with a chalkboard, desks and chairs in a school building. We think of students writing in note books with pencils and paper, taking exams, entering and leaving classes at specific times marked by bells and clocks. The primary skills associated with this type of education are language and literacy skills and, to a somewhat lesser extent, numeracy skills. The "right to education" is normally understood as the right to formal, Western-style, education.

However, at its broadest, most basic level, education is a socialization process that is a natural part of any culture. Children in any setting must learn to function and survive in the community and environment in which they live; they are, in effect, "programmed" to learn. Education is about learning *skills, knowledge* and appropriate *social behaviour*. The way these are passed from one generation to another is the *method of transmission*. All of these things will vary depending upon culture, physical and social setting, size of the community, what kinds of skills and knowledge must be acquired, and various other factors. When we define it broadly like this, we can say that all communities have education, and that formal education as we think of it is just one type. Whether education is effective or not depends primarily upon the extent to which it prepares learners for participation in their communities and larger social groups, and whether it provides them with what they need to survive and thrive in their environment.

Spring (2000) notes that the World Conference on Education for All was "characterized by an array of conflicting educational purposes". This conflict is reflected in the vagueness with which education is defined within the World Declaration on Education for All.[15] The closest the document comes to defining "education" is in Clause 1 of Article 1, which says that every person has the right "to benefit from educational opportunities designed to meet their basic learning needs":

> *These needs comprise both essential learning tools (such as literacy, oral expression, numeracy and problem solving) and the basic learning content (such as knowledge, skills, values and attitudes) required by human beings to be able to survive, to develop their full capacities, to live and work in dignity, to participate fully in development, to improve the quality of their lives, to make informed decisions, and to continue learning. **The scope of basic learning needs and how they should be met varies with individual countries and cultures, and inevitably, changes with the passage of time** (cited in Spring 2000:6; emphasis added).*

As a definition, the above is very broad and encompasses a range of educational possibilities. It also suggests the need for flexibility in determining how these "basic learning needs" should be met. In practice, however, definitions of education are often very narrow, and usually do not take into consideration local knowledge, expertise or economic realities. Many researchers have pointed out that in the current climate of "globalization of education", even purportedly "bilingual" or "multicultural" programs usually rely uncritically on models designed in the West.[16]

Some of the most profound mismatches between the educational ideals of global education discourses, and local social and economic realities, occur among indigenous communities around the world. Spring (2000:4) says that the "most daunting problem" of the Jomtien conference was "reconciling a universal declaration of the right to education with cultural differences, particularly those of indigenous peoples". The section below will highlight the experiences of indigenous peoples in education worldwide, and re-examine the notion of the "right to education" as it is defined in documents that emphasise the rights of indigenous peoples.

Indigenous Peoples and "Education for All"

Indigenous peoples worldwide share certain experiences in formal education systems. A large body of literature points to several broad historical parallels, including (1) separation of children from their families while they attend schools (often boarding schools far from their communities), (2) where they are taught foreign systems of knowledge, (3) in a language or language variety other than their own, (4) by teachers from cultures that are different from, and dominant to, their own, (5) and who use instruction and disciplinary styles that do not match that of the students' home life. Probably as a result of some combination of the above factors and others, indigenous peoples experience (6) overall poor performance in formal education systems, accompanied by high drop-out rates (Hays 1999).

The experience of schooling for indigenous children frequently gets set up as a no-win situation. Those who remain in school often experience alienation and/or physical separation from their communities. The generation gap that occurs when children go to government schools - especially when these are boarding schools - can effectively halt the transmission of knowledge that is normally passed on orally from one generation to another. Due to biases inherent in Western education systems, however, indigenous children frequently do not succeed, and often return to their communities having been taught that the way they live is inferior to the rest of society. Formal education systems tend to emphasize what indigenous students "cannot do or do not know, rather than what they can do or do know" (Moraes 1996:121).[17] Furthermore, the standards by which students are judged in schools often directly contradict values and standards of the home community. For example, while most indigenous communities value cooperation and reinforce mutual respect, school environments usually reward competition and self-promotion.

In addition to being foreign to students, and thus more difficult for them to participate in, the systems of evaluation themselves serve to effectively bar the participation of large numbers of indigenous children. Evaluation systems that rank students individually and hierarchically ensure that there will always be some at the bottom. Research among various minority groups in schools around the world has shown that the power and status relations between students' communities and the rest of society are one of the strongest determinants of "success" or "failure" in school.[18] Around the world, indigenous minorities like the San are at the bottom of the socio-economic hierarchy, and this is matched by their experiences in school. In other words, the educational model that is being promoted for *all* is based upon a model in which it is virtually impossible for *all* to succeed, and in which indigenous peoples are the most disadvantaged.

A policy guided by the aim of *Education for All* that sees educational success only as success within the formal education system does not allow for legitimate alternatives for those who do not function well within this system. Students who experience barriers to their success in school - as indigenous peoples often do - or who otherwise choose, for whatever reason, not to participate, are defined as *failures*. Likewise, an understanding of *Educational Rights* that focuses only upon access to formal, state-based education without recognizing the validity of traditional knowledge and teaching methods is more than just an incomplete recognition of indigenous rights. Such approaches practically guarantee the "failure" of indigenous peoples across the world.

These facts have not gone unnoticed by indigenous peoples. The World Indigenous Peoples' Conference on Education (WIPCE 1999) has outlined in *The Coolangatta Statement On Indigenous Peoples' Rights in Education* the effects that formal education—often compulsory—has had upon indigenous communities:

> *Historically, Indigenous peoples have insisted upon the right of access to education. Invariably the nature, and consequently the outcome, of this education has been constructed through and measured by non-Indigenous standards, values and philosophies. Ultimately the purpose of this education has been to assimilate Indigenous peoples into non-Indigenous cultures and societies. Volumes of studies, research and reports dealing with Indigenous peoples in non-Indigenous educational systems paint a familiar picture of failure and despair. When measured in non-Indigenous terms, the educational outcomes of Indigenous peoples are still far below that of non-Indigenous peoples. This fact exists not because Indigenous peoples are less intelligent, but because educational theories and practices are developed and controlled by non-Indigenous peoples.* (Coolangatta Statement 1999, section 1.3.1)

The statement goes on to say that, where the rights of indigenous peoples to education are recognized, they "are often interpreted to read that Indigenous peoples only want access to non-Indigenous education" (Section 1.3.2). The Coolangatta Statement insists upon the right of Indigenous peoples to Self-Determination, which embodies the right, among other things,

> to control/govern Indigenous education systems; to establish schools and other learning facilities that recognize, respect and promote Indigenous values, philosophies and ideologies; [and] to promote the use of Indigenous languages in education (Section 2.2.4)

Other international documents also assert that indigenous peoples have, in addition to the right of access to all levels and forms of state education, the right to establish their own educational systems. Article 15 of the UN Draft Declaration on the Rights of Indigenous Peoples states that:

> Indigenous peoples have the right to an education in their own languages and cultures, using indigenous teaching methods.

The Preamble to the World Declaration on Education for All includes the recognition that:

> traditional knowledge and indigenous cultural heritage have a value and validity in their own right and a capacity to both define and promote development. (Cited in Spring 2000:5)

The Coolangatta Statement notes that, despite the barriers:

> Indigenous peoples across the world are demanding and, in some cases, achieving the establishment of systems of education which reflect, respect and embrace Indigenous cultural values, philosophies and ideologies.

Indigenous peoples around the world are claiming, in addition to the right to participate in formal education systems if they so choose, the right *not* to be assimilated into other cultural systems through the education system, and the right to establish their own systems of education. Many San in southern Africa also express the desire for education closer to their homes, in their own language, and which respects and values their culture. So far, for the vast majority, such education is not available.

In the Nyae Nyae Conservancy of eastern Namibia, however, substantial resources have been invested in the creation of a unique project that integrates "traditional" and culturally appropriate, mother-tongue education with formal education. *The Nyae Nyae Village Schools Project* is illustrative in many ways. It provides an example of the potential to establish mother- tongue, community-based education for San communities but also of the difficulties in doing so. The project and the experience of the Nyae Nyae community as a whole with education also illustrate the problems of narrow educational goals, where "success" is measured primarily as success within the formal education system. The following sections explore the notions of *Education for All* and *Educational Rights* in the context of the Nyae Nyae community.

The Nyae Nyae Jul'hoansi and the Village Schools Project

The Ju|'hoansi of Nyae Nyae, unlike most San in the region, still live on part of their ancestral land, and thus have the opportunity to practise their traditional subsistence activities of hunting and gathering. The Nyae Nyae Conservancy, situated on the eastern side of the Tsumkwe district, covers an area of approximately 6,300 square kilometres. Close to the geographical centre of the area is Tsumkwe, the main town. With a population of approximately 1000, the town is the administrative and economic centre of the Nyae Nyae area, and is the location of the government school. There are between 30-35 smaller villages, with a combined population of approximately 1000, for a total population of approximately 2000 within the conservancy boundaries.[19] Almost all of the village residents are Ju|'hoansi, but in Tsumkwe town there are a variety of ethnic groups, with most of the positions of influence and income occupied by non-Ju|'hoansi.

The *Village Schools Project* (VSP) grew out of a collaborative effort between local NGOs and Namibia's (then) Ministry of Education and Culture in the early 1990s, as a response to Ju|'hoan children's lack of participation in the government schools of Tsumkwe District East. The Village Schools are meant to create a safer, more familiar and more comfortable environment in which the children can learn in their own languages about things relevant to their lives for the first three years of school. In the Village Schools, currently operating in four of the larger villages of the Nyae Nyae Conservancy, children are taught in the Ju|'hoan language, by members of their own speech community, making the project one of the only places in southern Africa where San children have access to formal education in their mother tongue.[20] The ultimate goal is to increase the self-confidence of both learners and the communities, so that Ju|'hoan children can enter the government schools in Grade 4 as "critical thinkers" with the basic skills necessary to succeed in those schools, and a firm grounding in their own culture.

While the focus is on providing schooling closer to home that incorporates the language, knowledge and skills from their communities, from the outset, the goal of ultimately preparing children to be success-

Young teachers on their way to a Village School (Nyae Nyae). Photo: Diana Vinding

ful in the government schools has been central to the project. Although very many children attend the Village Schools, most of these do not attend the government school in Tsumkwe (which they are supposed to start in Grade 4) for very long.[21] The reasons children give for dropping out are numerous, the most common being reports of abuse and/or teasing from other children and the teachers; theft of property; lack of food; not having the proper clothes and/or toiletries; and missing their parents and family. Often children will simply shrug and say that the school was "not good". Still others simply express a preference for staying in the bush and a desire to hunt, gather and make crafts. Since the success of the Village Schools Project is measured by non-Ju|'hoan stakeholders in terms of how many children carry on with their education at Tsumkwe school, and since the vast majority do not go on, the conclusion is often drawn that the project is "failing".

Interestingly, the Ju|'hoansi themselves do not seem to see it this way. One of the most striking characteristics of the Ju|'hoansi's responses to questions about education is that there does not seem to be an assumption that the same solution will work for all individuals. When asked what they think should happen with their children's schooling, Ju|'hoan parents almost always emphasize that there should be different options, and that individuals will decide for themselves what they want to do. People often suggested that the Village Schools should go beyond Grade 3, to higher grades. Then, they say, those children that want to go on with schooling but stay in the village will be able to do so, and those that want to leave and go elsewhere for school will also have that option. The strongly express a desire for *flexibility* within their educational options.

There thus seems to be a gap between the way in which the Ju|'hoansi themselves view the Village School Project and their educational goals, and a government policy guided by a goal of *Education for All*. A lack of recognition of these differences in perspective has made it difficult for those involved to fully understand and address the educational problems in the area. The over-emphasis on formal education places a strain on the individuals who *do* achieve success within this system, as well as on those who do not and on the community as a whole. It also leads to a lack of appreciation for the validity of the skills that people in the area possess, their method of transmission, and the immediate economic realities of survival in the area. The remainder of this chapter will briefly explore these dynamics.

Education as an Individual Right?

The Ju|'hoansi, like many hunting and gathering groups, are frequently defined in both the academic and popular literature as "egalitarian". The full impact of such firmly embedded social ideals is often underestimated, however. Also underestimated is the difficulty of creating an education project that simultaneously recognizes egalitarian community ideals *and* prepares students for participation in an education system based upon competition. Whether students drop out or succeed, the contrast between the value systems presents major problems for students. While the problem is most often understood to be the poor showing of Ju|'hoan students in the formal education system, those who do well in the government schools face a whole new set of problems. In a community that values equality and non-competitive approaches to learning, those who succeed in a system based upon hierarchy and competition have, at some point, had to contradict the cultural values of their upbringing.

The advantages that education is supposed to bring are most often associated with elevated status and material gain; however only a very few have so far achieved the skills and benefits of formal education. The ways in which a recent tradition of strict equality, and related understandings of fairness, express themselves in circumstances of increasing *inequality*, in which a few individuals are promoted above others, can create enormous difficulties for the community as a whole, and particularly for those who are "successful".[22] Reactions to such individuals often include jealousy, expressed as resentment, as overt or subtle refusal to co-operate, or as increased pressure to share food or material wealth. The pressure that formally educated individuals experience is not only financial; the weight of the hopes and expectations of the communities—and often of the outsiders who have invested in training and support for these individuals—is also resting on their shoulders. At the same time, many express a feeling of having sacrificed a sense of *belonging* to their larger community, something that can be extremely painful and in some cases destructive. Some express frustration in the sense that they no longer are allowed to make their own decisions about their lives. In this context to talk about education simply as a "right" on an individual level seems to overlook other deep, important issues.

Education for All as a Community Right?

At the community level, the emphasis on formal education has led to a de-valuation of the skills and educational approaches of the Ju|'hoansi. Earlier this chapter argued that formal education is merely one type of education, that all communities can be said to educate their children, and that the effectiveness of education is measured by the extent to which it allows students to survive and thrive in their physical and social environments. As Liebenberg (1990) and others have persuasively argued, San communities have been able to survive in a harsh environment for generations through enormous skill, depending upon their intimate knowledge of the *veld* (bush) and the animals that live in it. Such survival skills are not innate; they are learned, passed down from generation to generation in very specific ways. Generations of San children have had to learn the skills and flexibility necessary to survive in their particular circumstances. San children have also had to learn the appropriate behaviours to be accepted within their community. We can thus understand San communities as *educating* their children.

The method of information transmission employed for this type of education is very different from the didactic classroom method associated with formal schools today, so different that it is often not even recognized as such. However, some current educationalists argue that the Ju|'hoan method of education is in fact ideal in many ways. Heckler (1992), for example, notes that the Ju|'hoansi follow an educational strategy characterised by a high adult to child ratio, constant activities that never exclude children, willing participation on the part of children (it is they who seek or reject participation) and a level of respect accorded to the moods of a child that is equal to that of adults. Formal education, by contrast, is typified by a high child to teacher ratio, children divided into categories based on age, and prescribed activities for specific units of time, regardless of the desire of the children to actually participate in that activity. In these ways, formal education is not only a foreign system to Ju|'hoan (and other San) children, but it is questionable whether it is the way that "all" children from *any* culture will learn best. The main point here is that the superiority of formal education, based as it so often is upon Western models of education, is not a given.[23]

Furthermore, the method of transmission employed by the Ju|'hoansi is *necessarily* different from that employed in formal education, for the knowledge itself is of a different character. Scott (1998) describes "indigenous knowledge"[24] as a knowledge based on years of accumulated exposure to and experience in a particular environment, and generations upon generations of orally transmitted information. Confined to a general geographic area that is nonetheless variable, and unrestricted by the permanence of written records, it is intimately specific to place, and yet also entirely flexible (ibid.). Wilmer (1993) proposes that indigenous peoples' knowledge of the natural world can be understood as an "'inner technology' of heightened consciousness"; a specific awareness of the intricate ecosystem they depend upon for survival. This type of knowledge, he argues, cannot be acquired in a laboratory setting in a few decades, it "can only be acquired over time if it is the sort of knowledge considered valuable" (1993:208). These authors describe a form of knowledge that cannot be divided into discrete units and taught for an hour in a class at school. The information that forms the basis of such knowledge must be communicated over sustained periods of close contact with the environment and with the community made up of the bearers of this knowledge. It is largely through the formal education system that this kind of knowledge is destroyed, as children are separated from their communities and the transmission is halted.

The argument for the need to preserve indigenous knowledge can be, and often is, based upon its general value for humanity. However, such knowledge, and the skills that accompany it, can only survive if communities themselves choose, and are able, to pass it on. This, in turn, will only happen if they, themselves, perceive it as valuable. In the past, the information and skills transmitted within San communities were crucial to group and individual survival; the question relevant here is whether or not they are valuable today. Clearly, we can no longer make the argument that *only* knowing how to survive in the bush, and in social isolation, is education enough for San people; that option is rapidly diminishing. San people everywhere in southern Africa are caught in a process of transition and are struggling to adapt to rapidly changing circumstances. Skills, knowledge and a familiarity with the ways of other social groups gained through the formal education system must be available for San communities as they are for others.

However, for the Ju|'hoansi, as well as many other San groups, "traditional" skills are *also* still important to survival in several ways. Most people in the Nyae Nyae area still gain a large proportion of their subsistence from hunting and gathering. Unless and until other means of obtaining food are secure, the skills that allow them to live from the *veld* are crucial to their survival. These skills can also provide cash income; there is a small but growing market within the tourism industry for hunting and gathering trips. Also importantly, people simply *like* to practise these skills. This was expressed by everyone, from the old men and women who tell endless stories about their experiences in the bush, to the children and young men and women who cite "going out into the bush" as either a reason for not attending school, or a viable alternative as a lifestyle choice. Those who were successful in school sometimes lament the fact that they never really learned how to hunt properly, because they were away or too busy with formal education.

When asked about the importance of formal education versus traditional skills such as hunting and gathering, people almost invariably replied that these two things are *both* important. While parents do want their children to learn how to read and write and to speak English, they also want them to learn how to track and hunt animals and to be able to gather plant foods, and to make crafts. People explained that they depend upon all of these things for survival.

The responses of the Ju|'hoansi suggest that what is often interpreted as a rejection of the formal education system, or perhaps an incomplete acceptance, is in part the result of strategic decisions based upon an assessment of realistic options. San individuals and communities are, in fact, choosing to remain flexible in their educational options, and their subsistence strategies. This does not mean that Ju|'hoan and other San groups are necessarily content with the choices that are available to them; many would like to have improved educational facilities, better teachers, schools closer to home, adult literacy classes. They would also like to have more secure access to land and other resources, and for their culture and land rights to be respected by other groups. But, in the face of rapid change and insecurity, people are seeking to lessen their vulnerability and are *actively* making educational decisions with this in mind. Insisting upon formal education, as it exists in southern Africa today, for *all* of a community's children would ultimately result in the loss of a unique knowledge base, upon which some groups, such as the Ju|'hoansi, still depend for survival.

I suggested at the beginning of this chapter that education - by which is understood formal education based on Western ideals - is put forth as a sort of panacea that will solve the problems of disadvantaged communities. This discourse is absorbed by San individuals and communities, who also often internalise the supposed superiority of such education. However, after weighing up a variety of economic, cultural and personal considerations, many San children and youth decline to participate in this system and choose instead to pursue other subsistence options and lifestyles. At best, a superficial discourse about *Educational Rights* and *Education for All* that only considers formal education fails to recognize and respect these realities, and the strategic choices that people make to confront them, and thus fails to meet people's actual needs. At worst, these discourses, and policies, planning and implementation based upon them, serve to further marginalize San populations and contribute to social breakdown.

Conclusion

A simple goal of *Education for All* in which "education" means only formal, classroom-based education has at least three detrimental consequences among many San groups. First, the aim seems to have become simply pushing as many children as possible into and through a system whose values often directly contradict those of the home; this contributes to community breakdown. Secondly, the enormous value placed on formal education automatically *devalues* other sorts of learning, thus resulting in a group of people who, despite the legitimate and valuable skills they do possess, are labelled as "ignorant" and "uneducated". Third, the devaluation of these skills in tracking, hunting and gathering may be leading to a decrease in their transmission, and thus the loss of a potential source of subsistence and income generation.

San groups must have the right to access formal education, especially when they themselves demand this right. However, we must also begin to interrogate the virtually unquestioned emphasis on formal education and the ways in which education is defined. These definitions, and the assumptions that underlie them, are part of much larger national, regional and global power structures of which San communities, and other hunting and gathering populations, fall at the very bottom. In order to challenge these structures, then, it is not enough to simply talk of providing access to education. Rather we must look carefully at what education is, what it means to peoples like the Ju|'hoansi, and what options are actually available to them. Then we should ask whether these options are something that they should have a right *to* - or if they are, perhaps, something that they should have the right to refuse or to accept. ❏

Notes

1   See Kann, Hitchcock & Mbere, 1990; Kann, 1991; Mendelsohn, Swarts and Avenstrup, 1995; Le Roux, 1999; Siegrühn & Hays, 2000; Nyati-Ramahobo, 2003; Polelo 2003.

2   There are also San people living in Zimbabwe, Zambia and Angola. Until recently, however, little was known about their circumstances. The Working Group of Indigenous Minorities in Southern Africa (WIMSA) has recently funded surveys in Zambia and Angola. In both countries, San children report that they do not go to school because they are abused there.

3   The vast majority of San in South Africa live in the Northern Cape Province.

4   The National Khoe and San Language Body (NKSLB), under the Pan South African Language Board (PanSALB) is responsible for the development of these languages (see Chennells and du Toit, this volume).

5   In Namibia, the Nama are not considered to be a marginalized group as they are in South Africa, and a fully developed range of learning materials are available in their language, Khoekhoegowab.

6   The !Xun and Khwe are now in the process of moving to Platfontein where a new school is being built and is expected to be ready for occupation by the end of 2004.

7   In 2002 Schmidtsdrift School had a 75% pass rate, and in 2003 there were twelve Grade 12 learners (Jonkers, Jomo, Principal, personal communication by fax 15 November 2003).

8   There is currently a move to begin instruction in English as early as Standard 2, but this has yet to be implemented everywhere in the country. This earlier introduction of English instruction creates even more difficulties for minority language children, especially as the method of language introduction was designed for Setswana-speaking children (Willemien le Roux, personal communication, 09 January 2004)

9   Of 65 RAD settlements, 57 have schools; 15 of these have hostels. The other 25 hostels for the RAD children are not in the settlements, but actually serve farms and other dispersed populations where no remote area dweller community has been established (Sheldon Weeks, personal communication, 07 January 2004).

10 Kweneng West, North West (Ngamiland), Ghanzi, and Kgalagadi North, which together contain 54.7 percent of RAD settlements (Botswana, 2003a).

11 Sheldon Weeks, personal communication, 07 January 2004.

12 Khwedam is the language of the Khwe. –Ed.

13 The other two are the Ovahimba and the children of farm workers, many of whom are San.

14 The Wimsa Regional Education Coordinator reports that in Namibia, statistics on ethnic groups in schools are often gathered from forms the students fill out, where they are asked to identify their home language by choosing from a list. Although "San" might be a choice on the list, not all "San" students use this identity marker. Their specific languages (i.e. Hai‖om, Ju|'hoansi, !Kung) are generally not included as a choice. (Yvonne Pickering, personal communication, 08 October 2003)

15 The document unanimously adopted by the conference delegates.

16 See Aikman, 1996; Freeland, 1996; Brady, 1997; Fitzsimons, 2000.

17 See also Saugestad, 1996; McGovern, 1999.

18 Cummins, 1986; Ogbu, 1993; Aikman, 1997.

19 These numbers are rough estimates; the detailed statistics from the census conducted in 2001 are not yet available. Furthermore, there is still a fair amount of mobility among villages and between villages and Tsumkwe, and sometimes entire villages will move or disperse.

20 The number of village schools fluctuates somewhat. There were originally three schools, this number later increased to five, and schools periodically close and reopen depending upon water and food availability, movements of elephants, and other factors.

21 Ironically, those who first attend the Village Schools actually drop out at a higher rate than those who attend the government school in Tsumkwe from Grade 1. Reasons for this probably have to do with the contradiction discussed in the text of this paper, but it may also be because those who start at Tsumkwe School from Grade 1 usually do so because their parents or other family members are living and working in Tsumkwe, and they thus have family support. It may also be that they have lived in Tsumkwe prior to attending school there, and are more accustomed to life in the town.

22 See also Biesele, 1993.

23 In fact, even in Western cultures there is a growing movement that rejects formal education as inadequate, evidenced by the growing numbers of alternative education systems and parents who choose to home school their children.

24 There is no commonly accepted term to refer to this type of knowledge, and, as Scott (1998) has pointed out, terms that are used often connote inferiority to "modern" or "scientific" understandings of the world. In this paper I simply use the term "indigenous knowledge".

APPENDIX

APPENDIX

Sidsel Saugestad

Khoe-San Languages: an Overview

K hoe-San languages are most easily recognised by the unique and pho-
netically complex click sounds. Originally spoken over the whole
of southern Africa, they belong to three main families of languages,
as different from each other as e.g. Indo-European from Finno-Ugri-
an. Within each family of languages some languages are mutually un-
intelligible, while others are so close that it could be deemed arbitrary
as to whether they are called languages or dialects.

There is as yet no authoritative vocabulary of southern African indigenous language names, and there is a need for standardised generic
terms and for easy-to-use orthographies that adequately represent the
complexity of the languages. But a standardisation process is underway.
A meeting in Namibia in 2000, under the auspices of WIMSA, brought
together San language, oral history and education specialists from the region and produced the *Penduka Declaration on the Standardisation of Ju and
Khoe Languages* (WIMSA 2001:94-96). The present overview follows these
recommendations, as well as the standards set by Anthony Traill (1995),
and the recommendations made by Andersson and Janson (1997).

The JU (Northern Khoe-San) family of languages is basically a dialect continuum with a high degree of mutual intelligibility. *Ju* languages are
spoken in Botswana, in the Ngamiland District and the northern part
of Ghanzi District, and in north-eastern Namibia/southern Angola. The
largest language in this group is *Ju|'hoan*, spoken by some 4,000 of Na-
mibia's San population, and by perhaps the same number in Botswana.
!Kung is a well-known dialect of this language.

The KHOE (Central Khoe-San) branch comprises maybe thirty or more
different languages and major dialects. They are spoken in an area extending from Zimbabwe in the north-east, across the Central District
and Central Kalahari Game Reserve, including Kweneng and Ghanzi Districts in Botswana, to large parts of Namibia in the west. Among
the best known are *Naro*, spoken by some 8,000 people in Ghanzi, *G|ui*
and *G||ana* (spoken in the Central Kalahari Game Reserve). *Tshwa* and
Shua are spoken in the central and eastern part of Botswana. These are
the least documented of the San languages, and it is unclear how many
of the main dialects should be termed separate languages. Some 20,000
people speak or have recently spoken these languages, but this is also

the area with the most severe language loss. The related languages *Khwe*, *Bugakhwe* and ‖*Anikhwe*, are spoken in Caprivi and Okavango.

Khoekhoegowab, previously called Nama, is a cover term for a language continuum covering most of Namibia, the north-western part of South Africa and some small pockets in Botswana, with the related *Hai‖om* spoken in northern Namibia (originally in the region of Etosha). In terms of speakers, this is the largest of the Khoe languages.

The *Southern Khoe-San* branch comprises the Taa and !Ui families of languages that were probably once spoken over the whole of South Africa and the south-western part of Botswana. One language, *!Xóo*, remains, spoken by some 3 to 4,000 people in the southern part of Ghanzi and in the Kalahari District extending into South Africa.

Most Khoe-San languages were already extinct before a scholarly interest in them began to develop. This may in fact still be the case with a number of languages/dialects in the largely unknown areas of the Okavango, Central District and Eastern Botswana. Interestingly, while languages disappear in Botswana, in South Africa indigenous mobilisation has led to the discovery of a dozen speakers of a language called N|u that was assumed to have been extinct, spoken by people identifying themselves within the broader socio-linguistic category of ‡Khomani.

*Main languages/speech communities:**

Ju (Northern) languages:
> **!Xun** (formerly !Xû): the language and the people
> (in Namibia and South Africa)
> **Ju|'hoansi**: the language and the people
> **Ju|'hoan:** used only as an adjective
> **!Kung**: the language and the people
> **=Kx'au‖e**

Khoe (Central) Languages
> **Khoekhoegowab** (formerly Nama): language of the
> Hai‖om, Nama and Damara people
> **Khwedam**: language of the Khwe people
> **Khwe**: the people (formerly Kxoe) (in Namibia, Botswana and
> South Africa)
> **‖Anikhwe**: part of the Khwe people, mostly in Botswana
> **Bugakhwe**
> **|Anda**
> **Shua** (Deti, |Xaise, Danisi, Cara, Ts'ixa)

Tshwa (Hiechware, Kua, Tsua)
Naro: the language and the people
G|ui (or **Cgui**): the language and the people
G||ana (or **Xgana**): the language and the people

Taa and !Ui (Southern) Languages
!Xóo: the language and the people (mostly in Botswana)
N|u: the language of the southern Kalahari
N||n‡e: speakers of N|u
‡Khomani: people who used to speak N|u and |'Auo
|Xam: extinct language.

*   The various symbols used in San orthography (||, ‡, !, |) refer
to some of the click sounds, which are so characteristic of San
languages. -Ed.

ACRONYMS, ABBREVIATIONS AND TERMS

ACRONYMS, ABBREVIATIONS AND TERMS

AIDS	Acquired Immune Deficiency Syndrome
ANC	African National Congress (South Africa)
AU	African Union
Basarwa	San – name used in Botswana. (*Mosarwa*, sing.)
Batswana	the people of Botswana. (*Motswana*, sing.)
BGI	Botswana Game Industries
Bogwera	initiation for young males (Setswana)
Botlhanka	serfs, slaves (Setswana) (*motlhanka*, sing.), also taken to mean inferior status
CAMPFIRE	Communal Areas Management Program for Indigenous Resources
CBNRM	Community-Based Natural Resource Management
CBO	Community-Based Organisation
CCHA	Community-Controlled Hunting Area (Botswana)
CCT	Constitutional Court (South Africa)
CEDAW	Convention on the Elimination of All Forms of Discrimination against Women
CKGR	Central Kalahari Game Reserve
Conservancy	a legally defined area in Namibia in which communities have decision-making power with regard to wildlife resources
DITSHWANELO	The Botswana Centre for Human Rights
DWNP	Department of Wildlife and National Parks (Botswana)
EMIS	Education Management Information Services (Namibia)
EU	European Union
FAA	Angolan Armed Forces
FPK	First People of the Kalahari (Botswana)
GIS	Geographic Information Systems
GPS	Global Positioning System
HIV	Human Immuno-deficiency Virus
IBRD	International Bank for Reconstruction and Development (World Bank)
ILO	International Labour Organization
IMF	International Monetary Fund
IPACC	Indigenous Peoples of Africa Coordinating Committee
IUCN	International Union for the Conservation of Nature and Natural Resources (World Conservation Union)

IWGIA	International Work Group for Indigenous Affairs (Copenhagen)
Ju|'hoansi	San people (Ju|'hoan, adjective)
Kgosi	leader, headman (Setswana) (*dikgosi*, plural), sometimes used to refer to a chief among the Tswana
Kgotla	council place (Setswana), locality where public meetings are held
Khwa ttu	the San Cultural Centre, South Africa
Khwe	also known as Kxoe (San people)
Khwedam	the language of the Khwe
!Kung	today also known as Ju|'hoansi
LAC	Legal Assistance Centre (Namibia)
LCC	Land Claim Court (South Africa)
LRC	Legal Resources Centre (South Africa)
Mafisa	a cattle loan system, where the benefits of the cattle, milk, dung, and draught power, are exchanged for management and oversight
MBESC	Ministry of Basic Education, Sport and Culture (Namibia)
MET	Ministry of Environment and Tourism (Namibia)
Modisa	manager or herder (Setswana)
Mong	Master (Setswana)
Morafe	those who accept the authority of a *kgosi*, (Setswana) (*merafe*, plural), sometimes used to refer to a tribe or social unit
NGO	Non-Governmental Organisation
NIED	National Institute for Educational Development (Namibia)
NNC	Nyae Nyae Conservancy (Namibia)
NNDFN	Nyae Nyae Development Foundation of Namibia
N|oakwe	"the red people" – Naro term of self-reference
NORAD	Norwegian Agency for Development Cooperation
N!ore	territory, resource area (Ju|'hoan) (*n!oresi*, plural)
N!ore kxausi	Traditional Ju|'hoan land manager
NRMP	Natural Resource Management Project
NUFU	Norwegian Council for Higher Education
Nyatsi	Concubines (Setswana)
OAU	Organization of African Union
OHCHR	Office of the High Commissioner for Human Rights
PanSLB	Pan South African Language Board (South Africa)
PTA	Parent Teacher Association (Botswana)
Pula (P)	Botswana currency. Pula means "rain".
RAD	Remote Area Dweller (Botswana)
RADO	Remote Area Development Officer (Botswana)

RADP	Remote Area Development Program (Botswana)
SADC	Southern African Development Community
SADF	South African Defence Forces
SASI	South African San Institute
SCA	Supreme Court of Appeal (South Africa)
Setswana	the national language spoken in Botswana
SGL	Special Game License (Botswana)
SI	Survival International
STD	Sexually Transmitted Diseases
SWAPO	South West Africa People's Organization (Namibia)
TGLP	Tribal Grazing Land Policy (Botswana)
TOCaDI	Trust for Okavango Cultural and Development Initiatives (Botswana NGO)
UB	University of Botswana
UN	United Nations
UNDP	United Nations Development Program
UNEP	United Nations Environment Program
UNESCO	United Nations Education, Cultural, and Scientific Oganisation
UNHCR	United Nations High Commissioner for Refugees
UNICEF	United Nations Children's Fund
UNITA	União Nacional para a Independência Total de Angola
USAID	United States Agency for International Development
VDC	Village Development Committee (Botswana)
Veld/Veldt	open area of land typical for southern Africa (the bush)
VSP	Village School Project (Nyae Nyae, Namibia)
WGIP	Working Group on Indigenous Populations (United Nations)
WHO	World Health Organisation
WIMSA	Working Group of Indigenous Minorities in Southern Africa
WIPCE	The World Indigenous Peoples' Conference on Education
WMA	Wildlife Management Area (Botswana)
WTO	World Trade Organisation
WWF	World Wildlife Fund (USA), World Wide Fund for Nature
!Xu	also known as Vasekele, San people now in Angola, Namibia, and South Africa

BIBLIOGRAPHY

BIBLIOGRAPHY

Adams, Fiona and Wolfgang Werner
1990   *The Land Issue in Namibia: An Inquiry*. Windhoek: University of Namibia, Namibia Institute for Social and Economic Research.

Adams, Martin and Paul Devitt
1992   *Grappling with Land Reform in Pastoral Namibia*. Research paper series, 32a. London: Pastoral Development Network.

Africa Watch
1989   *Zimbabwe: A Break with the Past? Human Rights and Political Unity*. Washington, D.C. and New York: Africa Watch.

Aikman, Sheila
1996   The Globalization of Intercultural Education. *Compare* 26(2):153.
1997   Interculturality and Intercultural Education: A Challenge for Democracy. *International Review of Education* 43(5-6):462-479.

Alexander, Jocelyn, Joanne McGregor and Terence Ranger
2000   *Violence and Memory: One Hundred Years in the "Dark Forests of Matabeleland"*. London: Heinemann.

Anaya, S. James
1996   *Indigenous Peoples in International Law*. New York and Oxford: Oxford University Press.

Andersson, Lars Gunnar and Tore Janson
1997   *Languages in Botswana*. Gaborone: Longman Botswana.

Bank, Andrew, ed.
1998   *The Proceedings of the Khoisan Identities and Cultural Heritage Conference*. Cape Town: Institute for Historical Research, University of the Western Cape and Infosource.

Barnard, Alan
1992   *Hunters and Herders of Southern Africa*. Cambridge: Cambridge University Press.
2003   *Diverse People Unite. Two Lectures on Khoisan Imagery and the State*. Occasional Papers No. 94. Edinburgh: Centre of African Studies, University of Edinburgh.

Barnard, Alan and Justin Kenrick, eds.
2001   *Africa's Indigenous Peoples: 'First Peoples' or Marginalized Minorities*. Edinburgh: Centre of African Studies, University of Edinburgh.

Barnard, Alan and Michael Taylor
2002   The complexities of association and assimilation: an ethnographic overview. In *Ethnicity, Hunter-gatherers and the "Other": Association or Assimilation?* ed. Susan Kent. Washington: Smithsonian Institution Press.

Barume, Albert Kwokwo
2001   *Heading Towards Extinction? Indigenous Rights in Africa: The Case of the Twa of the Kahuzi-Biega National Park, Democratic Republic of Congo.* Document 101. Copenhagen: International Work Group for Indigenous Affairs (IWGIA).

Becker, Heike
2002   The Least Sexist Society? Perspectives on Gender, Change and Violence among Southern African San. *Journal of Southern African Studies* 29(1):5-23.

Beinart, William and Joanne McGregor
2003   *Social History and African Environments.* Cape Town: David Philip and Athens, Ohio: University of Ohio Press.

Bennett, T.W. and C.H. Powell
1999   Aboriginal Title in South Africa Revisited. *South African Journal of Human Rights,* Vol. 15: 449, 450.

Berger, Dhyani J., in consultation with Kxao Moses #Oma, Hosabe / Honeb and Wendy Viall
2003   *"The Making of a Conservancy": The Evolution of the Nyae Nyae Conservancy. Restoring Human Dignity with Wildlife Wealth 1997-2002.* Windhoek: Eco-Development Education and Training and WWF/LIFE Program.

Biesele, Megan
1993   "Eating Crow in the Kalahari: Levelling Lessons Taught by the Ju|'hoan Bushmen to their NGO." Paper Presented at Annual Meeting of the American Anthropological Association. Manuscript in possession of author.

Biesele, Megan and Robert K. Hitchcock
2000   The Ju/'hoansi San under Two States: Impacts of the South West African Administration and the Government of the Republic of Namibia. In *Hunters and Gatherers in the Modern World: Conflict, Resistance and Self-Determination,* ed. Peter S. Schweitzer, Megan Biesele and Robert K. Hitchcock, 305-326. Providence, RI and London: Berghahn Books.

Bishop, Kristyna
1998   Squatters on Their Own Land: Khwe Territoriality in Western-Botswana. *Comparative and International Law Journal of Southern Africa* 31:92-121.

Bodley, John H.
1999   *Victims of Progress.* Fourth edition. Mountain View, California: Mayfield Publishing Company.

Bollig, Michael
1997   *Resource manage and Pastoral Production in the Epupa Project Area. Social impact assessment of the Epupa Project.* Windhoek: Legal Assistance Centre.

Bollig, Michael, Robert K. Hitchcock, Cordelia Nduku
    and Jan Reynders
   2000   *At the Crossroads: The Future of a Development Initiative. Eval-
          uation of KDT, Kuru Development Trust, Ghanzi and Ngamiland
          Districts of Botswana.* The Hague: Hivos.
Boonzaier, Emile, Candy Malherbe, Andy Smith and Penny Berens
   1996   *The Cape Herders: A History of the Khoikhoi of Southern Africa.*
          Cape Town and Johannesburg: David Philip.
Botswana, Republic of
   1975a *Customary Courts Act.* Gaborone: Government Printer.
   1975b *National Policy on Tribal Grazing Land.* Gaborone: Government
          Printer.
   1984a *Citizenship Act.* Gaborone: Government Printer.
   1984b *Tribal Grazing Land Policy Guidelines.* Gaborone: Government
          Printer.
   1986   *Wildlife Conservation Policy.* Gaborone: Government Printer.
   1987   *Chieftainship Act.* CAP. 41:01. Gaborone: Government Printer.
   1994a *Revised National Policy on Education.* Gaborone: Government
          Printer.
   1994b *Ostrich Management Plan Policy of 1994.* Government Paper
          No.1 of 1994. Gaborone: Government Printer.
   1994c *Evaluation of the RAD Programme.* Gaborone: Government
          Printer.
   1995   *Game Farming, 3. Ostrich.* Department of Wildlife and Nation-
          al Parks, Botswana File WP UTI, Vol. VI,2.
   1997   *National Development Plan 8, 1997/98 - 2002/2003.* Gaborone:
          Government Printer.
   1999   *Draft Botswana Cultural Policy.* Gaborone: Ministry of Local
          Government, Lands & Housing.
   2003a *Education Statistics 2001.* Gaborone: Government Printer.
   2003b *National Census 2001.* Gaborone: Government Printer.
   n.d.   *Report of the Second Regional Conference on Development Pro-
          grammes for Africa's San Populations, October 11-13, 1993.* Ga-
          borone: Government Printer.
Brady, Wendy
   1997   Indigenous Australian Education and Globalization. *Interna-
          tional Review of Education* 43(5-6):413-422.
Bredekamp, Henry C. Jatti
   2001   Khoisan Revivalism and the Indigenous Peoples' Issue in Post-
          Apartheid South Africa. In *Africa's Indigenous Peoples: 'First
          Peoples' or Marginalized Minorities,* ed. Alan Barnard and Justin
          Kenrick, 191-209. Edinburgh: Centre of African Studies, Uni-
          versity of Edinburgh.

Brenzinger, Matthias
1997 *Moving to survive: Kxoe communities in Arid Land.* Cologne, Germany: University of Cologne.
2000 *San Communities in Angola and Zambia.* Windhoek: The Legal Assistance Centre.
2001 Angola and Zambia. In *An Assessment of the Status of the San in South Africa, Angola, Zambia and Zimbabwe,* ed. Steven Robins, Elias Madzudzo and Mathias Brenzinger. Windhoek, Namibia: Legal Assistance Center.

Britz, Rudolf G. et al.
1999 *A Concise History of the Behoboth Basters Until 1990.* Windhoek: Klaus Hess Publishers.

Burger, Julian
1987 *Report from the Frontier: The State of the World's Indigenous Peoples.* London: Zed Press.

Casdhan, Elizabeth
1979 "Trade and Reciprocity among the River Bushmen of Northern Botswana". Ph.D. Dissertation, University of New Mexico, Albuquerque.

Cassidy, Lin, Ken Good, Isaac Mazonde and Roberta Rivers
2001 *An Assessment of the Status of San in Botswana.* Windhoek: Legal Assistance Centre.

Chaskalson et al.
1996 (1999) *Constitutional Law of South Africa.* Cape Town: Juta.

Child, Graham
1995 *Wildlife and People: The Zimbabwean Success.* Harare and New York: Wisdom Foundation.

Corbett, Andrew
1999 "Presentation on behalf of the Himba traditional leadership". Paper presented at the World Commission on Dams, Geneva, July 1999.

Cummins, Jim
1986 Empowering Minority Students: A Framework for Intervention. *Harvard Educational Review* 56(1):18-37.

Davies, Caitlin
2003 *The Return of El Negro.* Cape Town: Penguin Books (South Africa).

Davis, Shelton H. and Lars T. Soefestad
1995 *Participation and Indigenous Peoples.* World Bank Environment Department Papers 021. Washington, D.C.: The World Bank.

Derwent, Sue
1999 *Guide to Cultural Tourism in South Africa.* Cape Town and London: Struik Publishers.

d'Errico, Francesco, Christopher Henshilwood and Peter Nilssen

2001   An Engraved Bone Fragment from c. 70,000-year-old Middle Stone Age Levels at Blombos Cave, South Africa: Implications for the origin of symbolism and languages. *Antiquity* 75:309-18.

DITSHWANELO (the Botswana Centre for Human Rights)

1996   When will this moving stop? Report on a fact-finding mission to the Central Kgalagadi Game Reserve, April 10-14 1996. Unpublished report by DITSHWANELO, Gaborone.

Dowson, Thomas

1992   *Rock Engravings of Southern Africa*. Johannesburg: Witwatersrand University Press.

Draper, Patricia

1975a   !Kung Women: Contrasts in Sex Role Egalitarianism in the Foraging and Sedentary Contexts. In *Toward an Anthropology of Women*, ed. Rayna Reiter, 77-109. New York: Monthly Review Press.

1975b   Cultural Pressure on Sex Differences. *American Ethnologist* 2:602-16.

1978   Learning Environment for Aggression and Anti-social Behavior among the !Kung. In *Learning Non-Aggression*, ed. Ashley Montagu, 31-53. New York: Oxford University Press.

Draper, Patricia and Nancy Howell

1997   "Some Demographic Correlates of Sedentary Status: Ju/'hoansi in the 1960s". Paper presented at the 97th Annual Meetings ofthe American Anthropological Association, Philadelphia, Pennsylvania, 1998.

Durning, Alan

1992   *Guardians of the Land: Indigenous Peoples and the Health of the Earth*. Washington, D.C.: WorldWatch Institute.

Education Management Information Systems (EMIS)

1999   *Education Statistics*. Windhoek, Namibia: Ministry of Basic Education and Culture.

Estermann, C.

1976   *The Ethnography of Southwestern Angola, Volume I: The Non-Bantu Peoples – The Ambo Ethnic Group*, ed. Gordon Gibson. London: Holmes and Meier.

Ezzell, Carol

2001   The Himba and the Dam. *Scientific American*, June 2001.

Felton, Silke and Heike Becker

2001   *A Gender Perspective on the Status of the San in Southern Africa*. Windhoek, Namibia: Legal Assistance Center.

Finlayson, J.D., Bruce Rigsby and H.J. Bek

1998   *Connections in Native Title: Genealogies, Kinship, and Groups*. CAEPR Research Monograph No. 13. Canberra: Aboriginal Economic Policy Research, Australian National University.

Fisch, Maria
1999   *The Secessionist Movement in the Caprivi: A Historical Perspective.*
        Windhoek: Namibian Scientific Society.
Fitzsimons, Patrick
2000   Changing Conceptions of Globalization: Changing concep-
        tions of Education. *Educational Theory* 50(4):505-520.
Freeland, Jane
1996   The Global, the National and the Local: forces in the develop-
        ment of education for indigenous peoples - the case of Peru.
        Compare 26(2)167-195.
Gaeses, Elfriede
1998   Violence against San Women. In *Out of the Shadows: The First
        African Indigenous Women's Conference,* ed. Angelina von Ach-
        terburg, 92-98. Amsterdam: Netherlands Center for Indigenous
        Peoples.
Gibson, Clark C.
1999   *Politicians and Poachers: The Political Economy of Wildlife Policy
        in Africa.* Cambridge: Cambridge University Press.
Good, Kenneth
1992   Interpreting the Exceptionality of Botswana. *Journal of Modern
        African Studies* 30(1):69-95.
1999   *Review of Government Policy.* Consultancy to the European Un-
        ion on the Condition of the San in Botswana. Gaborone.
Gordon, Robert
1992   *The Bushman Myth. The Making of a Namibian Underclass.* Boul-
        der: Westview Press.
Grimes, Barbara A., ed.
2000   *Ethnologue: Languages of the World.* Volume 1. Fourteenth Edi-
        tion. Dallas: SIL International.
Hamalengwa, M. C. Flinterman and E.V.O. Dankwa, compilers
1988   *The International Law of Human Rights in Africa: Basic Docu-
        ments and Annotated Bibliography.* Dordrecht, Boston and Lon-
        don: Martinus Nijhoff Publishers for the United Nations In-
        stitute for Training and Research.
Hasler, Richard
1996   *Agriculture, Foraging and Wildlife Resource Use in Africa: Cultural
        and Political Dynamics in the Zambezi Valley.* London and New
        York: Kegan Paul International
Hahn, C.H.L, H. Vedder and L. Fourie
1928   *The Native Tribes of South West Africa.* London: Frank Cass and
        Co, Ltd.
Harring, Sidney L.
1996   The Constitution of Namibia and the "Rights and Freedoms"
        Guaranteed Communal Land Holders: Resolving the Incon-

sistency Between Article 16, Article 100 and Schedule 5. *South African Journal on Human Rights* 12 (3): 467-484.

2001   God Gave Us This Land: The OvaHimba, the Proposed Epupa Dam, the Independent Namibian State, and Law and Development in Africa. *Georgetown International Environmental Law Review* 15 (35).

Harring, Sidney L. and Willem Odendaal

2002   *One Day We Will All be Equal: A Socio-legal Perspective on the Namibian Land Reform and Resettlement Process.* Windhoek: Legal Assistance Centre.

Hays, Jennifer

1999   Global Problems, Local Solutions: An overview of Indigenous Peoples in education systems worldwide. In *Torn Apart: San Children as Change Agents in a Process of Assimilation* by Willemien le Roux, Appendix IV: xvi-xxii. Windhoek: Working Group of Indigenous Minorities in Southern Africa.

Heckler, Melissa

1992   *Oh Place Where we Have Played, Stay Well: An indigenous village learning environment. Report on 1990 pre-school pilot project, /Aotcha, Namibia.* Windhoek: Nyae Nyae Development Foundation in Namibia.

Hitchcock, Robert K.

1978   *Kalahari cattle posts: a regional study of hunter-gatherers, pastoralists and agriculturalists in the western sandveld region, Central District, Botswana.* 2 vols. Gaborone: Ministry of Local Government and Lands.

1988   Settlement, Seasonality and Subsistence Stress among the Tyua of Northern Botswana. In *Coping with Seasonal Constraints*, ed. Rebecca Huss-Ashmore with John J. Curry and Robert K. Hitchcock, 64-85. Philadelphia: Museum Applied Science Center for Archaeology, the University Museum, University of Pennsylvania.

1994   International Human Rights, the Environment and Indigenous Peoples. *Colorado Journal of International Environmental Law and Policy* 5(1):1-24.

1995   Centralization, Resource Depletion and Coercive Conservation among the Tyua of the Northeastern Kalahari. *Human Ecology* 23(2):169-198.

1996   *Kalahari Communities: Bushmen and the politics of the environment in southern Africa.* IWGIA Document 79. Copenhagen: IWGIA.

1997   African Wildlife: Conservation and Conflict. In *Life and Death Matters: Human Rights and the Environment at the End of the Millennium*, ed. Barbara Rose Johnston, 146-166. Thousand Oaks, California: AltaMira Press.

1999a Introduction: Africa. In *The Cambridge Encyclopaedia of Hunters and Gatherers*, ed. Richard Lee and Richard Daly. Cambridge: Cambridge University Press.

1999b Tyua. In *The Cambridge Encyclopaedia of Hunters and Gatherers*, ed. Richard B. Lee and Richard Daly, 225-229. Cambridge: Cambridge University Press.

2000 *Decentralization, Development and Natural Resource Management in the Northwestern Kalahari Desert, Botswana.* Washington, D.C.: Biodiversity Support Program (BSP).

2001 "Hunting Is Our Heritage": The Struggle for Hunting and Gathering Rights among the San of Southern Africa. In *Parks, Property and Power: Managing Hunting Practice and Identity Within State Policy Regimes,* ed. David G. Anderson and Kazunobu Ikeya, 139-158. Osaka, Japan: National Museum of Ethnology.

2004 Human Rights and Anthropological Activism Among the San. In *Human Rights: The Scholar as an Activist,* ed. Carole Nagengast and Carlos G. Velez-Ibañez, 169-191. Norman, Oklahoma: Society for Applied Anthropology.

Hitchcock, Robert K. and Rosinah Rose B. Masilo

1995 *Subsistence Hunting and Resource Rights in Botswana.* Gaborone, Botswana: Natural Resources Management Project, Department of Wildlife and National Parks.

Hitchcock, Robert K. and Tara M. Twedt

1997 Physical and Cultural Genocide of Various Indigenous Peoples. In *Century of Genocide: Eyewitness Accounts and Critical Views,* ed. Sam Totten, William S. Parsons, and Israel W. Charny, 372-407. New York and London: Garland Publishing.

Hodgson, Dorothy L

2002 Introduction: Comparative Perspectives on the Indigenous Rights Movement in Africa and the Americas. *American Anthropologist* 104(4):1037-1049.

Hoq, Leboni Amena

2002 Note, Land Restitution and the Doctrine of Aboriginal Title: *Richtersveld Community v Alexkor Ltd and Another. South African Journal of Human Rights,* Vol.18: 421, 421.

Horn, Frank, ed.

1996 *Minorities and Their Right of Political Participation.* Rovaniemi, Finland: Northern Institute for Environmental and Minority Law at the University of Lapland.

Hulme, David and Marshall Murphree, eds.

2001 *African Wildlife and Livelihoods: The Promise and Performance of Community Conservation.* London: James Currey.

Human Rights Watch/Africa
 1995   *Violence against Women in South Africa: State Response to Domestic Violence and Rape.* New York and Washington, D.C.: Human Rights Watch/Africa.

Hunter, Malcolm L., Robert K. Hitchcock and Barbara Wyckoff Baird
 1990   Women and Wildlife in Southern Africa. *Conservation Biology* 4(4):449-451.

International Labor Organization
 1989   *The Indigenous and Tribal Peoples' Convention No. 169 of 1989.* Geneva, Switzerland: ILO.

 1999   *Indigenous peoples of South Africa: Current trends.* Geneva: ILO.

IPACC - Indigenous Peoples of Africa Co-ordinating Committee
 2003   *Indigenous Peoples of Africa.* Booklet. Cape Town: IPACC.

IWGIA - International Work Group for Indigenous Affairs
 2003   *The Indigenous World 2002-2003.* Copenhagen: IWGIA.

Jacob, Evelyn and Cathie Jordan, eds.
 1993   *Minority Education: Anthropological Perspectives.* Norwood: Ablex Publishing Corporation.

Kann, Ulla
 1991   Where the Sand is the Book: Education for everyone in the Nyae Nyae area. Consultancy report for the Nyae Nyae Development Foundation in Namibia (NNDFN) and the Swedish International Development Authority (SIDA), Windhoek.

Kann, Ulla, D. Mapolelo and P. Nleya
 1989   *The Missing Children: Achieving Universal Basic Education in Botswana. The Barriers, and Some Suggestions for Overcoming Them.* Gaborone, Botswana; National Institute of Development Research and Documentation, University of Botswana.

Kann, Ulla, Robert K. Hitchcock and Nomtuse Mbere
 1990   *Let them Talk: A Review of the Accelerated Remote Area Development Programme.* Gaborone: Ministry of Local Government and Lands and Oslo: Norwegian Agency for Development and Co-operation.

Kenrick, J. and J. Lewis
 2004   Indigenous Peoples' rights and the politics of the term "indigenous". *Anthropology Today*, 20 (2):4-9.

Kipuri, Naomi
 1999   The Human Rights Situation of Indigenous Peoples in Africa. *Indigenous Affairs*, no.1 (January/March 1999):18-24. Copenhagen: IWGIA.

Kuper, Adam
 2003   Return of the native. *Current Anthropology* 44 (3):389:402.

Lee, Richard B.
1979   *The !Kung San: Men, Women and Work in a Foraging Society.* Cambridge, MA: Harvard University Press.

Lee, Richard B. and Irven DeVore, eds.
1976   *Kalahari Hunter-Gatherers: Studies of the !Kung San and Their Neighbours.* Cambridge: Harvard University Press.

Lee, Richard B. and Richard Daly, eds.
1999   *The Cambridge Encyclopaedia of Hunters and Gatherers.* Cambridge: Cambridge University Press.

Lehmann, Karin
2004   Aboriginal Title, Indigenous Rights and the Right to Culture. *South African Journal of Human Rights*, Vol. 20:86.

Le Roux, Willemien
1999   *Torn Apart: San Children as Change Agents in a Process of Acculturation. A Report on the Educational Situation of Children in Southern Africa.* Ghanzi: Kuru Development Trust and Windhoek: Working Group of Indigenous Minorities in Southern Africa.

Liebenberg, Louis
1990   *The Art of Tracking: The Origin of Science.* Cape Town: David Philip.

Madzudzo, Elias
2001   Zimbabwe. In *An Assessment of the Status of the San in South Africa, Angola, Zambia and Zimbabwe*, ed. Steven Robins, Elias Madzudzo and Mathias Brenzinger. Windhoek, Namibia: Legal Assistance Center.

Malan, J.S.
1995   *Peoples of Namibia.* Wingate Park, S.A.: Rhino Publishers.

Marshall, Lorna
1976   *The !Kung of Nyae Nyae.* Cambridge, MA: Harvard University Press.

Masilo-Rakgoasi, Rosinah
2002   "An Assessment of the Community-Based Natural Resource Management Approach and Its Impacts on the Basarwa: Case Study of Xaixai and Gudigwa Communities". M.A. Thesis in Development Studies, University of Botswana, Gaborone, Botswana.

Mberengwa, Ignatius
2000   "The Communal Areas Management Program for Indigenous Resources (CAMPFIRE) and Rural Development in Zimbabwe's Marginal Areas: A Study in Sustainability". Ph.D. Dissertation, University of Nebraska-Lincoln, Lincoln, Nebraska.
2001   "The Vadema of Chapoto Ward, Guruve, Zimbabwe". Manuscript on file at the University of Nebraska-Lincoln.

McGovern, Seana
1999   *Education, Modern Development and Indigenous Knowledge: An Analysis of Academic Knowledge Production.* New York: Garland Publishing, Inc.

Mendelsohn, John M., Patti Swarts and Roger Avenstrup
1995   Marginalisation in education: The case of Bushman-speaking people. In *EMIS Bulletin* 3 (June 1995), ed. Management Information Systems Division. Windhoek: Ministry of Basic Education and Culture.

Mendelsohn, John and Carole Roberts
1998   *An Environmental Profile and Atlas of Caprivi.* Windhoek: Gamsberg-Macmillan.

Minority Rights Group International
1997   *World Directory of Minorities.* London: Minority Rights Group International.

Moeletsi, B.
1993   "The Tribal Land Act of Botswana: Does it have a place for Basarwa?" Paper presented at the Workshop for the Promotion of Basarwa Research and Studies, University of Botswana, 17-18 December 1993.

Moraes, Marcia
1996   *Bilingual Education: A Dialogue with the Bakhtin Circle.* Albany: State University of New York Press.

Musters, C. J. M., H. J. de Graaf and W. J. ter Keurs
2000   Can Protected Areas Be Expanded in Africa? *Science* 287:1759-1760.

Naldi, Gino J.
2003   Land Reform in Zimbabwe: Some Legal Aspects. *Journal of Modern African Studies* 31(4):585-600.

Namibia, Republic of
1992   *Regional Conference on Development Programmes for Africa's San Populations, Windhoek, Namibia, 16-18 June 1992.* Windhoek: Ministry of Lands, Resettlement and Rehabilitation.

1997   *Toward Education for All - A Development Brief for Education, Culture and Training.* Windhoek: Gamsberg MacMillan for the Ministry of Basic Education, Sport and Culture.

2000   *National Policy Options for Educationally Marginalised Children.* Windhoek: Ministry of Basic Education, Sport and Culture.

Namibian Economic Policy Research Unit (NEPRU)
1991   Papers from the National Land Conference. Windhoek: Government of Namibia.

Nettheim, Garth, Gary D. Meyers and Donna Craig
2002   *Indigenous Peoples and Governance Structures: A Comparative Analysis of Land and Resource Management Rights.* Canberra, Australia: Australian Institute of Aboriginal and Torres Strait Islander Press.

Ng'ong'ola, C.

1993   "Legal recognition of traditional land rights: research notes and agenda". Paper presented at the Workshop for the Promotion of Basarwa Research and Studies, University of Botswana, 17-18 December 1993.

Nkelekang, M.

2003   "The Current Situation of Basarwa". Paper Presented at a Workshop held in preparation for the International Khoisan Conference, Gaborone, September 2003.

Nyati-Ramahobo, Lydia

2003   "Culture in Education for the San People". Paper presented at the Khoe and San Development Conference, University of Botswana, 10-12 September 2003.

Ogbu, John

1993   Variability in Minority School Performance: A problem in Search of an Explanation. In *Minority Education: Anthropological Perspectives* ed. Jacob and Jordan, 83-112. Norwood: Ablex Publishing Corporation.

OHCHR

2004   *Status of Ratifications of the Principal International Human Rights Treaties as of 9 June 2004.* Geneva: Office of the United Nations High Commissioner for Human Rights.

Pakleppa, Richard and Americo Kwononoka

2003   *Where the First Are Last: San Communities Fighting for Survival in Southern Angola.* Windhoek, Namibia: Trócaire Angola, the Working Group of Indigenous Minorities in Southern Africa and OCADEC.

Pankhurst, Donna

1996   *A Resolvable Conflict? The Politics of Land in Namibia.* Bedford, U.K.: University of Bedford.

Panos Oral Testimony Programme

1998   A Project on the Social and Individual Impact of Resettlement. Oral Testimony with the Kalahari San. n.p.

Parsons, Neil, ed.

2002   El Negro and the Hottentot Venus: Issues of Repatriation. Special Issue of *Pula: Botswana Journal of African Studies*, Vol 16 (2).

Perkins, J.S.

1991   Drought, cattle-keeping and range degradation in the Kalahari, Botswana. In *Pastoral Economies in Africa and Long Term Responses to Drought,* ed. J.C. Stone. Aberdeen: Aberdeen University African Studies Group.

Peters, Y.J.D.

1993   "On the Discrimination of the Rehoboth Basters: An Indigenous People in the Republic of Namibia". Paper submitted to the Working Group on Indigenous Populations, Geneva, July-August 1993.

Polelo, Mopati
2003   "Minorities On the Margins: School Dropout in Remote Areas of Western Botswana". Paper presented at the Khoe and San Development Conference, University of Botswana, 10-12 September 2003.

Reynolds, E.
1999   The Dobe Files. Manuscript. N.p.

Rivers, Roberta
1999   *People of the Wind: The Political Status of the San in Botswana. Consultancy on the Condition of the San in Botswana.* Brussels: European Union.

Robins, Steven, Elias Madzudzo and Matthias Brenzinger
2001   *An Assessment of the Status of the San in South Africa, Angola, Zambia and Zimbabwe.* Windhoek, Namibia: Legal Assistance Center.

Rohde, Richard
1993   *Afternoons in Damaraland: Common Land and Common Sense in One of Namibia's Former Homelands.* Occasional Publication no. 41. Edinburgh: Centre of African Studies, University of Edinburgh.

Rozemeijer, Nico, ed.
2001   *Community-Based Tourism in Botswana: The SNV Experience in Three Community Tourism Projects.* Gaborone: SNV (Netherlands Development Organization).

SASI - South African San Institute
2001   *SASI Annual Report 2000-2001.* Cape Town: SASI.
2002   *SASI Annual Report 2001-2002.* Cape Town: SASI.

Saugestad, Sidsel
1996   Setting History Straight: Bushmen Encounters in Cape Town. *Indigenous Affairs* (IWGIA) No. 4:4-11.
1997   The San of Southern Africa – Aspects of a Minority Situation. Annex to the San Regional Assessment Inception Report to the European Commission. Tromsø.
1998   *The Inconvenient Indigenous. Remote Area Development In Botswana, Donor Assistance and the First People of the Kalahari.* Tromsø: Faculty of Social Science, University of Tromsø.
2001a   *The Inconvenient Indigenous: Remote Area Development in Botswana, Donor Assistance and the First People of the Kalahari.* Uppsala: Nordic Africa Institute.
2001b   Contested Images: 'First Peoples' or 'Marginalised Minorities' in Africa? In *Africa's Indigenous Peoples: 'First Peoples' or 'Marginalised Minorities'*, ed. Alan Barnard and Justin Kenrick. Edinburgh: Centre of African Studies, University of Edinburgh.

Schapera, Isaac

1930   *The Khoisan Peoples of South Africa: Bushmen and Hottentots.* London: Routledge and Kegan Paul.

1938   *A Handbook of Tswana Law and Custom.* London: Frank Cass.

1943   *Native Land tenure in the Bechuanaland Protectorate.* Alice, South Africa: Lovedale Press.

Schoenberger, Karl

2000   *Levi's Children: Coming to Terms with Human Rights in the Global Marketplace.* New York: Grove Press.

Scoones, Ian, ed.

1995   *Living with Uncertainty: New Directions in Pastoral Development in Africa.* London: Intermediate Technology Publications.

Scott, James C.

1998   *Seeing Like a State: How Certain Schemes to Improve the Human Condition Have Failed.* New Haven: Yale University Press.

Selolwane, O.D.

1995   "Silence of the lambs? Ineffectual NGO influence on policy on the fencing of Botswana's communal rangelands". Unpublished paper, Centre for Continuing Education, University of Botswana.

1998   Equality of Citizenship and the Gendering of Democracy In Botswana. In *Botswana: Politics and Society,* ed. W.A. Edge and M.H. Lekorwe, 397-411. Pretoria: J.L. Van Schaik.

Siegrühn, Amanda, and Jennifer Hays

2001   Implementation Plan for Pilot Projects for the Khoe and San Languages in Schools in the Northern Cape Province. Submitted to the Northern Cape Education Department.

Skotnes, Pippa, ed.

1996   *Miscast: Negotiating the Presence of the Bushmen.* University of Cape Town Press.

Smith, Andy

1999   Archaeology and evolution of hunters and gatherers. In *The Cambridge Encyclopaedia of Hunters and Gatherers,* ed. Richard B. Lee and Richard Daly. Cambridge: Cambridge University Press.

Spring, Joel

2000   *The Universal Right to Education: Justification, Definition and Guidelines.* Mahwah: Lawrence Erlbaum Associates.

Souindola, Simao

1981   Angola: Genocide of the Bosquimanos. *IWGIA Newsletter* 31-32: 66-68.

Stander, P.E., //. Ghau, D. Tsisaba, //. /Oma, and // Ui

1997   Tracking and the Interpretation of Spoor: A Scientifically Sound Method in Ecology. *Journal of the Zoological Society of London* 242:329-341.

Sullivan, Sian

1996   *The 'Communalization' of Former Commercial Farmland: Perspectives from Damaraland and Implications for Land Reform.* SSD Research Report no. 25. Windhoek: University of Namibia, Multi-Disciplinary Research Centre.

Sutton, Imre, ed.

1985   *Irredeemable America: The Indians' Estate and Land Claims.* Albuquerque: University of New Mexico Press.

Suzman, James

2001a   *An Introduction to the Regional Assessment of the Status of the San in Southern Africa.* Windhoek, Namibia: Legal Assistance Centre.

2001b   *An Assessment of the Status of San in Namibia.* Windhoek, Namibia: Legal Assistance Centre.

Sylvain, Renee

2004   San Women Today: Inequality and Dependency in a Post-Foraging World. *Indigenous Affairs* 1-2/04:8-13.

Taylor, Michael

2000   "Life, Land and Power: Contesting development in northern Botswana". PhD thesis, University of Edinburgh, Department of Social Anthropology.

2001   Narratives of identity and assertions of legitimacy: Basarwa in northern Botswana. *Senri Ethnological studies* 59:157-181.

2002   Looking for life in the Okavango Delta: government policy and popular values affecting San livelihood strategies. *Development and Change* 33(3):467-488.

2003   Of wilderness, "Bushmen" and development. In *San and the State,* ed. Michael Bollig. Cologne: University of Cologne.

Tlou, Thomas, and Alec Campbell

1984   *History of Botswana.* Gaborone: Macmillan Boleswa.

Traill, Anthony

1985   *Phonetic and Phonological Studies of !Xoo Bushman.* Hamburg, Germany: Helmut Buske Verlag.

1995   The Khoesan languages of South Africa. In *Language and Social History. Studies in South African Sociolinguistics,* ed. R. Mesthrie. Cape Town: David Philip.

Twyman, C.

1998   Rethinking Community Resource Management: Managing Resources or Managing People in Western Botswana? *Third World Quarterly* 19, no. 4: 745-770.

UNDP

1998   *Namibia Human Development Report 1998.* Windhoek: United Nations Development Programme.

2003   *Human Development Report 2002: Millennium Development Goals: A Compact among Nations to End Human Poverty*. New York and Oxford: Oxford University Press.

UNHCR
  1998   *The State of the World's Refugees*. Geneva: U.N. High Commissioner for Refugees.

UNICEF
  1999   Project Proposal to Determine the Appropriate Curriculum for Remote Area Dweller Children in Western Botswana. Gaborone: United Nations International Childrens Emergency Fond.

United States Department of State
  2003   *Country Reports on Human Rights Practices for 2002*. Washington, D.C.: U.S. Government Printing Office.

United States Indian Health Service
  1991   *Trends in Indian Health*. Rockville, Maryland: U.S. Indian Health Service.

Van der Merwe, J.H.
  1983   *National Atlas of South West Africa (Namibia)*. Goodwood, S.A.: National Book Printers.

Weaver, Larry Chris and Patricia Skyer
  2003   "Conservancies: Integrating Wildlife Land-use Options into the Livelihood, Development and Conservation Strategies of Namibian Communities" Paper presented at the Fifth World Parks Congress to the Animal Health and Development Forum, Durban, South Africa, September 2003.

Wellmer, Gottfried
  2001   "Implications of the Red Line on the Namibian Economy". Paper presented at the Civil Society Conference on Land Reform, Windhoek, October 2001.

Werbner, P.
  1999   *Women, Citizenship and Difference*. London and New York: Zed Books.

Werner, Wolfgang
  1977   *Land Reform in Namibia: The First Seven Years*. Afrika Bibliographien Working Paper, No. 5. Basel: Basler Afrika Bibliographien.

White, Richard
  1993   *Livestock development and pastoral production on communal rangeland in Botswana*. Gaborone: Botswana Society.

Widlok, Thomas
  1999   *Living on Mangetti: "Bushman" Autonomy and Namibian Independence*. Oxford: Oxford University Press.

Wilmer, Franke
  1993   *The Indigenous Voice in World Politics: Since Time Immemorial*. Newbury Park: Sage Publications.

Wilmsen, Edwin N.
1989   *Land Filled with Flies: A Political Economy of the Kalahari.* Chicago: Chicago University Press.

Wily, Elizabeth
1976   *"Bere and Ka/gae".* Unpublished Manuscript, Botswana National Archives MICRO 809, 24pp.

WIMSA - Working Group of Indigenous Minorities in Southern Africa
1998   *Report on Activities April 1998 to March 1999.* Windhoek, Namibia: WIMSA.
2001   *Report from the First Regional San Education Conference in Okahandja, Namibia, May 7-11, 2001.* Windhoek: Wimsa.
2003   *Report on Activities April 2002 to March 2003.* Windhoek, Namibia: WIMSA.
2004   *Report on Activities April 2003 to March 2004.* Windhoek, Namibia: WIMSA.

WIPCE
1999   "Coolangatta Statement On Indigenous Peoples' Rights in Education." World Indigenous Peoples' Conference on Education, Hilo, Hawai'i, August 6, 1999.

Woodburn, James
1997   Indigenous discrimination: the ideological basis for local discrimination against hunter-gatherer minorities in Sub-Saharan Africa. *Ethnic and Racial Studies* 20(2):345-61.

Wyckoff-Baird, Barbara
2000   Environmental Governance: Lessons from the Ju | 'hoan Bushmen in Northeastern Namibia. In *Indigenous Peoples and Conservation Organizations: Experiences in Collaboration*, ed. Ron Weber, John Butler and Patty Larson, 113-135. Washington, D.C.: Biodiversity Support Program.

Wylie, Diana
1991   *A Little God: the Twilight of Patriarchy in a Southern African Chiefdom.* Johannesburg: Witwatersrand University Press.

Wynne, Susan
1989   "The Land Boards of Botswana: A Problem in Institutional Design". Ph.D. Dissertation, Indiana University, Bloomington, Indiana.

Young, Elspeth
1995   *Third World in the First: Indigenous Peoples and Development.* London: Routledge.

CONTRIBUTORS

CONTRIBUTORS

Joseph Akpan is a Nigerian political scientist who completed his Ph.D. at the University of Nebraska-Lincoln (USA) in 1992. He is currently working as a development consultant and also teaches African history, politics and development at various universities in Nebraska, including the University of Nebraska-Lincoln, Nebraska Wesleyan University and Peru State College.

Tung Chan is a lawyer and member of the New York bar. Her interest for, and knowledge of, the Richtersveld case stems from 1997 when she carried out research work for the Legal Resources Centre (Cape Town, South Africa) on constitutional and statutory provisions regarding provincial land and assisting in litigation of aboriginal title claim in Namaqualand. During 2000-2001, she worked with Justice Richard J. Goldstone, of the Constitutional Court of South Africa, on issues of the constitutional law of the United States and South Africa. She is currently serving on the Board of Directors of the Southern African Legal Services and Legal Education Project.

Roger Chennells is a South African lawyer and senior partner in the Stellenbosch law firm Chennells Albertyn. He is legal advisor to the South African San Institute (SASI), which he co-founded in 1996, as well as to the Working Group of Indigenous Minorities in Southern Africa (WIMSA) and IPACC (Indigenous Peoples of Africa Coordinating Committee), which he helped establish in 1997. Mr. Chennells was part of the team that negotiated the ‡Khomani land claim with the government of South Africa, the result of which was a settlement giving the ‡Khomani land and resource rights in the Kgalagadi Transfrontier Park area.

Clement Daniel is a Namibian lawyer and has for many years been associated with the Legal Assistance Center in Windhoek, Namibia, working as a Legal Practitioner / Manager from 1996 to 1998, and as the Center's director from 2000 to June 2004. He is a Labour Law lecturer at the University of Stellenbosch, South Africa, and has published extensively on labour law, freedom of speech, land rights, rights of indigenous minorities, and political parties and elections.

Aymone du Toit received a Bachelor of Law (LLB) *cum laude* in 1998 from the University of Cape Town. During 2001 she worked as a researcher for the Community Agency of Social Enquiry (CASE) on projects commissioned by the International Labour Office (ILO) and the Danish Ministry of Foreign Affairs (DANIDA) in the areas of economic development and legal aid policy. She also participated in reports for the National Treasury and the European Union Parliamentary Support Programme (EUPSP) on parliament's role in the national budgetary process, and in the new constitutional democracy. She is currently practising as an Advocate at the Cape Bar.

Christine Haney is a post-graduate anthropology student at the University of Nebraska-Lincoln (USA) where she is in the process of completing her Master's degree on San women's issues.

Sidney L. Harring is a Professor of Law at Queens College of the City University of New York (CUNY). He has worked on indigenous peoples' rights issues, including those of Native Americans and Namibians. In 1995, he served as a Fulbright Professor teaching international human rights law at the University of Namibia and his current research and writing is on communal land rights and land reform in Namibia.

Jennifer Hays is an anthropologist with a strong interest in minority rights and education issues. She currently lives in Namibia where she is writing her dissertation for a Ph.D. from the State University of New York at Albany based on fieldwork with the Nyae Nyae Juǀ'hoansi and other San communities of southern Africa. She has worked extensively in both Namibia and Botswana in conjunction with the Working Group of Indigenous Minorities in Southern Africa.

Robert Hitchcock is an anthropologist and coordinator of African Studies in the Department of Anthropology and Geography of the University of Nebraska-Lincoln (USA). He also serves on the board of the Kalahari Peoples Fund, a non-profit organization aimed at assisting the San and other peoples of southern Africa.

Melvin Johnson is an anthropologist-geographer who is currently completing his PhD in human geography at the University of Nebraska-Lincoln. He teaches anthropology, business and geography at the University of Nebraska - Lincoln and the Nebraska Wesleyan University (USA).

Thomas Edward Koperski is a humanities area researcher specializing in political science, sociology and psychology at the University of Nebraska-Lincoln (USA).

Isaac Mazonde is a Motswana anthropologist with a Ph.D. from the University of Manchester (UK). He is currently an Associate Professor of Geography in the Research and Development Office of the University of Botswana. His research interests include cultural/ethnicity studies and conflict management and resolution.

Ignatius Mberengwa is a Zimbabwean geographer who received his Ph.D. in Geography from the University of Nebraska-Lincoln (USA) in 2000. He is currently teaching environmental science at Bindura University of Science Education, Bindura, Zimbabwe.

Richard Pakleppa is a film-maker and development consultant who has worked on San human rights issues in Namibia and Angola with the Working Group of Indigenous Minorities in Southern Africa (WIMSA).

Sidsel Saugestad is an anthropologist with a Ph.D. from Tromsø University in Tromsø, Norway. She has undertaken field work and worked in Botswana, and is currently coordinating the University of Tromsø-University of Botswana San/Basarwa Research Project.

Michael Taylor is an anthropologist with a Ph.D. from Edinburgh University who currently works for the government of Botswana on a common property management program with the Ministry of Agriculture.

Diana Vinding is an anthropologist at the International Work Group of Indigenous Affairs (IWGIA) in Copenhagen, Denmark and is the coordinating editor of *The Indigenous World*, the annual publication on indigenous peoples world-wide.

The Working Group of Indigenous Minorities in Southern Africa (WIMSA) is a regional San advocacy group based in Windhoek, Namibia. The WIMSA team consists of Axel Thoma, Joram /Useb and Magdalena Brormann.